# FORMULA 1 WORLD CHAMPIONS

|  |  |
|------|----------|
| **1950** | GIUSEPPE FARINA |
| **1951** | JUAN-MANUEL FANGIO |
| **1952** | ALBERTO ASCARI |
| **1953** | ALBERTO ASCARI |
| **1954** | JUAN-MANUEL FANGIO |
| **1955** | JUAN-MANUEL FANGIO |
| **1956** | JUAN-MANUEL FANGIO |
| **1957** | JUAN-MANUEL FANGIO |
| **1958** | MIKE HAWTHORN |
| **1959** | JACK BRABHAM |
| **1960** | JACK BRABHAM |
| **1961** | PHIL HILL |
| **1962** | GRAHAM HILL |
| **1963** | JIM CLARK |
| **1964** | JOHN SURTEES |
| **1965** | JIM CLARK |
| **1966** | JACK BRABHAM |
| **1967** | DENNY HULME |
| **1968** | GRAHAM HILL |
| **1969** | JACKIE STEWART |
| **1970** | JOCHEN RINDT |
| **1971** | JACKIE STEWART |
| **1972** | EMERSON FITTIPALDI |
| **1973** | JACKIE STEWART |
| **1974** | EMERSON FITTIPALDI |
| **1975** | NIKI LAUDA |
| **1976** | JAMES HUNT |
| **1977** | NIKI LAUDA |
| **1978** | MARIO ANDRETTI |
| **1979** | JODY SCHECKTER |
| **1980** | ALAN JONES |
| **1981** | NELSON PIQUET |
| **1982** | KEKE ROSBERG |
| **1983** | NELSON PIQUET |
| **1984** | NIKI LAUDA |
| **1985** | ALAIN PROST |
| **1986** | ALAIN PROST |
| **1987** | NELSON PIQUET |
| **1988** | AYRTON SENNA |
| **1989** | ALAIN PROST |
| **1990** | AYRTON SENNA |
| **1991** | AYRTON SENNA |
| **1992** | NIGEL MANSELL |
| **1993** | ALAIN PROST |
| **1994** | MICHAEL SCHUMACHER |
| **1995** | MICHAEL SCHUMACHER |
| **1996** | DAMON HILL |

# AUTOSPORT
# 1996 GRAND PRIX REVIEW

**EDITOR** Andy Hallbery **ART EDITOR** Peter Charles **ASSISTANT EDITOR** Andrew Benson **GRAND PRIX EDITOR** Nigel Roebuck
**EDITORIAL ASSISTANTS** Simon Strang, Jonathan Noble, Jim Holder **PHOTOGRAPHY** Martyn Elford/Autosport Photographic,
Sutton Photographic **ADDITIONAL PHOTOGRAPHY** Allsport, Brewer, Darren Heath, Colin McMaster, Bryn Williams
**ADVERTISING** Martin Nott **PUBLISHING MANAGER** Guy Nicholls **SENIOR PRODUCTION MANAGER** Meurig Evans
**PRODUCTION MANAGER** Jim Turner **PUBLISHER** Peter Foubister **PUBLISHING DIRECTOR** Tony Schulp

**GRAND PRIX REVIEW 1996 is an Autosport Special Project published by Haymarket Special Motoring Magazines Ltd,**
**38-42 Hampton Road, Teddington, Middlesex TW11 0JE, England**

**PRINTED IN ENGLAND BY:** Butler & Tanner **COLOUR ORIGINATION:** F1 Colour, Mitcham, Surrey
**A HAYMARKET PUBLICATION** reprinting in whole or in part is forbidden except with prior permission of the publisher

AUSTRALIAN GP

*Melbourne*   'I've never trashed a racing car in my life like that.   It's destroyed. Of course I'm lucky.'
Martin Brundle

INSIGHT
*Michael Schumacher*

# Ferrari

SCHUMACHER PLUS FERRARI EQUALS..?

Before the start of the 1996 season, Michael Schumacher, in his brand new Ferrari overalls, declared that he would not be a contender to retain his World Championship title. But, he said, 1997 would be another matter. TONY DODGINS assesses the first year

GERMAN GP
ROUND 11
*Hockenheim*

# HILL CLAIMS BERGER'S GLORY

Title favourite Damon Hill took his seventh Grand Prix win of the season in Germany – but only after Gerhard Berger's Benetton expired with less than three laps to the chequered flag

"I heard a strange noise from one of our engines, and I wasn't sure if it was Gerhard's or mine"
*Damon Hill*

HUNGARIAN GP
ROUND 12
*Hungaroring*

# VILLENEUVE PILES ON THE PRESSURE

It was the perfect result for Williams in Hungary, clinching them the constructors championship. But it wasn't for Damon Hill because, with four races to go, the world title was still up for grabs

"I knew that unless I made a mistake or got caught up in traffic, Damon wouldn't get past"
*Jacques Villeneuve*

HISTORY

*Team-mates*

# CIVIL WARS

Such was Williams-Renault's domination of the 1996 season, it was clear from mid-season that either Damon Hill or Jacques Villeneuve would be the world champion. ADAM COOPER looks at other inter-team title chases

Villeneuve logged up vital seconds and thirds and stayed in touch with winner Hill

*Monza*

'I made a mistake and put myself out.
No excuses, it's just one of those things'

Damon Hill

*Melbourne* 'I've never trashed a racing car in my life like tha

It's destroyed. Of course I'm lucky.'
**Martin Brundle**

One final look at the times before Schumacher
sets a scintillating pole position at Monaco

Michael Schumacher

After the race at Monza, Damon Hill had a

mountain to climb in his chase for the world title    *Monza*

*Damon Hill*

# JUST CHAMPION

Very much the worthy winner, Damon Hill had the British public in a state of nervous exhaustion. He slipped up at Monza and Estoril, but, fittingly, clinched the title in style – from the front. BY NIGEL ROEBUCK

In my youth, I remember vaguely, one of those life assurance companies ran ads aimed at scaring people into making provision for their later lives. There was a drawing of a young man, around 25, and beneath the words, 'They tell me my job doesn't provide me with a pension.' Progressively the drawings aged, and the messages grew more urgent; finally, at 60-ish, and with furrowed brow, he says, 'Without a pension, I really don't know what I shall do...'

This long-forgotten quarter-page came back to me during the closing weeks of the Formula 1 season, when it began to look as though Damon Hill, quite without a care through the first half of 1996, might yet find a way to lose the world championship. He made it in the end, happily, but what had for so long seemed like a stroll to the title ultimately became something of a sweat.

Hill began the season extravagantly, in the manner of Ayrton Senna in 1991, or Nigel Mansell the year after. In Melbourne, true, he was beaten to pole position by new Williams-Renault team mate Jacques Villeneuve, and spent most of the race behind the F1 rookie, but still he looked assured, potentially quicker, and when Jacques's engine

began to lose oil pressure towards the end, he took over the lead. Afterwards Williams personnel confirmed from their telemetry that he had indeed been using his car more temperately than his team mate. One down, 15 to go.

The South American races fell to Damon without protest. At Interlagos, in terrible conditions, he led all the way from pole position, giving a perfect demonstration of how to win in the wet. In Buenos Aires, it was dry, but here again he was effectively unopposed. Three races, three wins.

At the Nurburgring, the victory sequence ended. Villeneuve won his first race, pressured by Michael Schumacher, and Hill scratched a fourth place, having made a poor start - something later in the season we would come almost to expect of him. At Imola, though, he won as he liked, and Monte Carlo utterly dominated until his engine failed in the late stages.

Barcelona Damon made a mess of, and frankly admitted it. Quite why, on an afternoon of almost tropical rainfall, he opted - on the grid - to make 'compromise' set-up changes to his car remains known

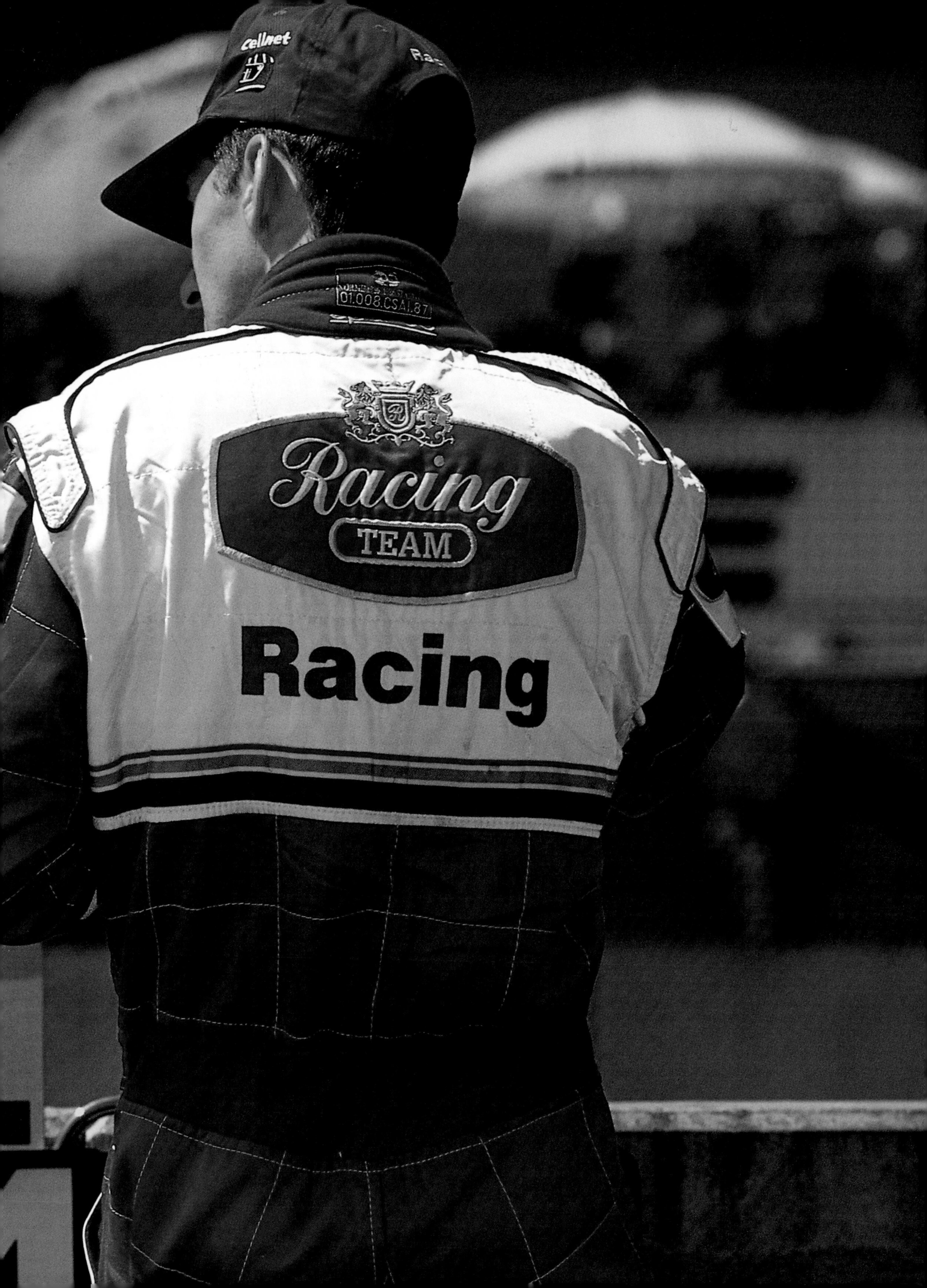
Cellnet
01.008.CSAI.87
Racing
TEAM
Racing

A model of concentration, Damon Hill prepared for 1996 like never before, and a breathtaking run of early season form was the launch pad for the 1996 world championship

only to him, but he found himself with a Williams near undriveable on the streaming track, which he left three times in the first 11 laps, on the last occasion for good.

All was back to normal again in Montreal, though, where he confidently outdrove Villeneuve. With eight of the 16 races run, Hill had won five times, and held a 21-point lead over Villeneuve – which went out to 25 after the French GP, where Damon again won with ease. At this stage of the game, it looked as though the world championship would be settled by the time of Spa or, at the latest, Monza. Hill was simply cantering to the title.

'I've been astonished,' said Bernie Ecclestone at Magny-Cours, 'at the way Damon has raised his game. He doesn't have the natural talent of Schumacher, but then neither does anyone else. What he's done is grow into a truly mature Grand Prix driver, and it's irrelevant that he's got the best car – the successful drivers have always had bloody good cars. You can't win all those races with bad cars, whoever you are.'

It is a strange phenomenon of F1, though, that one man rarely dominates – in terms of winning, winning, winning – an entire season. In 1992, Mansell and the overwhelmingly superior 'active' Williams FW14B won eight of the first 10 races, but although Nigel had clinched the title by the time of Budapest in mid-August, he was victorious only once in the last six Grands Prix. And the following year Alain Prost and FW15 took seven of the first 10, but never won thereafter.

Now, in 1996, Hill began to find himself in the same position. A loose wheel nut took him out of the British

Williams's pit
strategy was a
major element in
Hill's success,
having often played
second fiddle to
Benetton in 1995

Grand Prix, but again he had made a poor start, and
Villeneuve was able to lead all the way, scoring his second
victory. There was another win for Damon at Hockenheim,
but for once it owed something to luck, for he would
never have got by Gerhard Berger, had the Benetton-
Renault driver's engine not detonated in the closing laps.

Still, the championship lead over Villeneuve remained
healthy, at 21 points, and now there were only five races
to be run. Immediately ahead lay Budapest and Spa, two
circuits on which Hill had won before – and two more
circuits of which Villeneuve had no experience. All things
being equal, Damon's title would be assured before too
much longer.

Jacques won in Hungary, though. The foolishly sinuous
circuit may not have been to his taste, but he learned it
quickly, and took advantage of another slow start by the
championship favourite. As in Germany, Hill quickly closed
on the leader in the final laps, but Villeneuve's engine,
unlike Berger's, did not let him down, and the Canadian
was the unexpected victor. Now the gap was 17 points.

The looming threat from Villeneuve gained further
substance at Spa, a track he expected to adore, and did.
From pole position, he led the first part of the race, and
only pit stop confusion – which delayed both Williams
drivers – during a 'full course yellow' allowed Schumacher
to get ahead of him. Hill, after getting away badly once
more, managed to finish fifth, to Villeneuve's second, but it
could have been worse: without the pit stop screw-up he
would probably have been third, but Jacques would almost
certainly have won, closing the points gap by six, rather
than three. Damon now led by 13.

Before the next race, however, his life was to be turned
upside down, for Frank Williams informed him that his
services would not be required in 1997, that Heinz-Harald
Frentzen would be taking his place, alongside Villeneuve.

Hill, not surprisingly, was stunned. There had been
rumours for some time that Frentzen figured in Williams's
future plans – as early as June it was murmured that he
would replace Villeneuve, and by the time of Hockenheim
AUTOSPORT suggested, to general derision in the paddock,
that he would take over Hill's seat – but now the story was
firm: the world champion-elect was being dropped.

At Monza, Damon held a press conference, and his
answer to most questions was, 'You'll have to ask Frank
about that.' They had not fallen out over money, he
stressed, and he really didn't know why his contract was
not being renewed.

Only a handful of folk know the full facts, and probably
no two read them the same way. Some suggested that the
deal with Frentzen had been made months earlier, on the
heels of poor performances by Hill in the second half of
the 1995 season, others that Damon's manager was too
high-handed in his dealings with Williams, that he over-
played what was not an especially strong hand – every
other leading team was already committed on the driver
front, after all – and that Frank's patience simply snapped.
There were those, too, who pointed to Hill's tendency to
lose time in traffic; as a racer, they added, he was no
match for Schumacher, and while this had not mattered
too much in 1996, when Michael's Ferrari had usually kept
him from seriously threatening Williams, it might well be a
different story in the future.

Whatever, Damon's future was suddenly uncertain, and
while he mercifully handled the situation with his

customary dignity, and did not subject the world to a Mansellesque rant, it can have done little for his equilibrium as he went into the last three races of the season. On the line now, after all, was probably the last serious shot at the championship he would ever have.

Hill is as pleasant and well-balanced a human being as ever you will find in a paddock, and it was with some dismay that at Monza we noted, in addition to his normal entourage, the presence of an 'image consultant', for Damon's natural image would seem one of comparatively few in F1 which requires no outside assistance.

Still, it was his business, and in the race he seemed intent on giving his team bosses if not the finger, then at least the message that they had made a wrong decision.

Unable to come satisfactorily to terms with left-foot braking, Damon had retained a three-pedal layout in his FW18 throughout the season, and undoubtedly his conventional foot-operated clutch had been less effective for starting than had Villeneuve's hand-operated one. Poor getaways had cost him a great deal, and now he applied himself to improving them.

At Monza he started well – but not as well as Jean Alesi, against whom he drove an extraordinarily aggressive first lap, sitting it out side by side with the Benetton driver through the Ascari chicane, then clearly asserting himself. So you think I can't race...

It was all there for his taking in the Italian Grand Prix, for Villeneuve tagged a tyre corner marker after only a couple of laps, which bent his car's front suspension, and rendered him a backmarker for the rest of the day. Hill, pulling away consummately after six laps, had only to keep going, and the championship was over.

Therefore, it was in disbelief that we saw a Williams-Renault stalled in the middle of the road at the exit of the first chicane, watched its driver sprint for safety, then hang his head in angry frustration, only too aware of what he had chucked away. Like Jacques, Damon had clipped a wretched tyre corner marker.

In fact, though, his championship aspirations were still in better shape after Monza than before, for if he had blown the chance of clinching it, so also Villeneuve had missed the opportunity of closing on him. The gap stuck at 13 points, and now only Estoril and Suzuka remained.

Hill's Portuguese Grand Prix began as he might have dreamed. Only nine-thousandths of a second faster than Villeneuve, he took the 20th pole position of his career, and again robustly defended his lead against Alesi on the opening lap. With his championship rival trapped in fourth place, behind Schumacher, Damon disappeared into what seemed like a race of his own.

Then Jacques got by Michael in the overtaking manoeuvre of the year, and the game was on. By the time of their final pit stops, an inspired Villeneuve was up with Hill, and after them he was ahead, increasing his lead with every lap. A clutch problem in the late stages obliged Damon to back off, but – honest as ever – he sought no excuses: today, he said, he had simply been unable to stay with Villeneuve. Once more, the celebration party had to be postponed. Nine points between them, Suzuka to come.

And his reward came in Japan. A faultless drive saw him seal the world championship with his eighth win of the season. The fact that Villeneuve had retired from fourth place didn't matter. Damon was in front, controlling the race, and the destiny of the great prize.

**At Monza he started well, and drove an extraordinarily aggressive first lap**

It seemed to say much for Hill that, although his time with Williams was drawing to a close, the great majority of team members squarely hoped that he, rather than Villeneuve, would leave Japan as world champion. It was not they were against Jacques in any way, far from it, but that they felt that Damon had earned it, and not only for his work in 1996.

He had, after all, been a Williams-Renault driver for four years, in the course of them not only winning a huge number of races, but also 'coming through' in that terrible summer of 1994, following the death of team leader Ayrton Senna. He had paid his dues; he deserved this title.

There is an extrovert side to Hill's personality – putting a guitar in his hands is like putting Clark Kent in a 'phone box, but phlegmatic is his usual way, and his team always liked that about him. Mansell, wherever he was, had fresh problems flown in daily, which became wearisome over time, but for Hill, by contrast, the team's affection was obvious, and throughout the paddock the story is the same.

Perhaps there always lurked an impression, though, that at Williams his talents at the wheel were underrated, this perhaps a legacy of the manner of his arrival in the team, the promotion from mere test driver. Many a rival has pointed out, sometimes churlishly, that virtually throughout his F1 career Hill has had the best car at his disposal, but, as Bernie Ecclestone says, you still have to win the races, and that Damon has emphatically done. He may ultimately have made somewhat heavy weather of winning the world championship this year, but undoubtedly the title went to the right man. ■

On Sunday October 13 at Suzuka in Japan Damon climbed once again to the top of the finishers' podium and in so doing became, at last, the 1996 Formula One World Champion.

It was a superlative drive that firmly established Damon as one of the great British racing drivers, to rank along side Mansell, Hunt, Stewart et al.

Damon has focused himself on the Championship this year and he thoroughly deserves it. We at Grand Prix Legends congratulate him on his fine victory. And now it's time to celebrate with Damon's range of officially approved merchandise.

Some of it you may have seen before. Some of it you wont have.

The bomber jacket and rucksack are brand new as is the Flag T-Shirt.

Damon has also approved 2 exceptional prints from new artist, Neil Newnham. We think they are stunning.

Finally, the 'pièce de resistance' is a limited edition presentation of Damon's FW18 in 1:18 scale. Only 3000 will ever be produced. A real collectors' item.

So, join in the fun and send off for your officially approved Damon Hill merchandise now.

You wont be disappointed.

**COLLEGE JACKET (NM273)**
Wool mix jacket with leather sleeves and satin quilt lining. Black with blue sleeves.
M. L. XL.
£179.99

**DRIVER'S CAP (NM281)**
In our view the nicest of the Damon Hill caps.
£16.99

**HELMET BADGE (GF307)**
You won't find these anywhere else. We know because we bought them all! £7.99

**FW18 IN 1:43 SCALE (MC297)**
Die-cast in metal, 4" in length, this is a stunningly detailed replica of Damon's 1996 car. £16.99

**QUILTED JACKET (NM291)**
Rumoured to be a favourite with Damon's wife, Georgie, this is a must for those long, cold tyre testing sessions.
M. L. XL.
£89.99

**KEYRING (NM306)**
Suitable for Renaults and other cars.
£5.99

**RUCKSACK (NM299)**
Large enough to hold a helmet, racing suit, gloves and an F1A pass. Can be taken as hand luggage on international flights.
£29.99

**FLAG (NM289)**
If you were at Silverstone in July you probably bought one. If you weren't, this could be your last and only chance. (56cms x 30cms)
£14.99

**NEIL NEWNHAM PRINT (NN305)**
*Six-Point-One*
Neil Newnham has captured the drama of an F1 pit stop in quite stunning detail in this print, one of the finest F1 paintings we have seen. Limited to 500 examples, signed by Neil. (63.5cmx43.5cm)
£85

**NEIL NEWNHAM PRINT (NN303)**
*Winning Combination*
It's tough getting a print approved by Damon, and it doesn't surprise us that he's approved this one of the Williams FW18.
500 only examples signed by Neil. (63.5cmx43.5cm)
£85

**Grand Prix Legends**
FREEPOST LON 3270 London W10 6BR.
Tel: 0171 229 7399. Fax: 0171 727 8054.

# L MERCHANDISE RANGE

**FW18 – 1:18 Scale (MC295)**
Unique Limited Edition Tribute of 3000 pieces.
Damon's FW18 on plinth with celebratory plaque bearing Damon's signature and helmet. £49.99

**NEW**

**MINI HELMET (MC287)**
Cast in metal in 1:8 scale, about the size of a golfball, this highly detailed replica is a terrific momento. £9.99

**MY GRAND PRIX YEAR (MS301)**
The behind the scenes story of Damon's fight for the World Championship in 1996. Written by Damon. Hardback. £25.00

*Available mid-December*

**WHITE EYES T-SHIRT (NM293)**
Damon's brow, furrowed in concentration, has become his trademark. An unmistakeable T-shirt.
M. L. XL.
£19.99

**NEW**

**FLAG T-SHIRT (NM285)**
Celebrate Damon's 1996 F1 World Championship Victory with this T-shirt that flies the flag for Damon and for Britain.
M. L. XL.
£19.99

**BLACK CAR T-SHIRT (NM277)**
Damon at full tilt.
Very dramatic.
M. L. XL.
£19.99

**NAVY POLO SHIRT (NM279)**
A very dark blue, the colour of Damon's helmet, this polo bears his helmet design using the markings of the London Rowing Club.
M. L. XL.
£29.99

**DENIM SHIRT (NM275)**
Damon's favourite garment, when he's not in the cockpit, that is. M. L. XL. £49.99

**WAFFLE-KNIT T-SHIRT. (NM283)**
A distinctive 100% cotton T-shirt in heavy 'waffle' knit. About as thick as a sweatshirt.
M. L. XL.
£29.99

# APPROVED BY DAMON HILL

---

**DAMON HILL**

# PRIORITY ORDER FORM

## Tel: 0171 229 7399

Post to: Grand Prix Legends FREEPOST,
(No stamp required) LON 3270, London, W10 6BR.
Or Fax to us on: 0171 727 8054.

☐ I enclose a Cheque/PO
(payable to 'Grand Prix Legends)

I will pay by  Access ☐  Visa ☐  Amex ☐  Switch ☐

Card No:

| | | | | | | | | | | | | | | | |
|---|---|---|---|---|---|---|---|---|---|---|---|---|---|---|---|

Expiry Date: ☐☐☐   Switch Issue No: ☐☐

Signature:_____

Mr/Mrs/Ms: _____

Address:_____

_____

_____

Country: _____

Post Code: ☐☐☐ ☐☐☐     ASGPR/DPS

Tel:(Daytime) _____

**Please send me:**

| Ref No | Description | Size | Qty | Price |
|--------|-------------|------|-----|-------|
| | | | | |
| | | | | |
| | | | | |
| | | | | |
| | | | | |
| | | | | |
| | | | | |
| | | | | |
| | | | | |

| | |
|---|---|
| Postage & Packing (See Table) | £ |
| **TOTAL** | £ |

| Postage & Packaging Costs | | | |
|---|---|---|---|
| Total Cost of Order | UK | EC | Rest of World |
| Up to £30 | £3.50 | £6.00 | £10.00 |
| £30-£50 | £5.00 | £7.50 | £12.50 |
| £50-£75 | £6.50 | £10.00 | £15.00 |
| £75-£100 | £8.00 | £13.50 | £20.00 |
| £100-£150 | £10.00 | £15.00 | £25.00 |
| £150+ | £12.50 | £18.00 | £30.00 |

*Jackie Stewart*

# SCHOOL'S OUT

Triple world champion Jackie Stewart is well qualified to assess the current crop of F1 drivers. He'll be employing one of them for Stewart GP in 1997... By Alan Henry

**Main: Schumacher – 'the best racing driver in the world right now.' Hill – deserved to win title. Villeneuve – surpassed all expectations. Berger – life in the old dog yet?**

There are few men who know what makes a racing driver tick like Jackie Stewart. With 99 Grands Prix starts, 27 wins and three world championships to his credit, Stewart retired 23 years ago at the age of 33. Now he is poised to return to the F1 scene as co-founder of Stewart Grand Prix together with his son Paul.

Stewart knows what's needed to make the F1 Big Time behind the wheel. Approaching the eve of his new team's Grand Prix debut, we asked Jackie to comment on the Class of 1996. On who's hot and who's not. Drivers who may, at some stage in the not-too-distant future, be queuing up for a ride on F1's new Tartan Express.

There's no question about it, Jackie has a soft spot for world champion Damon Hill. It goes back to his own freshman F1 year when he partnered Damon's Dad at BRM in 1965 and frequently stayed with the family at their North London home. More than that; Stewart feels that Hill has matured beyond recognition throughout 1996.

'For me, Damon came of age at Imola,' he asserts. 'I was watching it on television at home and I suddenly saw a driver who knew what he had to do, and was comfortable in third place (during the opening stages).

'He was comfortable in the knowledge of when he was going to do it, how he was going to do it. For me, that suggested a tremendous feeling of recognition on Damon's part. So, I think he has matured enormously this year, becoming much more comfortable with himself generally.'

So does Jackie believe that Damon deserves to be World Champion in 1996? 'Yes, I do,' he replies firmly. 'But I don't think it was a *fait accompli*, although I think he's done everything to deserve his title.

'Believe me, I've never seen an unworthy world champion. It doesn't happen. For example, Denny Hulme only won the title once in 1967 when there were people who said that Jim Clark really deserved to win it. But there was a never a time that I did not regard Denny as one of the very best drivers in the world. Just as I do Damon.'

That said, Jackie confesses to being amazed by Jacques Villeneuve's potential. And, with the undistilled candour of a man confident enough to admit he might have been wrong – not a familiar trait in F1 circles – admits he was initially one of the doubters.

*Stewart on Schumacher*
**"1996 has reconfirmed the incredible scale of talent Michael has"**

## "It's a wonderful gift to get that drive, the greatest coup of his career"

'I think he has surpassed all expectations,' he concedes admiringly. 'I did not think that, even in a Williams, would he be able to accomplished those feats so confidently.

'To be honest, I was one of the people who was a bit surprised at Frank taking him on. I saw it very much as a risk, even having watched him closely in Indycars.

'But then again, I was in Melbourne and saw every inch of track in close proximity. Right there, Jacques produced the original copybook Grand Prix performance. Okay, I know that Giancarlo Baghetti won his very first Grand Prix, but Villeneuve was facing a difficult challenge on a difficult circuit, which he tackled with consummate ease. Total domination, in fact.

'Obviously in a Williams he probably had better downforce than the others. but he still had to drive the thing and he was driving on marbles for most of the time. I thought that was outstanding and the way he subsequently delivered the results was first class.

'Yet if he had become world champion, I'm not at all sure if it'd been the best thing for his career. I don't think he's ready to take the mantle as world champion.

'People may say 'don't be ridiculous, of course he should take it' but I'm not suggesting he avoided it. I'm just suggesting it would be more beneficial long-term to play another understudy year as world champion elect rather than reigning title holder.

'In a Williams for 1997, with a Renault engine, he might find himself in a position where the only person he needed to worry about on the horizon would be Michael Schumacher. Alright, so we don't know what Mika Hakkinen and David Coulthard are going to do, but in my view Schumacher would be Jacques's only threat.

'Damon is not going to be a threat with TWR Arrows, so therefore I feel that the world championship going to Damon is more appropriate. Having said that, however, the commercial considerations for all the suppliers and sponsors of the Williams team, for Damon to win the championship and for them not to be in a position to take advantage of that title is incredibly poor judgement in normal commercial terms.

'In any other business it would probably not be allowed to happen. It's crazy. Without being sceptical, that is a major issue in my mind.'

Talking of major issues brought the conversation round to Michael Schumacher. Stewart is modest about his own achievements, but when speaking about Schumacher his tone subtly changes. Perhaps it's a question of like recognising like.

'The 1996 season has again simply reconfirmed the incredible scale of talent Michael has,' says Jackie. 'He is the fittest man in Formula 1. No matter how anybody else works at it, Michael comes out of a car looking relaxed, untired and with an almost debonair physical aura surrounding him.

'It makes him look so fresh and unpressured. I think he's just got the key to the door. I believe he is the best racing driver in the world right now.'

By the same token, he feels that Eddie Irvine has performed with remarkable resilience in Maranello's unenviable supporting role.

'Being number two to the best is always a thankless task, but I think Eddie Irvine has dealt with it very well,' he asserts 'He's well suited to the role, in a way. He's got that air of acceptance about him, yet still looks comfortable and relaxed.

'I'm sure there must be moments when that's not the case, but he carries himself well. After all, it's not the worst job in the world he's got. He's driving for the Scuderia Ferrari and is getting well paid for it, I guess.'

Looking further afield at the Benetton squad, now populated by Ferrari refugees Jean Alesi and Gerhard Berger, a definite twinkle comes into Stewart's eye.

'Jean Alesi continues to impress and surprise,' he starts. Then comes the punch line. 'He impresses occasionally by the way he drives - and surprise in the sense that's taken him so long to get nothing more than a single win.

'You cannot be a supremely talented person - and for everybody else to be wrong all the time. I'm afraid there's something there that's not being understood correctly.'

And Berger? 'The ultimate journeyman driver. He

**Above:** Frentzen – pushed by Herbert in the latter half of the season. **Below:** Irvine – number two is a thankless task. Brundle - a journeyman driver. Hakkinen – the question in everyone's mind is "Will it come?"

Stewart on Alesi

## "There's something there that's not being understood"

**Above: Alesi – continues to impress and surprise. Below: Barrichello – car didn't work as well as it should. Salo – has shown some tremendous form. Panis – has done well this year**

sometimes surprises with a virtuosity which would appear to be coming out of the body of a younger man.

'Not an easy one to overtake and, I'm sure, probably getting to the point where he must consider how much longer he's got in top line racing.'

So how about the McLaren-Mercedes duo, David Coulthard and Mika Hakkinen? In particular, how does he rate the progress of his fellow Scot who started his serious professional single-seater career on the Paul Stewart Racing Staircase of Talent?

'I know David better than Mika,' he admits. 'He still suffers, to some extent, of being wonderful when the car is right, but somehow not at all comfortable when it's not.

'If he's going to step up to that next level, he's got to overcome that. He's either got to drive round the problems so that nobody really knows that the car is not right to the degree that he finds it unsuitable. Alternatively he's got to find a way of communicating more vividly the details of the car's problems.

'Somehow it hasn't come together as David would have wanted – or, indeed, as I would have wanted for David. He's a very complete driver both in and out of the cockpit – but the inside-the-cockpit stuff needs more work.'

'Mika has come back so well and so strongly from his Adelaide accident. That in itself is an enormous compliment to him, that he did it with such flair and confidence. But again, the water has run hot and cold. He's picked up several good finishes, but somehow it hasn't quite come alive yet. And the question in everybodys' mind is, I think, "will it come?"'

Looking further back in the pack, he has a degree of sympathy for the problems which seem to have afflicted Martin Brundle and Rubens Barrichello in the Jordan-Peugeot squad.

'Again, Brundle is a journeyman driver' he suggests, 'but with as good an objective mind as there is at the moment in F1. He's been with so many teams over so many years that he's a good analyst.

'Every now and again Martin can pull it together. It doesn't seem as though Jordan's chassis has been all that it

might have been and the team is no longer one of the newcomers. So I think if you consider the comparative skills of Martin and Rubens, one must conclude that that the car is perhaps not working as well as it should do. I think everybody is quite impressed by the engine, so that is a worry.'

Stewart won the Monaco Grand Prix on no fewer than three occasions, so it's perhaps not surprising that mention of Olivier Panis – this year's winner for Ligier – brought a sympathetic smile to his lips.

'Yes, well that was a kind of unusual victory,' he smiles. 'But, hey, when you win the Monaco Grand Prix, you take what you get. But he's done well this year, but how well I can't really comment.'

Next, what about the Sauber lads? You know, the guys who drive for the team whose Ford works engine contract you'll be taking over next year. Jackie ignores the forced jocularity of the question.

'Well, Heinz-Harald is going to Williams,' he ponders. 'A wonderful gift to get that drive, the greatest coup of his career. He's now got to confirm the confidence that Frank Williams has shown in him. But I suppose there should be some questions raised because of the Johnny Herbert resurgence in the last third of the season.

'I just think Johnny has always shown potential, but he's never quite come of age in terms of delivering that potential. But if he had been a real superstar, I think it would have emerged by now. But again, I think he's a very solid driver who will be good for Sauber and the stability of a two year deal will be good for Johnny.'

Elswhere on the F1 grid, and Stewart discreetly excuses himself from commenting. He doesn't want to judge those he admits he knows too little about.

Yet he does make some thoughtful observations about Mika Salo and Jos Verstappen. 'Salo has shown some tremendous form from time to time,' he says thoughtfully. 'He seems a very logical driver. Verstappen, on the other hand, has been struggling. Very difficult to judge.' Good enough for Stewart Grand Prix, perhaps? Young guns on the way up? Jackie isn't being drawn. Not yet, at least. ■

FIA
FORMULA 1
WORLD
CHAMPIONSHIP

10 - 13 July 1997 (provisional dates)

# 1997 British Grand Prix

**Book now to secure your places for the 1997 British Grand Prix - the year's only appearance in the UK of the world's most glamorous sporting championship.**

In 1997 the British Grand Prix meeting will be bigger than ever with the action now filling four days for the first time.

In view of exceptional demand in 1996, new and additional seating will be introduced for 1997 in a series of enclosures. But remember tickets will be limited to 90,000 per day.

- Sunday completely sold out in 1996 – in record time
- Buying a ticket in advance reduces pedestrian queuing and avoids disappointment
- Early bookers of centre transfer gain the opportunity to join in the Pit Road walkabout.
- Grandstand seats sold out 6 months prior to 1996 event!

To avoid disappointment…
**Book now!**

Use the official Advance Booking Form or call us on the Hotline:

**01327 857273**

# Silverstone
## THE HOME OF BRITISH MOTOR RACING

# SCHUMACHER

Before the start of the 1996 season, Michael Schumacher, in his brand new Ferrari overalls, declared that he would not be a contender to retain his World Championship title. But, he said, 1997 would be another matter. TONY DODGINS assesses the first year

**B**ack in March, I didn't hold with all those who said Damon Hill would waltz to the world championship. The logic was simple enough. Michael Schumacher had beaten him comfortably with an inferior car in 1995 and Schumacher was on his way to a Ferrari team which, according to Jean Alesi, had the best-handling car he'd ever driven. Schumacher's retainer was US$25 million. Surely Ferrari wouldn't pay that unless they were ready for him — the final piece in the world's most expensive jigsaw.

Just look at the armoury: the highly-regarded John Barnard designing, a top class management figure in Jean Todt, seemingly limitless finance and now indisputably the finest throttle jockey in the world. The principal worry was the all-new V10 engine and its reliability. If that held up, the question was: could Schumacher make the difference and become the first Ferrari driver's champion since Jody Scheckter a whole 17 years earlier?

He could have done but he didn't get the chance. Ferrari were late with the new car and, given the resources at their disposal, that's hard to defend. The F310 went to Melbourne untested. They had to hope it was quick out of the box and it wasn't. The new car was a serious disappointment to the world champion. Barnard critics started to ask why he hadn't simply chosen to develop the 412T2. Without, that is, understanding the complexities involved in a new engine installation.

'Last year's car was very stable. You could really drive it on the limit very easily,' Schumacher muses. 'But the new car was completely different and that was unexpected. We presumed we would have the same situation with better efficiency, but it just wasn't the case. Basically we had a worse car. Why, I don't know. The only person able to answer that is Barnard. I don't know how long he spent in the wind tunnel but you can be pretty sure he believed the F310 was better. If his data hadn't shown him that, he wouldn't have built it. Either there is something in the car which we didn't find, or else whatever he found in the wind tunnel did not translate onto the track.'

Then there were problems with the new carbon composite gearbox. Again questions were asked. Why had Ferrari complicated things? The team was forced into racing with the old box in South America, which also meant a hybrid car with the old rear end. When Hill won the first three races and Schumacher scored a mere four points, the task looked insurmountable.

# PLUS FERRARI EQUALS..?

The story of 1996 was all Williams, pre-season favourite Damon Hill versus newcomer Jacques Villeneuve

# THE WORLD'S A STAGE
## BUT THE REST

From far left: The F1 season in a blur. Jordan promised much but delivered little. Jean Todt's life became a little easier as Schumi shone. Forti's world turned upside-down

# FOR WILLIAMS
## ARE MERELY PLAYERS

**D**amon Hill deserved to win the 1996 Formula 1 World Championship for many reasons. He won more races than anyone else. He dominated the first half of the season, and out of all the 16 races was the most consistent front-runner in Grand Prix racing. He has made a substantial contribution to Williams-Renault's success over the last five years. And it will most likely be his last chance.

There may be those who argue that Jacques Villeneuve deserved to win the title more because the way he launched himself headlong at Hill in the second half of the season suggests he is the better driver. But Villeneuve himself would not agree, at least with the first part of that statement. 'The championship is about the whole season,' he said at the Japanese Grand Prix, 'and he did a better season than we did.'

In any case, there is no moral World Champion in F1. If there was, Michael Schumacher would right now be celebrating his third consecutive title, for there was no better demonstration that he is the outstanding talent of his generation than the heights he achieved with the recalcitrant Ferrari F310.

The World Drivers' Championship — outmoded though it may be to some extent, so crucial is the car's role in modern F1 — is won by the man who scores most points in one season. And that was Hill, who also won twice as many races in the season as his team mate.

It had always looked likely to turn out that way, and the first race, when Villeneuve set pole position and led most of the way, proved to be something of a false dawn. Villeneuve was unlucky not to win that day, but it is now clear that if Villeneuve was going no faster than he had to in Australia, so was Hill controlling his pace, short-shifting, content with the thought that he could go faster if necessary, and that six points would do nicely, thank you very much, in the first race of the season.

Within six months, the tables would have turned to such an extent that a Hill at full stretch with a 13-second lead at one-third distance in the Portuguese Grand Prix could not hold off the flying Villeneuve. But for now, Hill was comfortable.

He went on to make a walkover of the first half of the season. Three straight wins were followed at the Grand Prix of Europe by a show of vulnerability after a poor start (how often that would occur again in the late-summer), but he was soon back on the rails, and before we knew it, half the season had gone by and Hill, who had won five of the eight races, was looking unassailable.

Commentators were moved to talk about a new serene Hill, more relaxed and at ease with himself, less twitchy, more confident, and driving with an authority that almost made you forget the appalling blunders of 1995. But wiser people, including Hill, were counselling caution.

'Let's see how serene he is when he is under pressure,' muttered Williams technical director Patrick Head after his driver's consummate win in difficult wet-dry conditions in Brazil. 'It would be a mistake to consider the championship a foregone conclusion,' Hill said after winning in Canada, a race which he admitted he needed to win after spinning three times in nine laps in the wet of

*Top row, left to right: Minardi deserved more than the usual annual financial struggle; After a promising start, Verstappen covered rather too many miles by foot; Briatore wanted more girls in the pitlane, and Berger was only too happy with that; Right or wrong refuelling played its part in the spectacle*

Barcelona two weeks before. 'There is always a threat from one quarter or another. One slip-up and they can get you.'

At the time, it seemed this was merely a desire not to tempt fate. How wrong you can be. After inheriting a victory at the German Grand Prix thanks to a blown Renault engine in Gerhard Berger's Benetton, Hill was not to win again until Japan. And Hockenheim was also to mark the last race in which Villeneuve looked like a beginner.

By then, the Constructors' title was all-but locked up in favour of Williams-Renault, but the writing for a season of somewhat unexpected domination was on the wall from the beginning. Williams kept the full potential of the

FW18 hidden to a degree in pre-season testing, but in Melbourne it was clearly the best car in the field by some degree — with what remained the best all-round engine in F1 fitted to the back of it — and despite vain attempts by other teams to catch up it remained so for the entire season.

With hindsight, it will probably be remembered as one of history's great F1 cars, but the advantage it had caught even Williams off guard.

'We've been a bit surprised,' admitted chief designer Adrian Newey at the end of the season, searching for an explanation. 'Our black and white results last year did not reflect the potential of the car, and over the winter we took the car and developed and improved it. Others

**Above: Brio wasn't enough to earn Frentzen and Sauber their first victory on the streets of Monaco. Far left: It wasn't just a brush with the tyres, but nothing was stopping a Ferrari victory in Italy for Schumacher**

"There is a certain pressure from having the best car. If you win, it's normal. If you don't your the loser"

*Michael Schumacher*

Left: After an unreliable 1996 Irvine hopes this is the view his rivals will see more of in 1997. Below far left: Destination Damon. Arrows hopes for a brighter future in 1997; Centre: Devotion makes you do funny things... Left: Bingo! Panis provided the surprise of the season at Monaco

seemed to take a more sideways step, and some, particularly Ferrari... Well, it's questionable whether they improved their car very much at all.'

In Hungary in mid-August, Williams duly sewed up its fourth Constructors' title in five years, and if Schumacher is the driver of his generation, the Newey-Head combination must now be regarded without question as the design axis of the decade.

The car was not the only aspect of Williams that was improved over a heart-searching winter. The team was collectively badly exposed on strategy by Benetton and Schumacher in 1995, and it realised it needed to make some changes. And how they worked. Williams's strategy was for the most part flawless this year, several times making Benetton look flat-footed, about which several Williams team members admitted a considerable degree of quiet satisfaction.

With such a car and team at his disposal, Hill was always going to be a contender for the championship, as was reflected in his pre-season billing as favourite. But as the season wore on, he had more and more reason to be thankful for the electric beginning to his campaign.

The expected challenge from Schumacher and Ferrari never really materialised, even if the German did score three outstanding wins, but Villeneuve, who many were a little disappointed with in the first half of the season, established himself as a top-class Grand Prix driver in the second. The cool, steely Canadian struggled on tracks he did not know early on, something he explained was down to his relative inexperience with F1 and the way it and its cars work. As he struggled badly in Monaco and Hockenheim, however, there were many outsiders who doubted his word. Perhaps he was just not that good, they began to murmur.

They were wrong, and a test after the German GP proved the turning point. The team allowed him his head on set-up, and suddenly he was transformed. In Hungary, a twisty track he did not know, he won. At Spa, another new track to him, he excelled, and would have won had it not been for the mix-up with the team's radios. In Monza, both Williams drivers made fundamental mistakes. But then in Estoril, Jacques was nothing short of brilliant in the race, passing Schumacher with that sensational move around the outside at the last corner (see page 104), and going on to hunt down and humiliate a shell-shocked Hill.

All this time, Hill began to look less and less convincing. He made bad starts in Britain, Germany, Hungary and Belgium, and was outraced in Belgium and Portugal. And as Head had suggested all those months before, when he found himself running in the pack, his weaknesses were spotlighted.

Villeneuve is a true-blood racer, as he showed on numerous occasions: battling with Hill in Melbourne; re-passing Schumacher after a pit-stop in Germany and Alesi on the re-start in Belgium; and then there was Portugal.

Hill, though, proved yet again that he is uncomfortable in such a situation. He is less instinctive, and that means opportunities, when they are there, are sometimes allowed to slip through his grasp. And there was no better illustration than in Belgium, when he was alongside Martin Brundle's Jordan going into Les Combes, and still failed to claim the place. That this was the same man who feistily battled past Jean Alesi on the first lap in Monza just added to the belief that racing does not come naturally to him, even if driving fast does.

It is this sort of thing that makes people wonder whether he is true world championship material, but that would be unfair. In the final analysis, he won more races than anyone, exploited the best car in the field more effectively over a season than his team mate, and scored the most points. And when the pressure was really on in Japan, it was Villeneuve that made the mistake at the start. After that, the title was Hill's.

# RACING ILLUSTRATIONS
### By Simon P Taylor, AGMA

## Damon Hill
Leading Michael Schumacher at Imola, on the way
to perhaps his finest victory of 1996

## Michael Schumacher
Passing Villeneuve to take the lead at Barcelona,
for a brilliant first victory for Ferrari

These prints are from Simon Taylor's latest collection of driver portraits. Each print is signed and numbered by Simon Taylor, and printed on 250gsm paper, size 326x450mm.

Damon Hill - Ltd to just 350 copies. Price £45.00 plus £1.50 p&p.

Michael Schumacher - Ltd to just 350 copies. Price £45.00 plus £1.50 p&p.

Jacques Villeneuve - Ltd to 850 copies. Price £39.00 plus £1.50 p&p.

Alesi/Benetton - Ltd to 850 copies. Price £39.00 plus £1.50 p&p.

Irvine/Ferrari - Ltd to 850 copies. Price £39.00 plus £1.50 p&p.

Coulthard/McLaren - Ltd to 850 copies. Price £39.00 plus £1.50 p&p.

Many other titles available including Berger, Mansell, Prost, Senna. For a full colour brochure, please send two 1st class stamps to the address below.

— · — · — · — · — · —

To order, please send a cheque payable to "SIMON TAYLOR" with your order details to the address below. Please allow 28 days for delivery.

SIMON TAYLOR,
PO BOX 482, HIGH WYCOMBE,
BUCKS HP13 6XH.
TEL/FAX 01494 436947.

Associate Member

**Top left: The jury's still out, but Pedro Diniz went some way to silencing the critics. Top right: Herbert's struggle to re-establish his reputation was rewarded with a two-year deal from Sauber. Main photo: When the rain came Schumacher enhanced his peerless reputation as the best there is**

Even Schumacher gave his old rival approval of some kind. 'There have been a lot of stories that Damon has been a different person since the beginning of the season,' the reigning World Champion mused in Portugal. 'For me, that is not the case. Damon is Damon. To change completely? I don't see it. Nobody has done this, in my view, ever. Not me, not anybody else, not Damon, and this has become obvious through the season. Nevertheless, I think he has done a good job, and he deserves to win the championship. To win so many races, you have to drive. There is a certain pressure from having the best car. If you win, it's normal. If you don't you're the loser.'

For Schumacher, there was a different kind of pressure, the kind that comes with an entire nation expecting you to bring the glory days back to a legend.

If he did not quite manage to do that, he did not disappoint in any way. He was quite brilliant in an evil-handling car in Brazil and Argentina, and he maintained that form throughout the season. And all three of his wins were superb. From the utter dominance of Barcelona, to the mind-over-matter win at Spa, where he took on the world's greatest circuit in a car about the steering of which he had considerable doubts, to Monza, it was a great driver in a situation where greatness always shines — overcoming the deficiencies of a poor car. His team mate, Eddie Irvine (who bore well a difficult situation, where he was unable to grow used to the car because he was denied enough testing), is not a man who is easily impressed. But he was lost in admiration for Schumacher. 'The car is terrible,' Irvine would often say. 'How Michael does these

things, I just don't know.' As Berger said, Ferrari was in no
better situation than it had been in 1995, and arguably it
had taken a backward step. The difference was
Schumacher.

The only blemish on his record was Monaco, where he
made an elementary mistake on the first lap, but that
served only to remind us that he was human. Schumacher
started 1996 perceived as the best driver in the world, and
his reputation was enhanced no end in what was probably
his best season yet.

The same cannot be said, however, for either the team
he left or the one he joined. Ferrari was as chaotic as ever,
with an over-complex car failing to achieve what its
designers had aimed for from the start. It handled badly
and unpredictably, its titanium/carbon-fibre gearbox (a
wasteful and unnecessary expense, according to rival
designers) kept breaking, and then the car submitted to a
quite ridiculous run of appalling reliability mid-season.

In three races, Canada, France and Britain, Schumacher
and Irvine managed just 56 laps. It was laughable from the
outside, but clearly not when you were involved. 'I was
very angry at first,' Schumacher said after France, where
his engine failed on the warm-up lap. 'But at times like this
that you must control your emotions and stay cool and
rational. We must grit our teeth and continue to push on.'

Two weeks later, after retiring from the British GP after
just a handful of laps, the word he used to describe the
situation was 'absurd'.

But that was the end of the darkest days, and the rest of
the season served to remind you that as long as
Schumacher is there, Ferrari can never be discounted.

Which is what we used to say about Benetton. But it
had a tough time coming to terms with not having
Schumacher, and had its first winless season since 1988.
The B196 was probably the second best car in the field,
but without Schumacher that was not enough. The drivers
said the car was too nervous on the entry to corners, the
team worked hard to improve it. But despite fleeting
glimpses of competitiveness they fought for most of the
season for the minor podium places.

Boss Flavio Briatore was not amused, and all season
there were rumours that one or other of the drivers would
be replaced. By Silverstone, the man under pressure was
Alesi, of whose moods and temper fits the team was
apparently tiring. But moody or not, Alesi was generally by
far the most convincing Benetton driver on the track, and
talk of replacing him seemed faintly absurd. Whatever, he
and Berger will probably stay for 1997, when they will
hope for more from their car.

The same can be said of McLaren, which erased the
unhappy memories of 1995, but was still some way from a
return to form. The MP4/11 was much better than last
year's MP4/10, and at some tracks really quite good. David
Coulthard qualified just 0.5s from pole in Monaco, for
example, and either he or Mika Hakkinen would probably
have won on merit in Belgium had it not been for the
safety car.

But the team remained confused as to what made the
car slow. In fast corners it was good, but it struggled badly
in long, medium-speed bends and slow corners (it was
slower even than the Minardis in the middle part of the lap
at Estoril, a handling circuit), which would seem to
suggest a lack of grip. There was not much wrong, though,
with the Mercedes engine, as the trap speeds at
Hockenheim and Monza were to demonstrate.

Hakkinen and Coulthard proved evenly-matched, with
Coulthard quicker when he was confident in the rear of
the car, and Hakkinen on top when the Scot was not. As
boss Ron Dennis knows, give them a good car and they
will win races.

The rest were also-rans. Jordan was a disappointment,
falling back throughout the season after a promising start,
and suffering badly from the pains of trying to grow from

From right: Tyrrell
spent all season
searching for more
power and
reliability from
their Yamaha
alliance; Smile!
Panis samples the
joys of winning a
Grand Prix; There
were a number of
solutions to curb
cutting at Monza –
none worked
satisfactorily;
Middle row: Going
for gold. It was a
tough year for
Brundle and
Jordan; Flashes of
brilliance. When
Berger shone the
Benetton didn't

**Ligier's miraculous win at Monaco proved to be a flash in the pan**

Left: It's not all daggers at dawn stuff between Michael and Damon. Right: All the mod cons for Schumacher's new office. Far right: In between car problems Salo still impressed

**Hakkinen and Coulthard proved evenly-matched. Give them a good car and they'll win races**

Top: In the wake of a disappointing year Barrichello was left to ponder his options; Above right: Anyone for Hill? The Italians ponder their options. Main: One for the Christmas quiz... Coulthard wore one of Schumacher's helmets at Monaco after his own kept steaming up during warm-up

small team to big. But more people and equipment have been added and it hopes to continue throughout '97 the way it started '96. Of the drivers, both of whom can be quick, a terribly slow-starting Martin Brundle eventually got the upper hand on Rubens Barrichello.

Sauber's new Ford V10 was way down on power and rain was the only chance for Heinz-Harald Frentzen — against whom Johnny Herbert was able to re-establish his reputation — to demonstrate the talent he can display in a Williams next year; Ligier's miraculous Monaco win was a flash in the pan; and Arrows, like Jordan, went downhill after a promising start, with new owner Tom Walkinshaw investing nothing in the 1996 car, saving for his big push in1997, when he will have the Yamaha engine, whose appalling reliability wasted a good car at Tyrrell.

Many, though, think Walkinshaw will eventually make Arrows work, and Damon Hill, who feels he proved a point this season, is clearly one of them. The new World Champion felt Arrows was the best of a poor bunch of options for next year. But while Arrows may improve, at the front little is likely to change. Newey promises 'a few differences' on the FW19, which, one has to say, is likely to afford Williams another title courtesy of Villeneuve or Frentzen, with Schumacher providing the spoke in the wheels. The biggest point proved next year will probably be proved to Hill, and it will be the same lesson taught to the rest of F1 in 1996 — and that is exactly how good Williams-Renault really is. Damon, though, after crowning six years at the team with the biggest prize of all, probably does not need to be told. ■

# THE MOST COMPREHENSIVE FORMULA ONE MERCHANDISE CATALOGUE IN THE WORLD

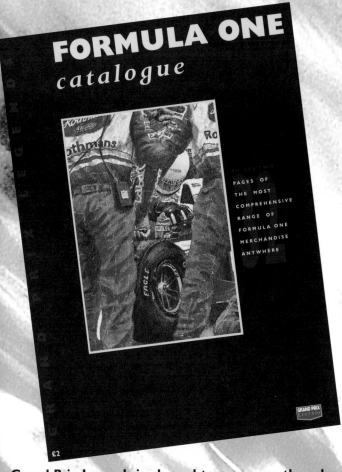

FORMULA ONE *catalogue*

PAGES OF THE MOST COMPREHENSIVE RANGE OF FORMULA ONE MERCHANDISE ANYWHERE

£2

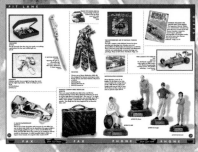

Grand Prix Legends is pleased to announce the release of the most comprehensive Formula One merchandise catalogue available anywhere.

From a Damon Hill keyring to a Sony Play Station complete with steering wheel and pedals, or even a Williams Italjet Scooter, this catalogue gives you access to a huge number of products celebrating Formula One, many of which cannot be found in the shops, even in those outlets supposedly dedicated to F1.

With something for everyone, be they six or 60, GPL's Formula One catalogue will retail at £2.00, but if you order yours before Christmas it is completely FREE. So order now unless you want to miss out on the most comprehensive array of F1 products. Anywhere.

Send coupon to Grand Prix Legends, FREEPOST *(No stamp required)*, LON 3270, London W10 6BR. Or call the Priority Tel Line: 0171 229 7399. Or send a Fax on: 0171 727 8054.

---

Please send me my FREE copy of the Grand Prix Legends Formula One Catalogue

Mr/Mrs/Ms :_____

Address :_____

_____

Postcode: ☐☐☐☐☐☐☐   Tel (Day):_____ (Evening:)_____   ASGPR/CAT

**Priority Tel Line**
**0171 229 7399**

**GRAND PRIX**
*LEGENDS*

# FORMULA 1 1996

*World Championship* AUSTRALIA  BRAZIL  ARGENTINA  EUROPE  SAN MARINO  MONAC

GRAND PRIX REPORTS **NIGEL ROEBUCK**

BRAZILIAN GP **ANDREW BENSON**
IN HINDSIGHT **ANDREW BENSON**

PHOTOGRAPHS **MARTYN ELFORD/
AUTOSPORT PHOTOGRAPHIC;
SUTTON MOTORSPORT IMAGES**

ADDITIONAL PHOTOGRAPHY BY
**BRYN WILLIAMS; COLIN McMASTER;
DARREN HEATH; ALLSPORT; BREWER**

CIRCUIT ILLUSTRATIONS **STEVE VILLIERS**

**SUTTON MOTORSPORT IMAGES**

# JACQUES LUCKS OUT AS HILL WINS

It looked like history was in the making in Melbourne as Jacques Villeneuve headed for victory in his first ever Grand Prix, but the win fell to his Williams team mate Damon Hill

There were five laps to go when they hung out a board from the Williams pit. At the top of it was the Canadian Maple Leaf, and beneath the word 'SLOW'. In the pressroom there were murmurings about team orders, but anyone with eyes to see knew otherwise: for 20 or more laps the white on Damon Hill's car had been turning yellow, which meant that Jacques Villeneuve's Renault V10 was losing oil.

Thus, the Australian Grand Prix lacked the fairytale ending for which most, to be honest, had hoped. Villeneuve, warned now that continuing at his present speed risked not finishing at all, backed off on the next straight, allowing Hill through to victory in the first race of the 1996 Formula 1 World Championship.

More significantly, it was the first Grand Prix of Jacques's career, and marked the most impressive debut anyone could remember. As it was, the young man started from pole position, which only Mario Andretti and Carlos Reutemann had done before, and he led calmly from the start, until the moment that board went out. When he crossed the line, second or not, the roof of the main grandstand nearly came off.

Such opposition as the Williams-Renault drivers faced on the marvellous new Melbourne park circuit came only from Ferrari. World champion Michael Schumacher ultimately retired with brake problems, but ran with Villeneuve and Hill for the first 20 laps, and Eddie Irvine then picked up the slack with an impressive third place. The rest, it would seem, have much to do.

'Can the kid take the heat?' broadly summed up the gossip in the paddock on Sunday morning. Villeneuve had stunned everyone with his performances in practice and qualifying, but there were those who muttered that the pressure of race day was a different matter. This was his first Grand Prix, after all, and he was on pole position, and there was a new starting procedure, and...

There were few who felt this way, however, who had watched Jacques in Indycars, or seen him in either pit or press room during the practice days. This is indeed a cool one.

Race morning, however, was rather less satisfactory than Jacques would have wished, for in the warm-up his Williams-Renault stopped out on the circuit, following the failure of a pipe in the hydraulic system. As a consequence the pole-sitter completed only eight laps. Ninth fastest, he was not too concerned.

The other FW18, Hill's car, duly set the best time, followed by the Benetton-Renaults of Alesi and Berger, both of whom were rather happier with their cars than in qualifying. Schumacher and Irvine were fourth and sixth with the Ferraris, sandwiching Frentzen's Sauber. To the fore, also, were Messrs Salo and

Verstappen, giving Tyrrell and Arrows a shout in the race.

Twenty cars only started the Australian Grand Prix, the lamentably slow Fortis having failed to qualify under the new '107%' rule. If this was a source of disappointment to the team's personnel, it was one of relief to the other drivers, who dreaded the presence of the yellow chicanes on a track refreshingly free of them.

Before the race, there was a degree of apprehension about the start, for not only was there a new man at the front of the grid, but also a new starting procedure. These fears were groundless, however, as the lights on the gantry flicked on, one by one, and then off, and Villeneuve, with just a touch of wheelspin, catapulted away into his first F1 lap, leading the pack.

The next concern had been the first corner, a tight right-hander, followed immediately by a left, which seemed like an invitation for closely-bunched cars to run into each other. Again, there was no problem, although Hill, who had not got away well, went in on a tight line and got out of shape, whereupon both Irvine and Schumacher zapped past him. 'At that moment,' Damon said, 'it was looking like a very long race...'

As it was, though, he was to get another chance, for at the end of the opening lap the red flag was out, the race stopped. Back at the second turn Martin Brundle was upside down, his Jordan-Peugeot effectively chopped in

Top: Mika Hakkinen was in the points on his much welcomed return to Grand Prix racing.
Above: Outside looking in. The start to the 1996 season is just minutes away. Right: Damon Hill's victorious Williams-Renault, stained by oil thrown out by Jacques Villeneuve's leaking Renault V10

"Today it happened to me, but another day it could happen to Damon or Eddie. It's part of racing"

*Jacques Villeneuve*

half. Despite the fact that the cockpit survival cell was plainly intact, it was with some incredulity that we watched him scramble from the wreckage, apparently without injury.

Brundle was the victim of a chain reaction accident, apparently triggered by his team mate Rubens Barrichello, who moved across Panis's Ligier in defence of his place, obliging Olivier to brake hard. Directly behind was Coulthard, and David believes his car was nudged from behind. Whatever, the McLaren swerved across the road, and hit Herbert's Sauber – which had Brundle's Jordan immediately behind. In a flash, the yellow car was tumbling over the pair of them, landing upside down, and skating along for a considerable distance, before coming to rest in a gravel trap.

Martin was brought back to the pits in an ambulance, and, once there, was seen to be running down the pitlane, in search of the race doctor, Sid Watkins. Just as Derek Warwick took the restart at Monza in 1990, after a fearful accident, so it was clear that Brundle had the same in mind.

'I felt absolutely fine,' he said. 'I knew the car was a write-off, but there was no way I'd travelled halfway round the world to watch the race...' Once 'Prof' had checked him over, pronounced him fit, Martin gave a thumbs-up to the crowd, then ran for the T-car. The accident had occurred at around 165mph. They are not normal, these people.

Elsewhere Coulthard was strapped into the spare McLaren, but for Herbert there was no such luxury. His car had been damaged beyond immediate repair, and now the spare Sauber was pressed into service for

Frentzen, whose original car had stopped with an electrical problem on the final parade lap.

Half an hour later came the restart – and again Villeneuve got it absolutely right, as also this time did Hill. Out of the first corner, the two Williams led from the two Ferraris, and then followed Alesi's Benetton, Hakkinen's McLaren, Barrichello, Frentzen, Berger and Salo.

On lap two, the unfortunate Brundle had another mishap – at the very same corner as before, albeit with less severe consequences. 'When you start from the pitlane, you don't get the final warm-up lap,' he explained, 'so of course the tyres are relatively cold. I was behind Diniz, and I simply couldn't believe how early he braked for the corner. Just slid into the back of him...' The Jordan stalled, and what Martin described as

**Above:** World championship leader Damon Hill offers his commiserations to Jacques Villeneuve as Williams celebrate a perfect result. **Below:** The season was just two corners old when Martin Brundle's spectacular crash brought out the red flags

# IN HINDSIGHT

Jacques Villeneuve made more of an impression than probably even he imagined on his Grand Prix debut in Melbourne.

His pole position was already earning him glowing praise after qualifying, with 1980 World Champion Alan Jones describing it as 'one of the most stunning displays I've ever witnessed in F1... (he has) the ability to establish himself as one of the greatest F1 drivers of all time.'

And after Jacques led team mate Damon Hill for most of the race, triple world champion Jackie Stewart (right) added his name to Villeneuve's ever-growing list of admirers. 'What we've seen here is the birth of a new superstar,' the Scot reckoned.

But as the season settled down, and a more rounded picture emerged, people began to wonder whether all that adulation had been heaped on the Indycar champion prematurely.

He's not as fast as Hill, the doubters began to mutter as Villeneuve struggled on many of the circuits new to him, and he's terribly slow at learning tracks. Perhaps he wasn't so good after all.

But by mid-summer it had become clear that his relative tardiness was only a result of the novelty of it all, and once he got to grips with F1, he turned out to be really rather good — as his stupendous drive in the Portuguese GP, and excellent pole at Spa-Francorchamps were to demonstrate. And Williams became ever more impressed with him the more the team grew to know him.

In the final analysis, then, perhaps not the new Ayrton Senna, but there are certainly many more years of success ahead.

'the weekend from hell' was over.

The Williams boys were having rather a good time of it, however. At the front, Villeneuve continued to lead from Hill, but the gap was never much more than a second, and usually less. Behind them, though, Schumacher had swiftly got by Irvine, and was moving up. At this stage of the game, indeed, it seemed that the Ferrari might genuinely challenge the Williams, although there was little doubt that Schumacher was right at the limit, his car noticeably more twitchy than the FW18s.

It is strong, though, the F310, as we came to appreciate on lap nine, when Irvine's car shrugged off a savaging from Alesi's Benetton. Once more the scene of the drama was turn two, and quite what Jean had in mind seems unclear. 'My lap times were quicker than Irvine's,' he said, 'and it was important to overtake, because the first three cars were getting away. I tried to pass, but it did not work...'

It did not. From impossibly far back, the Benetton lunged down the inside of the Ferrari, and the inevitable contact followed. 'With Alesi,' Eddie commented dryly, 'you never know what to expect.' The Ferrari continued without apparent damage, but the Benetton's left sidepod was in pieces.

Villeneuve, Hill and Schumacher continued to run up front, covered by a couple of seconds or so. Irvine, fourth, was now nearly 10 seconds adrift, and falling back all the time, albeit well clear of Hakkinen, driving a wonderful comeback race in a somewhat less than competitive McLaren. Right up with Mika were Barrichello, Berger and Salo. 'I should have been higher up.' said Gerhard, 'My first start was great, my second was terrible. And when you're in a bunch of cars here, it's difficult to get by. I decided to wait until the stops.'

These began in earnest on lap 20. Villeneuve, Hill and Schumacher had been trading new fastest laps, but Michael broke up the lead pattern by heading in for tyres and fuel. At 12.9 seconds, it was a good stop, and Irvine's, on lap 22, was quicker still,

but as the Williams duo continued to circulate, the true state of affairs in this race became apparent: Villeneuve and Hill would be stopping only once, their major rivals - notably Schumacher - twice. With a much lighter fuel load in the early stages, therefore, the Ferraris had flattered, but not to deceive for long.

Schumacher, moreover, was clearly in trouble after his stop, retaining his third place, but now losing seconds a lap to the leaders. The Ferrari was running out of brakes, and on lap 32 Michael came in. His mechanics attempted to bleed the front brakes, but the real problem lay with the rears, and immediately after rejoining the car ran briefly off the road. It didn't hit anything, but clearly there was no possibility of continuing, and Schumacher cruised gently back to the pits, where he retired. Michael is not accustomed to these things.

As the Ferrari departed, so the tussle at the front intensified. On lap 30 Villeneuve came in for his one and only stop, which, at 17.6 seconds, was not too speedy, but almost a second faster than Hill's, which followed two laps later. Despite that, Damon squeezed out of the pits marginally ahead of his team mate, and for half a lap the two blue cars were all but tangling as Jacques, his tyres fully up to temperature, sought a way by. This he finally found, and Hill correctly made no attempt to chop him. 'When you're racing against your own team mate,' he said, 'you obviously have to keep one eye on the team's results, as a whole.'

So Villeneuve was now back in the lead, but his Williams seemed to lack some of the fluency it had shown before its stop, and Jacques later confirmed that his second set of tyres had not the grip of the first. As well

Michael Schumacher plays hide and seek with Ferrari team mate Eddie Irvine

---

# AUSTRALIAN GP
## ROUND 1

**10 March 1996**
**FIA Formula 1 World Championship**

**Race data:** 58 laps of a 3.274 mile circuit
**Weather:** Dry and sunny
**Distance:** 189.9 miles

**Winner:** Damon Hill,
Williams-Renault FW18, 123.494mph
**Previous result:** N/A (new circuit)
**Fastest lap:** Jacques Villeneuve,
Williams-Renault FW18, 1m33.421s

## *Melbourne*

RESULTS © 1996 Federation Internationale de l'Automobile, 8 Place de la Concorde, Paris, 75008 France

## STARTING GRID

| | DRIVER | |
|---|---|---|
| 1 | Villeneuve | 1:32.371 |
| 2 | Hill | 1:32.509 |
| 3 | Irvine | 1:32.889 |
| 4 | Schumacher | 1:33.125 |
| 5 | Hakkinen | 1:34.054 |
| 6 | Alesi | 1:34.257 |
| 7 | Berger | 1:34.344 |
| 8 | Barrichello | 1:34.474 |
| 9 | Frentzen | 1:34.494 |
| 10 | Salo | 1:34.832 |
| 11 | Panis | 1:35.330 |
| 12 | Verstappen | 1:35.338 |
| 13 | Coulthard | 1:35.351 |
| 14 | Herbert | 1:35.453 |
| 15 | Katayama | 1:35.715 |
| 16 | Fisichella | 1:35.898 |
| 17 | Lamy | 1:36.109 |
| 18 | Rosset | 1:36.198 |
| 19 | Brundle | 1:36.286 |
| | Diniz | 1:36.298 |

Above: The kid took the heat. Below: A traffic jam with a difference in Melbourne

as that, he made a mistake, skating briefly off the road on lap 34, but holding on to his lead as he rejoined.

'It was my fault,' he frankly admitted. 'The car was heavy with fuel, and I left my braking too late. On the bumps it's easy to get the back wheels light under braking, and afterwards I was quite surprised to find myself actually pointing in the right direction...'

Hill was surprised, too. 'I really thought he'd lost it, and then I was worried that maybe he might clip me when he came back on the track, but fortunately it didn't happen. I had to lift off, though, and of course by the time I'd got back on the power, he'd gone!' Despite the occasional lurid moment, though, there was not a trace of animosity between the team mates afterwards, which bode well for the season ahead.

As Jacques and Damon continued

to battle, so Irvine's Ferrari began to catch them a little, but the local commentators, who got very excited by this, had perhaps overlooked the fact that Eddie would be stopping again for fuel and tyres, while the Williams pair would not. On lap 42, running 18 seconds adrift of Hill, the number 2 Ferrari was in, rejoining without losing its third place, but now running nearly 50 seconds from the front. Melbourne was strictly a fight between two drivers.

The last 15 laps were mesmeric. For some little time there had been the hint of trailing smoke from Villeneuve's car, and Hill's, close behind, was becoming grimier by the lap. 'I reckon Jacques started losing oil from about the time of our stops,' Damon said. 'I was getting covered in it - it was down my neck, and everything, and I'd used all my visor tear-offs, and was wiping my visor

with my glove, which just made visibility worse, of course. As well as that, I was worried that his engine might go bang, and we'd both go off on the oil...'

Thus we came to the closing laps, to the worsening oil smoke, to the board from the Williams pit to the leader. 'They were screaming in the radio for two laps,' Jacques said, 'so I understood that something was wrong. They could see the smoke, where I couldn't, and of course they had the telemetry as well. But then the red lights started coming on in the corners, and I knew the pressure was going down.'

It must have broken his heart to do it, but Villeneuve heeded the warning board, and surrendered his lead. 'Of course it was very disappointing, because the win was there. We had fought until those final laps, and, without the problem, it would have been a battle to the end. But, you know, second place in my first Grand Prix is great, so I still feel very happy.'

Over the last four laps, Jacques indeed rolled it off, aware of a considerable cushion to Irvine, and thinking - as Bernie Ecclestone had predicted of him - 'all the time in terms of winning a championship.' At the finish he was 38 seconds adrift of Hill, but could not have stood higher in the eyes of those who looked on. When the two of them stepped from their cars, their body language suggested that the battle had been fierce but fair.

No, Jacques said later, he didn't feel that he had been robbed. 'In racing, everything is pushed to the edge, and anything - car, engine, driver - can go wrong. Today it happened to me, but on another day it could happen to Damon or Eddie. It's part of racing.' He may be understandably weary of the constant comparisons with his famous father, but this good-natured honesty, this lack of guile, brought back to mind another Villeneuve we once knew.

Hill, leading the world championship for the first time in a year, was of course elated by victory, and quite reasonably so. It was also

evident that Irvine was agreeably surprised to finish third in his first race with Ferrari, and no surprise there, either, for this was a fine drive in an under-developed car with a brand new engine.

For Benetton, Melbourne was a disappointment, although Berger's fourth place at least yielded some points. Hakkinen took fifth for McLaren, but his expression afterwards suggested that the team still has a mountain to climb. Williams folk apart, perhaps the happiest face in the paddock was that of Harvey Postlethwaite, in whose under-financed Tyrrell 025 Mika Salo finished an excellent sixth.

Everyone in Australia, though, was talking about the new kid on the block. The young fresh-faced Canadian, who had arrived in Melbourne and so startled Formula 1, although, apparently, not himself. ∎

## RACE RESULTS

| | DRIVER | CAR | RACE | LAPS | RESULT |
|---|---|---|---|---|---|
| 1 | Damon Hill (GB) | Williams-Renault | 1m33.621s | 58 | 1h32m50.491s |
| 2 | Jacques Villeneuve (CDN) | Williams-Renault | 1m33.421s | 58 | 1h32m28.511s |
| 3 | Eddie Irvine (GB) | Ferrari | 1m34.533s | 58 | 1h33m53.062s |
| 4 | Gerhard Berger (A) | Benetton-Renault | 1m34.757s | 58 | 1h34m07.528s |
| 5 | Mika Hakkinen (FIN) | McLaren-Mercedes | 1m35.843s | 58 | 1h34m25.562s |
| 6 | Mika Salo (FIN) | Tyrrell-Yamaha | 1m35.280s | 57 | 1h33m03.181s |
| 7 | Olivier Panis (F) | Ligier-Mugen | 1m34.767s | 57 | 1h33m14.468s |
| 8 | Heinz-Harald Frentzen (D) | Sauber-Ford | 1m35.596s | 57 | 1h33m29.436s |
| 9 | Ricardo Rosset (BR) | Footwork-Hart | 1m36.557s | 56 | 1h33m21.629s |
| 10 | Pedro Diniz (BR) | Ligier-Mugen Honda | 1m37.024s | 56 | 1h33m25.689s |
| 11 | Ukyo Katayama (J) | Tyrrell-Yamaha | 1m36.373s | 55 | 1h32m51.827s |
| R | Pedro Lamy (P) | Minardi-Ford | 1m38.784s | 42 | Seat |
| R | Michael Schumacher (D) | Ferrari | 1m33.651s | 32 | Brakes |
| R | Giancarlo Fisichella (I) | Minardi-Ford | 1m38.077s | 32 | Clutch |
| R | Rubens Barrichello (BR) | Jordan-Peugeot | 1m35.064s | 29 | Engine |
| R | David Coulthard (GB) | McLaren-Mercedes | 1m37.746s | 24 | Stuck throttle |
| R | Jos Verstappen (NL) | Footwork-Hart | 1m36.649s | 15 | Engine |
| R | Jean Alesi (F) | Benetton-Renault | 1m35.519s | 9 | Accident |
| R | Martin Brundle (GB) | Jordan-Peugeot | 1m56.481s | 1 | Spin |

## CHAMPIONSHIP POSITIONS

| | DRIVER | PTS | CONSTRUCTOR | PTS |
|---|---|---|---|---|
| 1 | Hill | 10 | Williams-Renault | 16 |
| 2 | Villeneuve | 6 | Ferrari | 4 |
| 3 | Irvine | 4 | Benetton-Renault | 3 |
| 4 | Berger | 3 | McLaren-Mercedes | 2 |
| 5 | Hakkinen | 2 | Tyrrell-Yamaha | 1 |
| 6 | Salo | 1 | | |

FIA
FORMULA 1
WORLD
CHAMPIONSHIP

# CLASSY HILL SINGS IN THE RAIN

Damon Hill and Williams-Renault brought a touch of class to the Brazilian Grand Prix when the title favourite crushed his rivals in the torrential rain

## "It was a novel experience to go past Michael [Schumacher] with both of us staying apart and not going off the track"

*Damon Hill*

I think we're in very good shape for the race,' Damon Hill said on race morning, and he could not have been more right. Formula 1 drivers don't often like to make predictions as confident as that before a race, but in Brazil, it seemed as if nothing was going to stop Hill winning his third consecutive Grand Prix, including Adelaide last year.

On pole position by a clear second, Hill and his Williams-Renault were a country mile ahead of their opposition on the tricky, bumpy Interlagos track, and had the look of winners about them from the word go. If that level of superiority was not quite carried over into the race, Hill and Williams were still the quickest combination on the track.

The weather did its best to throw a spanner in the works, a torrential downpour drenched the track half an hour or so before the start which meant the race began in conditions so wet that the abnormally brave Jean Alesi was moved to say he was scared. But Hill made no mistakes at all in a race in which the track was changing lap by lap, just as he made none throughout the weekend, and cantered away to one of the most impressive victories of his career.

Behind him, Alesi was closest to making a fight of it; a feisty Rubens Barrichello was fast in qualifying and race, but eventually threw away the chance to climb onto the podium in front of his home fans; and Michael Schumacher drove what was probably one of his best ever races, in a Ferrari with handling something akin to a bucking bronco. Finally, the race weekend proved a humbling one for Jacques Villeneuve – the star of Melbourne – who dropped it while fending off Alesi for second place.

There were other noteworthy performances too, not least from Heinz-Harald Frentzen, but the day belonged to just one man. Damon Hill. Both he and Williams had them all guessing in Brazil.

The warm-up, like the practice days, was held in steamy Brazilian sunshine. Hill was down in seventh, 0.3s behind quickest man Martin Brundle, but Damon seemed unconcerned, chatting calmly in the garage in the break before the race.

And in the end it all meant nothing anyway. Rain was predicted for the afternoon, and sure enough, clouds had been gathering all morning. For a while, it looked like it may stay dry, but with 35 minutes to go, the heavens opened, and everyone's carefully-laid plans came to nothing.

When it rains in Brazil, it rains with a vengeance, and when the cars went out for the reconnaissance laps demanded by a change in track conditions, they could barely be seen for the huge rooster tails of spray.

The drivers were worried men. 'The rain started coming down again while we were actually sitting in the cars waiting to go out,' Schumacher said, 'so there could have been no discussion about not racing. But I told

my team to ask the race director to be very careful in those conditions, because it was undriveable and we could not have raced.'

Fortunately, however, the rain abated, and even if it did not cease completely for some time, it eased off enough for a race to go ahead. But even then, visibility in the early laps would be virtually non-existent.

Getting a good start would be all important on such a wet track, and this was the closest Hill came to a mistake on Sunday.

As the lights went out, Barrichello's Jordan, from his excellent second place on the grid, came looming up on the inside on the run down to the first corner. Hill dealt with that, only to find Villeneuve trying to make it

past around the outside. It was touch and go for a moment, but unlike in Melbourne three weeks before, Hill made it clear he was in no mood to trifle, and forced his team mate back into second place.

'The conditions were, shall we say, risky,' Hill said. 'Obviously I was in the best possible position, on a clear track, but even so there were rivers on the track and quite heavy rainfall even after the start. I can hardly imagine what it was like for the guys behind. I was eager to use that moment to get a gap.'

He was true to his word, and was soon streaking away at the front. After just three laps he had built up an astonishing 9.3s lead over Villeneuve, and he extended that to 15.5s after

ten laps. Driving smoothly and consistently, he appeared completely unruffled. Already, the race was seemingly looking won.

As Hill suspected though, his pursuers were having a torrid time in his wake. Alesi, who always excels in the wet, had made a cracking start and jumped up to third from fifth. 'I knew the visibility would be very difficult as soon as we got going,' he said, 'so I wanted to make some places at the start. After that, the visibility was so bad I was actually quite scared.'

# IN HINDSIGHT

Such was the ease with which Damon Hill dominated the Brazilian Grand Prix that people were already beginning to wonder how the Englishman could lose the world championship.

But the new 'serene' Hill, as many newspapers were beginning to see him, counselled caution. 'The car is good and I want to capitalise on that while I can,' he said, 'because for sure that will change during the season.'

It didn't, but the serenity did – to an extent.

As Williams technical director Patrick Head (pictured right) murmured at the time, it's very easy to be serene when you're dominating races, let's see how serene he is when he's under pressure.

And true enough, a few mistakes began to creep back into Hill's driving later in the season as the pressure from team mate Jacques Villeneuve mounted.

Out of the car, though, the mask of calm tended to stay resolutely in place, although it slipped somewhat at Hockenheim, when it was first written that he was to lose his Williams drive for 1997 (see *Hindsight*, German GP, page 88).

How much of the new serene, confident Hill, people were beginning to ask by September, was manufactured by a determined effort on his part to be more media-friendly? He had, after all, hired an image consultant over the winter, who became increasingly visible as the season went on.

But did it really matter? Hill was, is, and will remain one of the more down-to-earth of F1's superstars, and if he's found a more effective method of dealing with the pressures of the job, who can begrudge him that?

Schumacher had the same problem. 'I couldn't see anything. I was just trying to keep the car on the road.'

If anything, though, the rain was helping to produce a cracking race. Before long, there was a five-car battle for second place, with Villeneuve ahead of Alesi, Barrichello, Schumacher and the flying Frentzen.

At this early stage, Barrichello was doing his best to progress, but try as he might – and he swapped places with Alesi at the first corner several times – the Frenchman proved as tough a customer to pass as ever.

Frentzen, driving hard in the Sauber, was having a similar problem with Schumacher, although he passed his countryman briefly at the start of lap 17, only to be repassed before the end of the lap. The Saubers were tricky all weekend, but Frentzen said the car felt good in the race. He had to rely on an excellent Sauber pitstop to pass the Ferrari, but it was all for nought: engine failure put paid soon afterwards to yet another reminder of the German's talent.

Jos Verstappen, driving a blinding race in the Arrows, was another man on the move. The Dutchman looked for a time like he might join the battle for second place, and was the fastest man of all on the track on laps 10 and 14. Sadly however, by lap 19, his Hart engine had cried enough, putting an end to yet another extremely promising performance.

Up in second place, meanwhile, Villeneuve had settled into the tricky wet conditions and after about 10 laps he and Hill were circulating at a pretty similar pace. At the same time he was proving himself to be a tough customer in his battle with Alesi, but while Villeneuve got away with exuberance in Melbourne, Alesi was about to bring him down to earth with a bang after the dream start to the Canadian's Grand Prix season.

The Benetton drew alongside the Williams on the back straight on lap 26. Villeneuve rather naughtily squeezed him right over towards the grass on the inside, but Alesi forced him back towards the outside again, claiming the dry line. They went into the corner side by side, and Villeneuve, on the wet outside line, simply lost the car, the Williams pirouetting gently into the gravel trap and out of the race.

'Villeneuve had a problem with, I think, a Forti,' Alesi said, 'and he had to slow down before the straight. I was on the inside line for the next corner, so when I turned in he was already in trouble – and then I didn't see him anymore.'

Jacques, honest as ever, admitted the fault was his. 'I made a mistake,' he shrugged. 'I went a little bit wide, because Jean was on the inside and I didn't want to chop him off. I had two wheels on the wet and it slid more than I thought it was going to, and that was it.' Once clear of Villeneuve, Alesi began to carve into Hill's lead. He closed on the Williams by a second or so a lap, and to add extra spice to the situation, the track was beginning to dry, and the two of them, clearly on a one-stop strategy, as opposed to most behind them, had their pitstops looming.

No sooner did he look in with a shout, however, than Alesi was to make his task more difficult for himself. Having closed the gap from 17.5s to 13.1s from laps 27 to 31, he ran wide on to the grass, allowing Barrichello to pass him again.

Not one to be deterred easily, Jean set about all over again catching Damon, and the tension was heightened when it started to rain once more, and the Williams pit briefly readied more wets for Hill. Almost immediately, however, the rain stopped, and when Damon finally came in on lap 40 it was for slicks. It was, as Hill put it, 'a very difficult race to call'.

'We decided that the race was going to be wet,' he said, 'at least for the first part, and that meant a one-stop strategy. That worked absolutely perfectly and the stop fitted exactly into the window for the change-over to slicks. It was very good planning by the team.'

Alesi followed him in a lap later, and immediately the pair set about trading fastest laps. It looked like a no-holds-barred charge in an attempt at an against-all-odds victory by Alesi, but he had, he said, other things on his mind.

Rumours had been flying around the paddock during the weekend that Benetton had given Alesi a serious talking to after his ill-advised and ill-fated passing attempt on Eddie Irvine at Melbourne, and after the race, Alesi admitted unprompted that the rumours were true – the implication being that he had been told to finish at all costs.

'My car was very easy to drive in the wet here,' he said, 'but after the accident at Melbourne I was tied a little by the team, so I was being very careful to finish here. I was not in my best condition for this situation.'

Hill, as had looked likely all along, now had the race won, and his only remaining problem came with 15 laps to go, when he came up to lap fourth-placed Barrichello, who was storming along having dropped behind Schumacher after his second stop.

The World Champion made a lot of time up on the Jordan between the pair's first and second stops – both stayed on wet tyres on their first visits to the pits, but while Schumacher made his on lap 24, when the track was still pretty wet, Barrichello plumped for his second set of wets on lap 34, when the track was probably good for drys. He was back again, for slicks this time, only nine laps later, and when he came back onto the track, Schumacher was ahead.

Now, though, Barrichello was trying to make amends. The Jordan was clearly quicker than the Ferrari, and Barrichello was on Schumacher's tail by lap 55. Hill, meanwhile, was looming up behind Barrichello to lap him, and he still had Alesi charging along behind trying to make up the gap to the lead.

It was a tricky situation for Damon. Should he try for a way past both? Or with a 20-odd second lead over Alesi could he afford to wait and watch – a decision which could involve him in any accident should Barrichello be after glory at home at any cost.

He wanted a way past. 'I was most concerned about Jean,' Hill said. 'If I had seen an opportunity to get past Rubens cleanly, I would have taken it. Unfortunately, for Barrichello, it didn't come to that.'

Indeed not. On lap 60, Barrichello

---

# BRAZILIAN GP

## ROUND 2

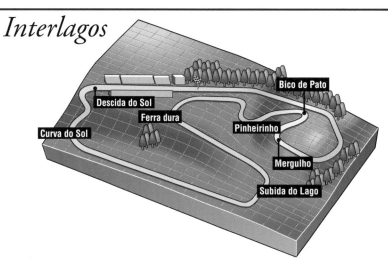

*Interlagos*

Track labels: Descida do Sol, Curva do Sol, Ferra dura, Bico de Pato, Pinheirinho, Mergulho, Subida do Lago

31 March 1996
FIA Formula 1 World Championship

**Race data:** 71 laps of a 2.687 mile circuit
**Weather:** Wet and drying
**Distance:** 190.825 miles

**Winner:** Damon Hill, Williams-Renault FW18, 104.19mph
**Previous result:** Michael Schumacher, Benetton-Renault B195, 116.15mph
**Fastest lap:** Damon Hill, Williams-Renault FW18, 1m21.547s

RESULTS © 1996 Federation Internationale de l'Automobile, 8 Place de la Concorde, Paris, 75008 France

## STARTING GRID

| | DRIVER | |
|---|---|---|
| 1 | Hill | 1:18.111 |
| 2 | Barrichello | 1:19.092 |
| 3 | Villeneuve | 1:19.254 |
| 4 | Schumacher | 1:19.474 |
| 5 | Alesi | 1:19.484 |
| 6 | Brundle | 1:19.519 |
| 7 | Hakkinen | 1:19.607 |
| 8 | Berger | 1:19.762 |
| 9 | Frentzen | 1:19.799 |
| 10 | Irvine | 1:19.951 |
| 11 | Salo | 1:20.000 |
| 12 | Herbert | 1:20.144 |
| 13 | Verstappen | 1:20.157 |
| 14 | Coulthard | 1:20.167 |
| 15 | Panis | 1:20.426 |
| 16 | Katayama | 1:20.427 |
| 17 | Rosset | 1:20.440 |
| 18 | Lamy | 1:21.491 |
| 19 | Badoer | 1:23.174 |
| 20 | Montermini | 1:23.454 |
| 21 | Marques | no time |
| 22 | Diniz | no time |

## "The Ferrari's handling is so bad you would not believe"

*Michael Schumacher*

lunged past Schumacher at the end of the pit straight, only to be repassed on the exit of the first corner. And further around the lap, Barrichello's chances of canonisation at home evaporated when he spun off at the end of the back straight. It looked like an unforced error, but Barrichello claimed that brakes had overheated in the passing attempt, which were a contributing factor to it.

Whatever the reason he was out of the race, and it had been a hairy moment for Hill. 'When Rubens lost it, I didn't know which way he was going,' he said. 'He started to go sideways and for a moment all I could see was a sideways Jordan in front of

me. Fortunately I had sufficient gap to wait before I went through.'

With that, Hill only had to lap Schumacher – 'that brought a wry smile,' Hill joked, 'it was a novel experience to go past Michael with both of us staying apart and not going off the track.' And that he duly did.

It was a fully deserving win, but behind him Alesi and particularly Schumacher drove excellent races. The reigning World Champion, in fact, will probably reflect with satisfaction on what was probably one of his best ever Grands Prix. The Ferrari was evil to drive in Interlagos, and he extracted every last ounce of performance out of it.

Both Mikas, Hakkinen and Salo, also shone, Hakkinen driving a sensible race in the tricky McLaren after a poor start, and Salo for the second race running being stuck behind it and unable to pass for a lack of power from the Yamaha in the Tyrrell. The pair spent most of the race dicing, as in their Formula 3 days, but when the track began to dry, the McLaren's Mercedes power advantage began to tell.

'We'd passed each other a few times after the pitstops but he always could pass me on the straight,' Salo said. 'I could only just hold on in his slipstream. Eventually, though, I just couldn't keep the same pace. I had a

**Despite this off in practice, Michael Schumacher drove one of his best races**

bit of a go at him, but I nearly lost it, so I dropped back, and from then on I was just concentrating on keeping ahead of Panis, who was catching me.'

A fascinating race, then, and some superb performances against the odds throughout the field. But for all that, really, the Grand Prix was about no one but the faultless Hill and his superb Williams-Renault. There was still a long way to go in the race for the World Championship, but on this evidence, it showed that the rest had a lot of work to do if anyone was to stop a Hill-Williams walkover. ■

## RACE RESULTS

| | DRIVER | CAR | RACE | LAPS | RESULT |
|---|---|---|---|---|---|
| 1 | Damon Hill (GB) | Williams-Renault | 1m21.547s | 71 | 1h49m52.976s |
| 2 | Jean Alesi (F) | Benetton-Renault | 1m21.866s | 71 | 1h50m10.958s |
| 3 | Michael Schumacher (D) | Ferrari | 1m22.889s | 70 | 1h50m00.569s |
| 4 | Mika Hakkinen (FIN) | McLaren-Mercedes | 1m22.283s | 70 | 1h50m16.004s |
| 5 | Mika Salo (FIN) | Tyrrell-Yamaha | 1m22.483s | 70 | 1h50m26.315s |
| 6 | Olivier Panis (F) | Ligier-Mugen Honda | 1m22.743s | 70 | 1h50m34.031s |
| 7 | Eddie Irvine (GB) | Ferrari | 1m23.062s | 70 | 1h51m11.438s |
| 8 | Pedro Diniz (BR) | Ligier-Mugen Honda | 1m23.576s | 69 | 1h50m27.806s |
| 9 | Ukyo Katayama (J) | Tyrrell-Yamaha | 1m22.722s | 69 | 1h51m00.929s |
| 10 | Pedro Lamy (P) | Minardi-Ford | 1m23.559s | 68 | 1h50m02.877s |
| 11 | Luca Badoer (I) | Forti-Ford | 1m25.627s | 67 | 1h50m52.957s |
| 12 | Martin Brundle (GB) | Jordan-Peugeot | 1m22.043s | 64 | Spin |
| R | Rubens Barrichello (BR) | Jordan-Peugeot | 1m22.359s | 59 | Spin |
| R | Heinz-Harald Frentzen (D) | Sauber-Ford | 1m36.166s | 36 | Engine |
| R | David Coulthard (GB) | McLaren-Mercedes | 1m36.245s | 29 | Spin |
| R | Johnny Herbert (GB) | Sauber-Ford | 1m38.127s | 28 | Electrics |
| R | Jacques Villeneuve (CDN) | Williams-Renault | 1m36.383s | 26 | Spin |
| R | Gerhard Berger (A) | Benetton-Renault | 1m36.998s | 26 | Hydraulics |
| R | Andrea Montermini (I) | Forti-Ford | 1m40.661s | 26 | Spin |
| R | Ricardo Rosset (BR) | Footwork-Hart | 1m36.981s | 24 | Accident |
| R | Jos Verstappen (NL) | Footwork-Hart | 1m35.435s | 19 | Engine |
| R | Tarso Marques (BR) | Minardi-Ford | | 0 | Spin |

## CHAMPIONSHIP POSITIONS

| | Driver | pts | Constructor | pts |
|---|---|---|---|---|
| 1 | Hill | 20 | Williams-Renault | 26 |
| 2 | Villeneuve | 6 | Benetton-Renault | 9 |
| 3 | Alesi | 6 | Ferrari | 8 |
| 4 | Hakkinen | 5 | McLaren-Mercedes | 5 |
| 5 | Irvine | 4 | Tyrrell-Yamaha | 3 |
| 6 | Schumacher | 4 | Ligier-Mugen-Honda | 1 |

FIA
FORMULA 1
WORLD
CHAMPIONSHIP

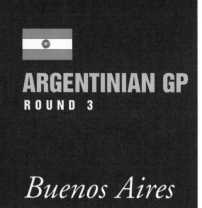
# HILL STRIKES AGAIN IN ARGENTINA

Damon Hill admitted that it couldn't get any better after he survived a dose of 'Buenos Aires belly' and a concerted threat from Michael Schumacher to take his third win in a row

> **"I feel I would have finished close to Damon, but I don't believe I could have beaten him"**
>
> *Michael Schumacher*

**Damon Hill may not have been the Argentinian fans' favourite, but he was undoubtedly the man of the moment**

He may have suffered from what may be discreetly termed 'an intestinal problem' in Buenos Aires, but that didn't stop Damon Hill taking his second flag-to-flag victory in a week, after starting, as at Interlagos, from the pole.

Going into the race, Hill had eaten almost nothing for two days, and was a little concerned about his strength and stamina, but afterwards he felt remarkably well, and paid tribute to his new fitness trainer. 'I definitely feel sharper this year,' Damon said, after another flawless performance.

Jacques Villeneuve, at another circuit new to him, made it a Williams-Renault one-two, and if it was another fine drive by the F1 rookie, he had reason to be pleased

with second place, for he made a dreadful start, and was back in ninth place on the opening lap. Swiftly, Villeneuve moved himself up to fifth after a determined effort, but by then the leaders were in the far distance, and he was fortunate to benefit from a 'yellow' period at mid-race, following an accident to Luca Badoer.

Third went to Jean Alesi, but the Benetton-Renault driver would surely have been second, had he not stalled during a fuel stop. Team mate Gerhard Berger was running second when his car's rear suspension failed, but there was some consolation for Jordan- Peugeot after the disappointments of Brazil, Rubens Barrichello finishing fourth, ahead of Eddie Irvine's Ferrari, which scrabbled

home narrowly ahead of Jos Verstappen's Arrows-Hart.

For McLaren-Mercedes, the Argentinian Grand Prix was an unmitigated disaster, and Michael Schumacher, too, came away empty-handed, albeit after inspired driving in both qualifying and race. The Ferrari's rear wing was damaged by accident debris flung up by Hill. Thus far, at least, the luck was riding with Damon in 1996, and deservedly so.

Conditions were beautiful on race morning, sunny and blue, but also cool, so that times in the warm-up were, in many cases, appreciably quicker than in the previous day's official qualifying session. Of these, the most dramatically improved were the Benettons of Alesi and Berger,

Martin Brundle and Tarso Marques blamed each other for this crash

both a couple of seconds inside their grid times.

There were, of course, murmurings that perhaps Jean and Gerhard had been running with very light fuel loads, but Benetton is a serious team. Undoubtedly, the lower temperatures made for a quicker track, but both drivers were much happier with the balance and grip of their cars than in qualifying, the team having worked all night on a series of set-up changes.

Schumacher's Ferrari set third fastest time, with the Williams duo next up, but neither Hill nor Villeneuve were looking to set dramatic times, instead making sure of their race set-ups.

Shortly before noon, there was a ceremony on the pit straight in honour of a nation's hero, Juan Manuel Fangio, who died the previous July. The Mercedes-Benz W196 from the Balcarce museum was on hand, and word was that Juan 'Manuelito', who raced Indycars this year for Dan Gurney, would take a lap in it. Ultimately, the straight-eight engine was never so much as started: the great man had been the last to drive the car, went the local wisdom, and would remain so. A less romantic explanation was that the W196, moribund in the museum for so many years, was no longer operational. Whatever, it was immensely touching to see the crowd rise in reverent applause as the lone silver car, pushed by four mechanics in Mercedes overalls, made its entrance.

Throughout the preceding week, there had been talk of mixed conditions on race day, but the sun continued to beat down as one o'clock approached. 'I definitely think this will be a race where strategy is important,' Schumacher had said, 'and for sure there will be a lot of retirements – this place is so slippery, and even worse if you get off line...' Michael planned on three stops for his Argentinian Grand Prix, but most of his rivals, notably the Williams and Benetton drivers, were going for two.

When the lights went out, Hill got away perfectly, and Schumacher went with him, but unfortunately Villeneuve, after exemplary getaways in Melbourne and Interlagos, squandered his hard-earned third qualifying slot. 'It was my own fault,' he said. 'I didn't release the clutch enough, so it slipped for a long time

before it grabbed. A lot of cars got past me before the first corner.'

There was no denying that. Jacques was ninth at the end of the first lap, struggling to get through a second group, comprising Coulthard, Barrichello, Verstappen and Hakkinen. The first group – Hill, Schumacher, Alesi and Berger – had already checked out, and after a single lap Villeneuve was already 8.4 seconds down on his team mate.

More to the point, the gap grew in chunks every time around, for Coulthard, although running fifth, was losing at least a second a lap to the leading quartet. It was not David's fault – he was in an unwieldy McLaren, after all – but he necessarily dictated the pace of those immediately behind him.

Jacques set to his task marvellously, passing Hakkinen on lap three, Verstappen on lap four, Barrichello on lap five, and Coulthard on lap eight. Now he had only the big four ahead of him, but Berger, the last of these,

**Above right:** A Renault Clio leads Damon Hill!
**Far right:** Jos Verstappen starred again on his way to sixth. **Below:** No luck again for Gerhard Berger

# IN HINDSIGHT

The horrific fiery accident that befell Ligier driver Pedro Diniz (below) in the Argentinian Grand Prix threw the spotlight vividly on the dangers of refuelling for the fourth time since the practice was re-introduced into Formula 1 for the 1994 season.

But in the wake of the accident caused by a breather valve jamming open on Diniz's car, and despite the vast majority of people expressing their concerns about the safety of the practice, there was no sign of a ban.

Max Mosley, the president of the sport's governing body, showed no sign of shifting from the view he expressed before the season started – that refuelling was a natural part of F1, that the risks were as minimised as they possibly could be, and that it added an extra cerebral dimension for spectators. This latter point was not seen at the time as an admission that the racing itself was boring, with little on-track action, but that's another story (see Canadian GP, page 74).

However, the thought that as much danger as possible was taken out of refuelling did little to change the views of those who are directly involved with it every other weekend. The rate of failures was too high, they said, and so far F1 has been lucky to have had only minor leaks.

As one engineer put it in Argentina: 'The whole thing is f***ing dangerous, but that's what they want, so we're stuck with it.'

was by now 15 seconds up the road. 'It was fun to fight with those guys, and overtake, but after that I was too far behind to catch up any more,' said Villeneuve.

For a little while it looked as though Schumacher really might make a race of it with Hill, for in the early stages he tailed the Williams closely, and it was not until lap seven that Damon established a clear second's lead. What had to be borne in mind, of course, was that the Ferrari was almost certainly going to make one more stop than the Williams, and was therefore running a lighter fuel load. As in the opening laps at Melbourne, however, Michael's sheer combativeness impressed.

Gradually, gradually, though, Hill started to sneak away, out of range, and Schumacher, his car ever looser, began to slip back towards the Benettons of Alesi and Berger. Jean, never more fired up than when he sees red ahead of him, closed to within a second by lap 11, only to make a mistake next time round, which meant starting the chase all over again.

On lap 19 Hakkinen brought his McLaren into the pits, but this was not the beginning of the planned first stops, for the mechanics quickly pushed the car into the garage. Never higher than eighth, Mika had been plagued by a throttle control problem almost from the start.

As expected, given the suspicion that he would be stopping three times, Schumacher was into the pits early, on lap 21, getting on his way in 7.1 seconds, and falling temporarily to fourth place. Next time round, Alesi was in, and although the stop was fractionally faster (6.8s), he just failed to get out in front of Schumacher. That battle recommenced.

Hill and Villeneuve made their stops on laps 24 and 25 respectively, and Berger, too, was in. With the front runners all fed and watered, the situation now was that Hill led Schumacher by five seconds, with Alesi another second back, then Berger, with Villeneuve still fifth, still out of touch with the leaders. But help - if such it may be called - was

at hand for Jacques, in the shape of the Safety Car, which came out on lap 27. A yellow car, Badoer's Forti, was off the road, upside down.

The Italian eventually scrambled free, quite unhurt, but Hill - the man with most to lose from the intervention of the Safety Car - was the first to agree that the decision to bring it out had been correct.

Badoer had tangled with Diniz, but if the Brazilian got out of that contretemps relatively unscathed, there was greater drama awaiting him. As the rest of the field tooled round, Pedro dashed into the pits, where his Ligier received a new nosecone, as well as fresh tyres and more fuel. When the hose was withdrawn, the return valve on the car's refuelling nozzle failed to close.

The consequence was a horrifying fire, albeit not, mercifully, in the pits. Diniz got back on the track, but the first time he put the brakes on hard, gasoline spewed on the hot engine, and instantly the back of the car was ablaze. Worse, the Ligier spun, so that the flames were fanned back over the cockpit area.

It seemed an agonisingly long time before Diniz got himself out of that car, but eventually he could be seen in the midst of the flames, and as he ran clear, fire marshals arrived. The car was a sorry mess afterwards, as was the driver's helmet which had been charred black. 'I realise,' Pedro said, 'that I'm fortunate to come away with just a slight burn to my left hand.' That seemed like a consummate understatement.

After five laps 'under yellow', the race restarted at the end of lap 32. 'I took it a little bit easily at first,' Hill said, 'because the pace car' - a Renault Clio - 'was driven so ridiculously slowly that not only did the tyres cool, but they also began to lose pressure. The bad bump into turn seven, for example, was suddenly much worse than it had been before.'

As in the opening laps of the race, Schumacher initially stayed with Hill, keeping within a second of him, but soon Damon once more eased away, and Alesi moved up to attack the Ferrari - which was now in trouble.

Soon after the restart, it transpired, Hill's Williams had run over a piece of

Above: Diniz in the oven. Below: Luca Badoer's attempts at burying his head in the ground brought out the Safety Car

debris (from the Badoer/Diniz incident), and flicked it back towards Schumacher. 'I saw something black flying towards me,' recounted Michael, 'and instinctively ducked, because I thought it was going to hit me in the face. Soon afterwards the car got so loose that I realised something was wrong.'

Alesi, close behind, knew more about it than Schumacher. 'I saw the Ferrari's rear wing suddenly bend,' he said, 'and I got on the radio to ask Flavio Briatore to tell Ferrari there was a problem with Michael's car, but maybe it was too difficult for him to hear me.'

On lap 40 Schumacher was into the pits for fuel and tyres, having revised his strategy in light of the 'yellow' period, and cut his planned stops from three to two. Although now back in eighth place, he was theoretically able to run through to the flag.

Alesi stopped on lap 44, took on fuel and tyres in seven seconds - and then stalled, which dropped him from second to eighth, immediately behind

---

## ARGENTINIAN GP

### ROUND 3

**7 April 1996**
**FIA Formula 1 World Championship**

**Race data:** 72 laps of a 2.645-mile circuit
**Weather:** Dry and sunny
**Distance:** 190.44 miles

**Winner:** Damon Hill,
Williams-Renault FW18, 99.427mph
**Previous result:** Michael Schumacher,
Benetton-Renault B195, 105.291mph
**Fastest lap:** Jean Alesi,
Benetton-Renault B196, 1m29.413s

## *Buenos Aires*

Horquilla
Senna
Entry to the esses
Confiteria
Ascari
Esses
Ombu
Curva Numero Uno
No8 Curvon
WATER

### STARTING GRID

| | DRIVER | |
|---|---|---|
| 1 | Hill | 1:30.346 |
| 2 | Schumacher | 1:30.598 |
| 3 | Villeneuve | 1:30.907 |
| 4 | Alesi | 1:31.038 |
| 5 | Berger | 1:31.262 |
| 6 | Barrichello | 1:31.404 |
| 7 | Verstappen | 1:31.615 |
| 8 | Hakkinen | 1:31.801 |
| 9 | Coulthard | 1:32.001 |
| 10 | Irvine | 1:32.058 |
| 11 | Frentzen | 1:32.130 |
| 12 | Panis | 1:32.407 |
| 13 | Katayama | 1:32.407 |
| 14 | Marques | 1:32.502 |
| 15 | Brundle | 1:32.696 |
| 16 | Salo | 1:32.903 |
| 17 | Herbert | 1:33.256 |
| 18 | Diniz | 1:33.424 |
| 19 | Lamy | 1:33.727 |
| 20 | Rosset | 1:33.752 |
| 21 | Badoer | 1:34.830 |
| 22 | Montermini | 1:35.651 |

Schumacher once more. Within two laps, he was by the Ferrari, into the first turn, and Michael, his car now near undriveable, retired to the pits forthwith. His rear wing, split by the initial impact of the flying debris, had by now begun to break up, its top plane gone altogether. A weekend's magnificent toil was shot to hell.

In all this concentration on the very front end of the field, it was easy to overlook developments and disappointments further down the order. Mika Salo, for example, whose Argentinian weekend had started with such promise, retired his Tyrrell-Yamaha, whose fly-by-wire throttle

was sticking, and Jos Verstappen, quite brilliant in the Arrows-Hart, fell from fifth to 11th after a very slow stop. He would recover splendidly by the end of the race.

The luckless Brundle was out, too, after a coming-together with Tarso Marques. The Brazilian youth was livid, claiming that he had been deliberately 'brake-tested'. 'I think he must have missed his braking point,' was how Martin saw it.

Now that Schumacher was gone, and Alesi delayed, Hill's horizon was clear. After the second round of stops, at the 50-lap mark, he continued to lead, with Berger now second, 12

seconds behind, and Villeneuve third. Initially, Jacques looked set to do battle with Gerhard, but lost three seconds in a single lap, delayed by Montermini in the wretchedly slow Forti. Villeneuve was comfortable, however, for Alesi, behind him, appeared rather to have gone to sleep in this period of the race.

That began to change on lap 56, when Berger unexpectedly came into the pits a third time. 'Under braking at the end of the straight,' he said, 'the car felt strange, and the right front wheel came off the ground. I came in because I thought I must have a puncture in the left rear.'

All was well with the tyre, however, and Gerhard was on his way again, after only six seconds, but at the fourth turn he pulled off, with rear suspension failure. 'I'm terribly disappointed,' he said, 'because the car was perfect up to that point, and I really needed a good result.'

What had been an assured second place now fell to Villeneuve, or so it seemed. But in the closing laps Alesi picked up the pace once more, suddenly turning in times as much as two seconds quicker than in his 'quiet' period, and setting the fastest lap of the afternoon. It never truly

looked as though he would catch Villeneuve, but he may regret that he did not begin the chase a little earlier.

The late laps were enlivened, too, by Verstappen's chase of Irvine's Ferrari. Already, on lap 60, there had been the once unimaginable sight of an Arrows passing a McLaren, as Jos calmly picked off the hapless Coulthard, and now there loomed the possibility of his going by a Ferrari.

On the very last lap, with Irvine's car now stuck in sixth gear, Verstappen went for it, but although he passed the Ferrari into a corner, his entry speed was simply too high, and he ran wide, surrendering the place once again. No matter: he made it home in the points.

The Williams-Renaults, though, got 16 of them, Hill and Villeneuve having scored their second one-two in three races. 'My radio didn't work from the very beginning,' Damon said, 'but otherwise the car was absolutely perfect. No complaints at all. I can't believe the way this season has started – it simply can't get any better than this, can it?'

Maybe it could. 'I feel I would have finished not that far from Damon,' said a muted Schumacher, 'but I don't believe I could have beaten him.' ■

## RACE RESULTS

| | DRIVER | CAR | RACE | LAPS | RESULT |
|---|---|---|---|---|---|
| 1 | Damon Hill (GB) | Williams-Renault | 1m29.653s | 72 | 1h54m55.322s |
| 2 | Jacques Villeneuve (CDN) | Williams-Renault | 1m30.163s | 72 | 1h55m07.489s |
| 3 | Jean Alesi (F) | Benetton-Renault | 1m29.413s | 72 | 1h55m10.076s |
| 4 | Rubens Barrichello (BR) | Jordan-Peugeot | 1m31.443s | 72 | 1h55m50.453s |
| 5 | Eddie Irvine (GB) | Ferrari | 1m31.372s | 72 | 1h56m00.313s |
| 6 | Jos Verstappen (NL) | Footwork-Hart | 1m31.099s | 72 | 1h56m04.235s |
| 7 | David Coulthard (GB) | McLaren-Mercedes | 1m31.408s | 72 | 1h56m08.722s |
| 8 | Olivier Panis (F) | Ligier-Mugen | 1m31.343s | 72 | 1h56m09.617s |
| 9 | Johnny Herbert (GB) | Sauber-Ford | 1m31.930s | 71 | 1h56m20.691s |
| 10 | Andrea Montermini (I) | Forti-Ford | 1m34.592s | 69 | 1h55m36.450s |
| R | Gerhard Berger (A) | Benetton-Renault | 1m30.104s | 56 | Suspension |
| R | Michael Schumacher (D) | Ferrari | 1m30.659s | 46 | Rear Wing |
| R | Pedro Lamy (P) | Minardi-Ford | 1m32.958s | 39 | CV Joint |
| R | Mika Salo (FIN) | Tyrrell-Yamaha | 1m31.930s | 36 | Sticking throttle |
| R | Martin Brundle (GB) | Jordan-Peugeot | 1m32.668s | 34 | Accident damage |
| R | Tarso Marques (BR) | Minardi-Ford | 1m32.925s | 33 | Accident |
| R | Heinz-Harald Frentzen (D) | Sauber-Ford | 1m31.005s | 32 | Spin |
| R | Pedro Diniz (BR) | Ligier-Mugen | 1m34.592s | 29 | Fire |
| R | Ukyo Katayama (J) | Tyrrell-Yamaha | 1m31.396s | 28 | Drive |
| R | Ricardo Rosset (BR) | Footwork-Hart | 1m33.606s | 24 | Fuel pump |
| R | Luca Badoer (I) | Forti-Ford | 1m35.893s | 24 | Accident |
| R | Mika Hakkinen (FIN) | McLaren-Mercedes | 1m32.369s | 19 | Throttle |

## CHAMPIONSHIP POSITIONS

| | DRIVER | PTS | CONSTRUCTOR | PTS |
|---|---|---|---|---|
| 1 | Hill | 30 | Williams-Renault | 42 |
| 2 | Villeneuve | 12 | Benetton-Renault | 13 |
| 3 | Alesi | 10 | Ferrari | 10 |
| 4 | Irvine | 6 | McLaren-Mercedes | 5 |
| 5 | Hakkinen | 5 | Tyrrell-Yamaha/Jordan-Peugeot | 3 |
| 6 | Schumacher | 4 | Footwork-Hart/Ligier-Mugen | 1 |

FIA

FORMULA 1
WORLD
CHAMPIONSHIP

# VILLENEUVE BEATS THE 'RINGMEISTER

Jacques Villeneuve stole the show with victory over local hero Michael Schumacher to take his debut victory in Formula 1 and bring an end to Damon Hill's perfect start to the season

> "At times he was too close to be comfortable but he made it fun – as long as I stayed in front"
>
> *Jacques Villeneuve*

The tension really started with five laps to go. Jacques Villeneuve had led from the start, but large in his mirrors for a long time had been Michael Schumacher. If the Williams-Renault had a performance advantage over the Ferrari, still this was the world champion on home ground – against a man in only his fourth Grand Prix, and the pair of them were fast closing on a gaggle of traffic. If the pressure was going to get to Villeneuve, it would surely be now.

There was not a hint of it, as Schumacher acknowledged afterwards. Jacques calmly picked his way through the backmarkers, and the issue was settled. At the flag the Williams was three-quarters of a second to the good, and the Canadian national anthem was played at a Grand Prix for the first time in 15 years. A comparable gap to the next time is not anticipated. 'I just did my job,' Villeneuve said. It seemed like consummate understatement.

More than anything, it was his absolute unflappability which impressed. He took the lead immediately, after team mate Damon Hill, again on pole position, made a mess of his start, and dropped to fifth place on the opening lap. It was not a memorable day for the world championship leader, one way and another, but at least he put three more points on the board.

Mercedes was praying for a decent result in Germany, and got it from David Coulthard, whose fine drive in the McLaren netted third place, a hair ahead of Hill, with the Jordan-Peugeots – very fast in a straight line – finishing fifth and sixth, Rubens Barrichello ahead of Martin Brundle.

Folk who have lived in the Eifel region all their lives said they could never recall late April weather like this. Three weeks before there had been thick snow on the ground, and at the very least everyone anticipated a freezing weekend, almost certainly accompanied by rain. From Wednesday through Sunday, though, the skies were clear, the temperature most acceptable. Goodyear people were especially happy about that.

Qualifying had indicated that, as usual, the Williams-Renaults were a class above the rest, with Hill handily quicker than Villeneuve, and in the race morning warm-up Damon once again headed the times, tailed by Jean Alesi and Gerhard Berger, whose Benettons felt substantially better than in practice. Mika Hakkinen, fourth,

Michael Schumacher closed in on Jacques Villeneuve in the final laps, but was denied the chance to repeat his Nurburgring victory of the year before

Clockwise from main: Jacques Villeneuve heads the field through the first corner. F1's latest winner enjoys his moment of glory. Jean Alesi's race lasted all of two laps. It was the pits for Mika Hakkinen

also felt more upbeat than at any previous race so far during the season, and Schumacher, fifth, devoted his session to fuel and tyre consumption work.

Villeneuve, initially concerned about a vibration in his Williams (which proved to be merely a tyre imbalance) was only eighth, but not concerned. 'I felt,' he said, 'we had a pretty good set-up for the race, and that was the main thing.'

It was to be put to the test from the start. When the lights went out, Hill did not get away well, and it was his team mate who took the lead – pressed into the first corner, amazingly, by Coulthard's McLaren-Mercedes, which had been sixth on the grid. 'It was one of those starts you always hope for,' David said. 'Revs right, just the right amount of wheelspin, and away you go.'

On the grid, Villeneuve's race engineer, Jock Clear, had warned him to watch for Schumacher at the start; this was the Nurburgring, after all. 'Wrong car, wrong car!' Jacques yelled into his radio, after the first corner. 'It was red and white...'

It was something no one had been expecting. In the midst of his dragster start, in fact, Coulthard had barely missed Alesi's Benetton, which crawled away, as did Berger's sister car. This seemed curious, but there was a logical explanation: the hand-brakes of both cars had jammed on. Yes, you read it right.

'That's what we call it, but in fact

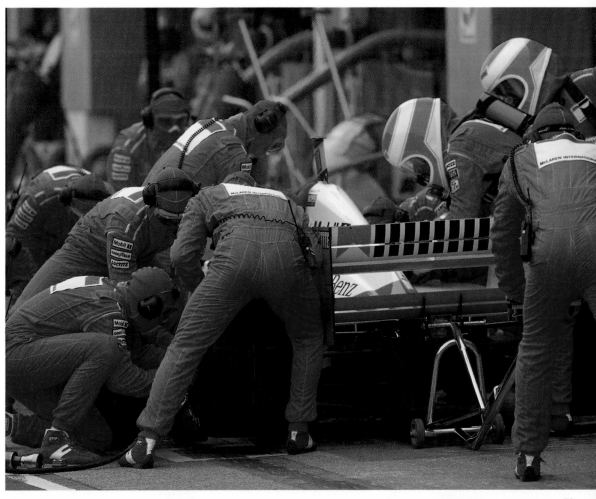

# IN HINDSIGHT

It was ironic that the weekend Ferrari president Luca di Montezemolo turned up at a race to pour oil on the team's troubled waters was the first race in which Michael Schumacher looked a real threat to Williams.

Not a threat to Damon Hill, but then he had taken himself out of the equation early on. But even to be faster than Jacques Villeneuve was an improvement after the fiasco of Ferrari's first three races.

The company's first V10 engine was mated to a too-complex car, with a high-tech gearbox that kept breaking, and suspect aerodynamics. Di Montezemolo was present to quell spiralling rumours that technical director John Barnard (right) was on his way out.

The race went some way to calming the speculation down, but it took a long time for Ferrari's season to look even semi-competent. An incredible mid-season catalogue of catastrophe saw Schumacher and Eddie Irvine complete only 54 laps between them in three Grands Prix – and Schumacher did 41 of those at Montreal.

Slowly, though, the car began to look half-decent – at least in Schumacher's hands – but still people began to wonder if Ferrari as set up in '96 could ever make a serious challenge for the world championship, as it professes to have as its target in 1997.

Rival designers, with a better record than Barnard's, wondered aloud what he was trying to achieve with the odd split sidepods, and others questioned why with Schumacher coming on board, the design team had not simply settled for an update of the user-friendly '95 car, and let Schumacher go out and ring its neck.

it's a button brake,' explained team operations manager Greg Field. 'On the grid the driver puts his foot on the brake, then puts his thumb on a button on the wheel, and takes his foot off the pedal. Now the brakes are controlled by his thumb. As he lets out the clutch, he releases the button, and he's on his way. We started using this as a means of controlling a car's 'creeping' on the grid – people were getting stop/go penalties for being just a few centimetres ahead of their mark.'

On this occasion, though, both 'button brakes' jammed on. Alesi's freed itself more readily than Berger's, but even Jean found himself down in 13th place on the opening lap – and that was to be the extent of his race. At the first corner of the second lap he took a run at Mika Salo's Tyrrell that was never even vaguely on. The cars touched, and disappeared into the gravel trap, from which Salo's emerged intact, but Alesi's did not. His team was not much impressed.

Berger, meantime, had covered the first 50 yards of the race with his right front wheel locked solid, which flat-spotted the tyre. Gerhard radioed to say he would be coming in for new rubber, but somehow his message never got through. When he stopped at his pit, the team was not ready. After rejoining, he ran quickly, and for a long time held the fastest lap, but it was always going to be a long afternoon back from 18th place. 'A pity,' Berger grimaced, 'because the car felt really good.'

At the front, Villeneuve found himself in a most enviable position. Not only had he got clear, but Schumacher and Hill were back in fourth and fifth places, with Coulthard's McLaren and Barrichello's Jordan to deal with. Every time around Jacques pulled away to the tune of half a second or more.

Into the first corner, on lap six, Hill passed Schumacher, which he said was the high point of his day. 'I made a mistake, and got too sideways at the previous corner,' Michael said, 'and that was that. The Williams was better on acceleration, anyway, so there was

nothing I could do.'

Damon, to the surprise of everyone, himself included, found Barrichello a tougher proposition, however, for the Jordan-Peugeot was prodigiously quick in a straight line, and while Rubens occasionally made a mess of a corner, his rival was unable to capitalise on it. Once Hill even tried on the outside of the last turn, but out of it the Williams was unable to keep pace. Peugeot have made remarkable progress since 1995.

Out by now were Irvine and Panis, who made contact at the chicane. At the time Eddie was heading for the pits, his Ferrari misfiring, and Olivier was not pleased by the incident: 'Irvine was obviously in some difficulty, but when I tried to pass him, he closed the door on me.' The Ligier was retired with damaged steering.

## "It was one of those starts you always hope for. Revs right and away you go"

*David Coulthard*

While Villeneuve continued serenely in the lead, the battle for second tightened up, and briefly Coulthard seemed to be delaying Barrichello, Hill and Schumacher. Soon, though, the McLaren had some breathing space, for Barrichello, in his efforts to keep Hill back, was making mistakes. And Damon began to suspect that something was awry with his car.

'It suddenly began to feel strange, as if I had a puncture or a broken anti-roll bar,' he said, 'and I radioed in to tell them. We decided to stop a few laps earlier than planned.' After falling back a bit from Barrichello, Hill pitted on lap 22. The Williams boys found nothing obviously wrong, but the check-over was costly in time, Damon getting on his way after 20.9 seconds, now back in 11th place.

A lap later, Schumacher was in –

and out again – in only 7.7s, so obviously this was a two-stop race for the Ferrari. Then followed Coulthard (9.8), Barrichello (12.5) and Hakkinen (6.6). Mika's stop was quick – too quick in fact, for he was swiftly informed of a 10-second stop/go penalty for speeding in the pitlane.

The crucial stop came on lap 26, and it passed without a hitch, Villeneuve being stationary for 8.9 seconds, and rejoining without losing his lead. Behind Jacques, though, a threat was beginning to materialise. Since taking on new tyres, Schumacher had been flying, putting together a sequence of extremely quick laps.

As well as that, Villeneuve found his Williams, on its new set of tyres, not handling as well as before. 'It got much colder towards the middle of the race,' he said, 'and perhaps the tyres were wrongly-pressured for the lower temperature, I don't know. But the car was sliding around more than before.'

Schumacher closed in at a rate which suggested he might be irresistible, the gap coming down by whole seconds a lap. By the 37th – with 30 still to go – the Ferrari was only six-tenths behind.

Getting up behind the Williams was one thing, getting by it quite another. Plainly, Michael was driving at the limit, but if Jacques felt any pressure he gave no indication of it. Lap in, lap out, his lines were immaculate, and he never locked a brake.

His team mate, meanwhile, was setting new fastest laps in his efforts to salvage something from a dire day which had originally promised so much. By now Hill was eighth, past Herbert's Sauber, and after Brundle's Jordan, but he had a bad moment on lap 28, scrabbling to get by Diniz. The Williams and Ligier touched, but both continued.

Frentzen's fifth-placed Sauber began the second round of stops, on lap 42, followed by Hill, Schumacher, Hakkinen and Barrichello. Unbelievably, Mika once again exceeded the pitlane limit on his way in. 'It wasn't that he forgot to press the limiter button on either occasion, or that the limiter wasn't set properly,' explained Ron Dennis. 'He hit the

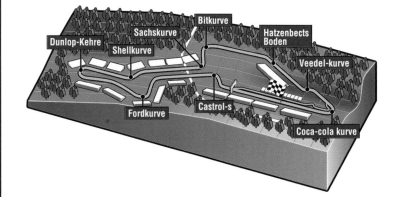

# EUROPEAN GP
## ROUND 4

**28 April 1996**
**FIA Formula 1 World Championship**

**Race data:** 67 laps of a 2.882-mile circuit
**Weather:** Dry and sunny
**Distance:** 189.07 miles

**Winner:** Jacques Villeneuve, Williams-Renault FW18, 120.03mph
**Previous result:** Michael Schumacher, Benetton-Renault B195, 113.83mph
**Fastest lap:** Damon Hill, Williams-Renault FW18, 1m21.363s

## *Nurburgring*

### STARTING GRID

| | DRIVER | |
|---|---|---|
| 1 | Hill | 1:18.941 |
| 2 | Villeneuve | 1:19.721 |
| 3 | Schumacher | 1:20.149 |
| 4 | Alesi | 1:20.711 |
| 5 | Barrichello | 1:20.818 |
| 6 | Coulthard | 1:20.888 |
| 7 | Irvine | 1:20.931 |
| 8 | Berger | 1:21.054 |
| 9 | Hakkinen | 1:21.078 |
| 10 | Frentzen | 1:21.113 |
| 11 | Brundle | 1:21.177 |
| 12 | Herbert | 1:21.210 |
| 13 | Verstappen | 1:21.367 |
| 14 | Salo | 1:21.458 |
| 15 | Panis | 1:21.509 |
| 16 | Katayama | 1:21.812 |
| 17 | Diniz | 1:22.733 |
| 18 | Fisichella | 1:22.921 |
| 19 | Lamy | 1:23.139 |
| 20 | Rosset | 1:23.620 |
| DNQ | Montermini | 1:25.053 |
| DNQ | Badoer | 1:25.840 |

RESULTS © 1996 Federation Internationale de l'Automobile, 8 Place de la Concorde, Paris, 75008 France

Martin Brundle put his early season troubles behind him to finish sixth and score his first world championship points for Jordan

button all right, but was going so fast that each time he was still a bit over the limit.'

Two stop/go penalties effectively put Hakkinen out of the reckoning, which was a great shame, for he would almost certainly have made the podium, given an uninterrupted run. 'Altogether, I guess those penalties cost me at least a minute,' he said. 'The car was terrific on the second set of tyres, and I think I might have had a chance to fight for the lead. Still, we've made progress since the last race, without a doubt.'

No argument there. Coulthard had been among the front runners from the very beginning, and drove an exceptionally good race throughout. It could not, as he said afterwards, have come at a better time, both for his team and himself.

Villeneuve came in for his last stop on lap 46, rejoining with a three-second lead over Schumacher. Again, the gap came quickly down, but again the Ferrari seemed able to get close, but no closer. 'All the time I was thinking about the 1995 race, when I was catching Alesi in the last few laps, and I was hoping that maybe a situation would come in which I could get past Jacques, as I did Jean.'

The closing laps were mesmeric, with never as much as a second separating the Williams and the Ferrari, but still Villeneuve looked unruffled, to the point that one suspected that, if it came to it, maybe he had a little in hand.

Nor was this the only fight in the playground. Half a minute behind the leaders ran Coulthard, but Hill, having found a way by Barrichello's fleet

Jordan, now wanted third place.

All was shaping up for a dramatic finale, therefore, and the sternest test was obviously of Villeneuve, pursued by the fastest driver in the world.

The bad news for Jacques - as for any leader - was that, with five laps to go, there was traffic on the horizon. 'I thought this might be my one chance,' Michael said, 'but he judged all the moves perfectly.'

Calmly, Villeneuve went by Salo, then Katayama, then Rosset, and the last car - Berger's Benetton - was quick enough not to be a problem. At the flag Jacques was three-quarters of a second to the good.

On the last lap, Hill made a final effort to separate Coulthard from third place, but David resolutely stuck to his line, and Damon's fourth place looked momentarily in jeopardy, for

right there on his tail was Barrichello. The three were covered by less than a second, and 21 seconds later Brundle came in to claim the last point.

Villeneuve, as Formula 1 has come to expect, was the essence of calm afterwards. 'We've worked hard to get to the top step of the podium, and it's good to be there so early.

'The car was much better than in qualifying, and particularly good on the last set of tyres - which was just as well because Michael was really going strongly, and we needed the car to be good at that point.

'As long as traffic wasn't going to be too much of a problem, I could keep an eye on him. At times he was too close to be comfortable, but he made it fun - as long as I stayed in front! I got a lot of satisfaction from today. I just did my job...' ■

## RACE RESULTS

| | DRIVER | CAR | RACE | LAPS | RESULT |
|---|---|---|---|---|---|
| 1 | Jacques Villeneuve (CDN) | Williams-Renault | 1m22.090s | 67 | 1h33m26.473s |
| 2 | Michael Schumacher (D) | Ferrari | 1m21.769s | 67 | 1h33m27.235s |
| 3 | David Coulthard (GB) | McLaren-Mercedes | 1m22.550s | 67 | 1h33m59.307s |
| 4 | Damon Hill (GB) | Williams-Renault | 1m21.363s | 67 | 1h33m59.984s |
| 5 | Rubens Barrichello (BR) | Jordan-Peugeot | 1m22.472s | 67 | 1h34m00.186s |
| 6 | Martin Brundle (GB) | Jordan-Peugeot | 1m22.815s | 67 | 1h34m22.040s |
| 7 | Johnny Herbert (GB) | Sauber-Ford | 1m23.225s | 67 | 1h34m44.500s |
| 8 | Mika Hakkinen (FIN) | McLaren-Mercedes | 1m22.078s | 67 | 1h34m44.911s |
| 9 | Gerhard Berger (AUT) | Benetton-Renault | 1m22.004s | 67 | 1h34m47.534s |
| dq | Mika Salo (FIN) | Tyrrell-Yamaha | 1m22.791s | 66 | 1h33m36.379s |
| 10 | Pedro Diniz (BR) | Ligier-Mugen Honda | 1m23.720s | 66 | 1h34m36.937s |
| dq | Ukyo Katayama (J) | Tyrrell-Yamaha | 1m22.602s | 65 | 1h33m31.599s |
| 11 | Ricardo Rosset (BR) | Footwork-Hart | 1m24.050s | 65 | 1h33m33.929s |
| 12 | Pedro Lamy (P) | Minardi-Ford | 1m24.369s | 65 | 1h34m03.416s |
| 13 | Giancarlo Fisichella (I) | Minardi-Ford | 1m24.660s | 65 | 1h34m25.170s |
| R | Heinz-Harald Frentzen (D) | Sauber-Ford | 1m22.697s | 59 | Accident |
| R | Jos Verstappen (NL) | Footwork-Hart | 1m23.233s | 38 | Gearbox |
| R | Olivier Panis (F) | Ligier-Mugen Honda | 1m24.168s | 6 | Accident |
| R | Eddie Irvine (GB) | Ferrari | 1m24.616s | 6 | Misfire |
| R | Jean Alesi (F) | Benetton-Renault | 1m36.595s | 1 | Accident |

## CHAMPIONSHIP POSITIONS

| | DRIVER | PTS | CONSTRUCTOR | PTS |
|---|---|---|---|---|
| 1 | Hill | 33 | Williams-Renault | 55 |
| 2 | Villeneuve | 22 | Ferrari | 16 |
| 3 | Alesi | 10 | Benetton-Renault | 13 |
| | Schumacher | | McLaren-Mercedes | 9 |
| 5 | Irvine | 6 | Jordan-Peugeot | 6 |
| 6 | Hakkinen/Barrichello | 5 | Tyrrell-Yamaha | 3 |

FORMULA 1 WORLD CHAMPIONSHIP

# BACK ON TOP AFTER COPYBOOK VICTORY

Damon Hill got everything right at Imola to score a fourth win in five races and put his title ambitions firmly back on track. Predictably Michael Schumacher was the only real threat in his first race on Ferrari's home turf

There were those, following Hill's disappointing race at the Nurburgring, who predicted that now, with his run of victories disturbed, Damon would start to crack, start to make mistakes, but at Imola he banished any such theories by scoring a copybook victory, his fourth in five races. The drive was perfectly judged, the team's tactical policy beyond reproach.

Hill was, however, beaten to pole position by an inspired Michael Schumacher, and, despite a brilliant showing by David Coulthard's McLaren-Mercedes in the early stages, again it was the Ferrari driver who posed the only semblance of a genuine threat to the Williams-Renault. Damon's team mate, Jacques Villeneuve, might have had something to say, but the Nurburgring winner was put out of the reckoning in the opening seconds by an errant Jean Alesi in his Benetton.

As ever, Schumacher put on a virtuoso display in a car which was not a match for the Williams, but as in Germany it was good only for the runner-up spot. Benetton, a team in some turmoil at the moment, got something from the day, Gerhard Berger finishing third, ahead of Eddie Irvine's Ferrari, Rubens Barrichello's Jordan-Peugeot and Alesi. As usual, though, it was essentially a matter of Hill and Schumacher.

By seven o'clock on race morning the hillsides around the Autodromo Enzo e Dino Ferrari were already packed tight with the fanatical tifosi. Not since 1981 had a Ferrari started from the pole at Imola, and on that occasion the driver was Gilles Villeneuve, the object of their reverence. They didn't yet feel that way about Schumacher, but clearly his inspired last-ditch pole position lap had had its effect.

Seconds after finishing the lap, however, Schumacher lost control at the Tamburello chicane, the car coming to rest in the gravel trap, its left rear wheel at an unusual angle. A track rod had pulled out, and during the night the Ferrari mechanics laboured away to modify the car's rear suspension mounting points, so as to preclude a possible recurrence. They finished work at 5.30am.

Michael had been understandably concerned by the failure: 'I never had

something like this happen before.' He was lucky indeed, not only that it happened after he had finished the quick lap, but also that it was at a chicane, rather than somewhere quick like Piratella.

For qualifying, Ferrari had used the new 'Evo 2' version of the V10, and Schumacher had been impressed, notably with its improved driveability, but while the team would almost certainly race it at Monte Carlo, the next race, at Imola it was considered a reliability risk, and older-spec motors were fitted for the race.

Michael set fourth fastest time in the warm-up, but team mate Eddie Irvine found his car twitchy at the rear, and was down in 16th. In rather greater trouble was Alesi, who went off at Piratella, and hit the tyre wall. Damage to the Benetton was lighter than might have been expected, and it was decided to attempt to repair it for the race. In the midst of a dreadful period for him, however, this was the last thing Jean needed.

David Coulthard and Mika Hakkinen, third and fifth, served further notice of McLaren's gradual return to prominence, changes to the front wing having markedly improved its balance. On their own, though, were the Williams-Renaults, Hill seven-tenths faster than Villeneuve, and both claiming entire satisfaction with their cars. 'It actually felt nicer this morning than in qualifying,' said Damon. Ominous for the rest.

On to two o'clock. It was difficult to imagine that Coulthard, who jumped to second at the beginning of the European Grand Prix, could improve on that at Imola, but improve he did. Into the first corner, the Tamburello chicane, David was in front, with Hill second, Schumacher third and Mika Salo an unaccustomed fourth for Tyrrell.

## "After the setback in Germany, it's great to get things back on course. The car was perfect"

*Damon Hill*

It led well, too. Schumacher squeezed by Hill on lap two, but although he later said that, yes, he was held up a bit by Coulthard, he also admitted there was no way he could pass him. Instead he would wait for the stops, he said, which sounded like a pretty good condemnation of the refuelling phenomenon. A more trenchant one by far would come later.

If Michael was not where he would liked to have been, in the lead, he was in far better shape than the man he pursued so relentlessly at the Nurburgring two weeks before. On the opening lap Villeneuve was last, and by a long way, his left rear tyre flat and breaking up. Into the pits he came, rejoining with more than 40 seconds to make up even on Luca Badoer's wretched Forti.

Soon after the start, Alesi's Benetton veered onto the grass, and clouted Jacques's front wheel as it rejoined the track. Not content with that, he clouted the Williams again at the next turn.

'At the first corner I was on the outside of Jean,' said Jacques, 'and he banged into me, front wheel to front wheel. I'm not sure why he did that, but I'm not saying he did it on purpose – probably not. That was OK, but at the next corner I was on the inside, a little in front of him, and he banged into my rear wheels...'

There ain't no justice. It was the Benetton, not the Williams, which came away apparently unscathed from the contretemps, although in fact Alesi's steering was to pull to the right for the duration of the race. Alesi said of the incident: 'Villeneuve moved over on me, and I had nowhere to go. His left rear wheel touched my right front, and after that the balance of the car felt all wrong.'

The remodelled Imola may be safer than the old, at which all of sound mind should rejoice, but as a circuit for Grand Prix racing it is now merely humdrum, presenting few opportunities for overtaking. On lap two Berger got by Salo, but thereafter no change in the order occurred until lap 14 – and then only because Olivier Panis brought his Ligier into the pits.

Still, the front runners circulated in reasonably close order, Coulthard keeping ahead of Schumacher, but

# IN HINDSIGHT

While Williams romped away with the 1996 season, its domination of the early races was making life very difficult for the team that humiliated it the previous season, Benetton.

The team that had been the centre of attention for the previous two years was finding life without Michael Schumacher far more difficult than it ever imagined.

Four consecutive races in which not only had they not won a race, but not even looked likely to, had got boss Flavio Briatore (right) jumpy. And in a tense team meeting before the San Marino Grand Prix he made his views clearly known — reputedly in words of one syllable.

The pressure was on the drivers, because the team was finding it difficult to cope with what it perceived to be the lack of speed and input compared to Schumacher, and on the team, because it was clearer than ever that the car was not as good as the Williams.

Berger and Alesi found the chassis nervous on the entry to a corner, and particularly difficult in qualifying, and while they made progress through the season, the drivers were never satisfied with it.

And, likewise, the pressure to perform never lifted. Rumours flew — Berger wanted to retire, Briatore wanted to ditch the emotional Alesi (below) — and even Berger's performance in Hockenheim, when he nearly won, did little to boost confidence — even that day the Williams was clearly faster.

The team's predicament was never better illustrated than when Damon Hill was ditched by Williams, and he was linked to Benetton to replace Alesi. There was no obvious performance advantage to the move, but Hill might come with the cachet of World Champion, and that would help satisfy the success-starved sponsors. How the mighty had fallen.

never by as much as a second. These two, indeed, began to edge slightly away from Hill, which suggested they were running less fuel than the Williams driver, and might well be working to a different race strategy. Damon looked unconcerned, and was driving with ease.

His team mate, on the other hand, was plainly charging. A little cold anger never hurt a racing driver's times, and Villeneuve, delayed, but now with an absolutely clear track before him, was generally the quickest man on the circuit, trading new fastest laps with Coulthard and Schumacher – and, by lap 13, Hill, who now began to trim back the advantage of the leading pair.

As the first stops neared, it was Coulthard, Schumacher, Hill, Berger, Salo, Barrichello, Alesi, Irvine, Brundle and Verstappen. On lap 20 the leading McLaren was in (8.2 seconds), and now Schumacher did his usual thing, popping in a scintillating lap, so that even though his stop, on lap 20, was a tad longer (9.5s) than Coulthard's, still he was able to scrabble out of the pits ahead of David, as he had planned.

Alesi update. On lap 19, after a long pitstop (19.5s), he exceeded the pitlane speed limit, which earned him a stop/go penalty. Flavio Briatore, on the pit wall, did not look in the mood

for levity.

Hill, who plainly had no intention of joining this early round of stops, now found himself in a comfortable lead, with Schumacher second, Coulthard third, and Berger fourth. On lap 24 came the first retirement, and very sadly it was that of Salo, in whose hands the Tyrrell-Yamaha had excelled, running as high as third at one point. 'The car had felt good from the start, and the first pitstop went perfectly. But then, just a lap later, the engine suddenly let go – otherwise I'm sure we'd have been on the podium.' A terribly unlucky day for Tyrrell, all told, for Ukyo Katayama's car was also on course for a points finish when its transmission failed late in the race.

Damon stayed out until lap 30, almost the halfway mark, which prompted many – including Schumacher – to wonder if he would be making but one stop. But as he was on his way again after only 7.6 seconds, it seemed somewhat unlikely that he had enough fuel to go the distance. Williams had played the strategy game superbly, however, their cars' superiority sufficient to allow them to start with more fuel than their rivals, yet run right on the pace.

'Just before the race,' said Hill, 'I admit that I said to Adrian Newey, "Are you sure this strategy is right?" But he said, yes, it seems to work out, so I said, "right, we'd go with that".

And, in fact, the tactics were perfect.'

When Hill went back out, he was still in the lead from Schumacher, albeit not by much. It was soon obvious, however, that Michael represented no real threat; he could keep station, but no more. And the Ferrari, Damon knew, would be making its second stop before long.

Shortly before it did, there was yet another refuelling-related incident in the pits – and this time a potentially catastrophic one. Jos Verstappen, victim of the original pit fire at Hockenheim in 1994, began to pull away from his pit before the fuel hose had been removed from his car. This pulled out at the tank end, and fuel began to spew out into the pitlane. Folk set to with paper towels, to soak it up, but the consequences of a single spark in that situation do not bear contemplation, for the tank was now open, of course. Yet another gypsy's warning to those who continue to advocate this absurdly perilous nonsense.

'We need to take a long hard look at what happened,' Verstappen said, 'to minimise the chances of this sort of thing happening again. I had the all-clear signal to leave the pits, but the fuel was still going in. I'm just happy that the injuries to Dave Lowe are not too serious.' The unfortunate Lowe was the man on the hose at the time of the incident, and initially it was thought his arm had been

McLaren enjoyed its most competitive performance of the year, with David Coulthard even leading the race

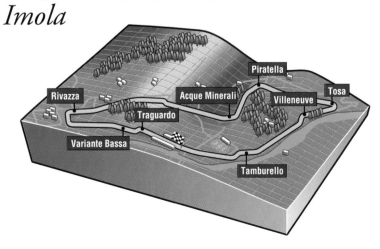

# SAN MARINO GP
## ROUND 5

5 May 1996
FIA Formula 1 World Championship

**Race data:** 63 laps of a 3.041-mile circuit
**Weather:** Dry and sunny
**Distance:** 191.583 miles

**Winner:** Damon Hill,
Williams-Renault FW18, 120.42mph
**Previous result:** Damon Hill,
Williams-Renault FW17, 113.04mph
**Fastest lap:** Damon Hill,
Williams-Renault FW18, 1m28.931s

## *Imola*

Piratella
Acque Minerali
Villeneuve
Tosa
Rivazza
Traguardo
Variante Bassa
Tamburello

RESULTS © 1996 Federation Internationale de l'Automobile, 8 Place de la Concorde, Paris, 75008 France

## STARTING GRID

| | DRIVER | |
|---|---|---|
| 1 | Schumacher | 1:26.890 |
| 2 | Hill | 1:27.105 |
| 3 | Villeneuve | 1:27.220 |
| 4 | Coulthard | 1:27.688 |
| 5 | Alesi | 1:28.009 |
| 6 | Irvine | 1:28.205 |
| 7 | Berger | 1:28.336 |
| 8 | Salo | 1:28.423 |
| 9 | Barrichello | 1:28.632 |
| 10 | Frentzen | 1:28.785 |
| 11 | Hakkinen | 1:29.079 |
| 12 | Brundle | 1:29.099 |
| 13 | Panis | 1:29.472 |
| 14 | Verstappen | 1:29.539 |
| 15 | Herbert | 1:29.541 |
| 16 | Katayama | 1:29.892 |
| 17 | Diniz | 1:29.989 |
| 18 | Lamy | 1:30.471 |
| 19 | Fisichella | 1:30.814 |
| 20 | Rosset | 1:31.316 |
| 21 | Badoer | 1:32.037 |
| DNQ | Montermini | 1:33.685 |

broken; an X-ray revealed that he had suffered a dislocated shoulder.

All of this was going on when Schumacher made his second stop, on lap 40. Stationary for 11.7 seconds, he rejoined without losing second place, but knew there was little prospect of improving on that – particularly when, on lap 43, he came upon Diniz and Hakkinen, who were disputing 10th place. In five laps behind them, the gap between Hill and himself increased from 25 to 39 seconds, and ultimately, when waved blue flags had failed to have any effect, he was reduced to shaking his fist at them, a most un-Schumacher-like thing.

Ultimately, both Hakkinen and Diniz were given stop/go penalties for ignoring the blue flags, and most observers thought the punishment well-deserved. In the McLaren pit, they were far more dismayed by the retirement, on lap 45, of Coulthard, with a loss of pressure in the hydraulic system. 'At my second stop I stalled,' David said, 'and I think that may have had something to do with the problem. Since the middle of the race the gearbox had started to feel a bit lazy on the downshift. The hydraulic pressure dropped, and eventually the car just stopped out on the circuit.' For the second weekend running, Coulthard had been very much McLaren's star.

Alesi update. On lap 47 he misjudged an attempted pass of Panis, hit the Ligier, spun, continued.

After the race Hill was cagey about whether or not he could have made the finish without a second stop. The general belief was that he could not, but, whatever, he came in on lap 50. It was pure routine, efficiently carried out in 8.3 seconds, and afterwards Schumacher was still more than 20 seconds adrift. Now it was an easy run to the finish.

In the late stages the Williams-Renaults ran in close formation, Hill now having lapped Villeneuve, who had hauled himself up to sixth, and looked like scoring a deserved point. It was not to be, however. At the end of lap 58, with five to the flag, Jacques came into the pits, and immediately cut the engine. The right rear suspension had broken.

There were no problems for the

**Right: Ricardo Rosset was forced to retire at his second stop following Jos Verstappen's pit-lane accident**

other Williams-Renault, however, Hill coming in to score his fourth victory of the season, and extend his world championship points lead to 21. It was another consummately professional and faultless race, in which both he and the team got everything right. 'After the setback in Germany,' Damon said, 'it's great to get things back on course.' And the car? 'The car was perfect, no problems at all.'

You couldn't say that of Schumacher's Ferrari. Halfway round the last lap, its right front brake disc exploded, and the front wheel locked solid. With smoke pouring from the tyre, Michael fought the car to the line, and suddenly the Italians saw a hero in this cool German, cheering him to the echo, and immediately invading the track. Immediately before the Tamburello chicane, Michael pulled off and parked it, returning to the pits in a course car, waving all the while.

'Before coming here, I would have thought that second place was impossible for us,' Schumacher said, 'because Imola is bumpy, and our car has not worked so well on bumps. But actually it was perfect from the beginning, although not fast enough to run with the Williams. Not yet, anyway.'

Berger was obviously relieved at achieving a good finish after a dismal start to the season, but he showed no signs of real elation. 'It's nice to get some points, but really at the moment the car is just how I hate it, nervous and pointy, with too much oversteer when I turn in. Still, considering the car's potential this weekend, I am happy with the result.'

Without Schumacher, Benetton looked like an ordinary team so far; with him, Ferrari looked a stronger force than at any time since 1990. Monte Carlo was next, where Michael had won for the last two years, and where Damon wanted to win more than anywhere else. The one and only qualifying session in the principality would be something else again. ■

## RACE RESULTS

| | DRIVER | CAR | RACE | LAPS | RESULT |
|---|---|---|---|---|---|
| 1 | Damon Hill (GB) | Williams-Renault | 1m28.931s | 63 | 1h35m26.156s |
| 2 | Michael Schumacher (D) | Ferrari | 1m28.966s | 63 | 1h35m42.616s |
| 3 | Gerhard Berger (A) | Benetton-Renault | 1m29.667s | 63 | 1h36m13.047s |
| 4 | Eddie Irvine (IRL) | Ferrari | 1m29.503s | 63 | 1h36m27.739s |
| 5 | Rubens Barrichello (BR) | Jordan-Peugeot | 1m29.888s | 63 | 1h36m44.646s |
| 6 | Jean Alesi (F) | Benetton-Renault | 1m29.542s | 62 | 1h35m43.597s |
| 7 | Pedro Diniz (BR) | Ligier-Mugen Honda | 1m30.852s | 62 | 1h36m33.333s |
| 8 | Mika Hakkinen (FIN) | McLaren-Mercedes | 1m30.192s | 61 | 1h34m49.164s |
| 9 | Pedro Lamy (P) | Minardi-Ford | 1m31.897s | 61 | 1h36m59.418s |
| 10 | Luca Badoer (I) | Forti-Ford | 1m32.426s | 59 | 1h36m10.706s |
| 11 | Jacques Villeneuve (CDN) | Williams-Renault | 1m29.226s | 57 | 1h27m49.134s |
| 12 | Olivier Panis (F) | Ligier Mugen-Honda | 1m30.184s | 54 | Gearbox |
| 13 | Ukyo Katayama (J) | Tyrrell-Yamaha | 1m30.772s | 45 | Lost drive |
| 14 | David Coulthard (GB) | McLaren-Mercedes | 1m29.480s | 44 | Hydraulics |
| 15 | Ricardo Rosset (BR) | Footwork-Hart | 1m32.169s | 40 | Pitstop |
| 16 | Jos Verstappen (NL) | Footwork-Hart | 1m30.479s | 38 | Pitstop |
| 17 | Martin Brundle (GB) | Jordan-Peugeot | 1m30.000s | 36 | Spin |
| R | Heinz-Harald Frentzen (D) | Sauber-Ford | 1m31.092s | 32 | Brakes |
| R | Giancarlo Fisichella (I) | Minardi-Ford | 1m31.633s | 30 | Engine |
| R | Johnny Herbert (GB) | Sauber-Ford | 1m30.811s | 25 | Misfire |
| R | Mika Salo (FIN) | Tyrrell-Yamaha | 1m29.997s | 23 | Engine |

## CHAMPIONSHIP POSITIONS

| | DRIVER | PTS | CONSTRUCTOR | PTS |
|---|---|---|---|---|
| 1 | Hill | 43 | Williams-Renault | 65 |
| 2 | Villeneuve | 22 | Ferrari | 25 |
| 3 | Schumacher | 16 | Benetton-Renault | 18 |
| 4 | Alesi | 11 | McLaren-Mercedes | 9 |
| 5 | Irvine | 9 | Jordan-Peugeot | 8 |
| 6 | Barrichello/Berger | 7 | Tyrrell-Yamaha | 3 |

**FIA FORMULA 1 WORLD CHAMPIONSHIP**

# PANIS WINS THE FANTASY GP

Even the bookies couldn't have forecast this one. No win for Damon Hill, Michael Schumacher or Jean Alesi... but a debut victory for Ligier's Olivier Panis

Olivier Panis brings Ligier their first Grand Prix victory for 15 years

> ## "I have nothing to regret about having won this way because I pushed hard to bring home a Ligier victory"
>
> *Olivier Panis*

A curiosity, this, even by Monaco standards. After two days of practice and qualifying in the dry, on Sunday morning there was torrential rain, and although it had stopped by race time, the track remained wet and slick. Two hours later, Olivier Panis and the Ligier-Mugen Honda took the chequered flag, and if he never wins another Grand Prix, he, like Jean-Pierre Beltoise 24 years before him, will still have had his day of days.

The fact that Panis and Ligier won suggests a race of attrition, and

indeed it was so, by any standards. But if Olivier was perhaps fortunate to make the top step of the podium, a high finish was always his due, after a magnificent drive in a less-than-fancied car. In the late stages David Coulthard – again McLaren's main man – gave spirited chase, before settling for second, and the only other cars around at the end were the Sauber-Fords of Johnny Herbert and Heinz-Harald Frentzen. The two Mikas, Salo and Hakkinen, were classified fifth and sixth, despite crashing out five laps from the flag.

Yes, it was that kind of race.

Until the halfway point, the Monaco Grand Prix belonged decisively to the Williams of Damon Hill, who beat pole man Michael Schumacher away from the grid, and was serenely out on his own – Schumacher having crashed out on lap one! – until his Renault V10 most untypically blew up on lap 41, the cruellest fortune in this, the race Hill wanted above all others. Thereafter Jean Alesi, very much on form this time, led until lap 60, when the Benetton-Renault suffered a broken

rear spring. And thus it was Panis who brought it home, a Tricolore fluttering from the cockpit on his slowing-down lap.

The forecast had always been for rain on Sunday, but they had said that about Saturday, too, and it had held off. But anyone familiar with the Cote d'Azur, and its mythically wondrous climate, looked at the mist that clung low to the mountains on race morning and had no doubts.

For the warm-up at least, however, the rain held off, and here was the first surprise. The second was that Panis's Ligier set the fastest time, but no one took too much notice of that, for the Frenchman admitted he had been running with a light fuel load. Second and fifth were the ever-improving McLaren-Mercedes of Hakkinen and Coulthard, with Schumacher's Ferrari third, Alesi's Benetton fourth, and Hill an unconcerned sixth.

By mid-morning, the rain was monsoon-like, and eventually it was announced that there would be an extra 'acclimatisation' session, from 1.15 to 1.30. Out they duly came to test the water, and in these treacherous conditions Hakkinen set the best time – and then parked his McLaren solidly against the fence at Tabac, which committed him to the T-car for the race.

Hill and Schumacher, rather more circumspect in a session in which times didn't matter at all, were eighth and ninth fastest, and undamaged. Irvine, whose Ferrari engine was being changed, had to miss the session altogether.

At 2.30 they came up to take the start, everyone on wets, save Verstappen, who reckoned there was little to be lost with a gamble on slicks. At the very first corner, he would have cause to reconsider.

Schumacher, by his own admission, made a poor getaway, and long before Ste Devote, Hill had assumed the lead, which he held confidently, and stretched, up the hill to Casino Square, and beyond. He must, as he pointed the Williams towards the tunnel, have expected to see red in his mirrors, but there was none. Schumacher, extraordinarily, had goofed at the right-hander after the Loews hairpin, getting halfway onto the inside kerb, then understeering off it into the guardrail on the outside.

The ice man had a terse expression on his face as he strode away from the car, but he made no excuses: 'I made a mistake at the start,' he said, 'and I made a mistake here, too. I'm very sorry for the team, and very angry with myself.' As Jean Todt put it, 'Michael accepts errors from others, but not from himself.' The converse of Nigel Mansell, if you will.

Out front, Damon found himself in a dream situation, with a clear road before him, and no Schumacher behind. There were, however, things on which to keep an eye, not least the bits of wreckage which already littered the track. Verstappen's slick-shod Arrows had gone off at the first

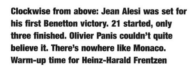

**Clockwise from above: Jean Alesi was set for his first Benetton victory. 21 started, only three finished. Olivier Panis couldn't quite believe it. There's nowhere like Monaco. Warm-up time for Heinz-Harald Frentzen**

corner (aided by Hakkinen), and the Minardis of Pedro Lamy and Giancarlo Fisichella had contrived to account for each other, the one naturally blaming the other.

Giancarlo Minardi, always refreshingly free of cant in this PR-dominated age, was crisp on the subject: 'We plan the race in detail, and it's annoying to see everything wasted by unbelievable mistakes by our drivers. We have to wait to see the telemetry, before deciding which one is responsible...'

Out, too, was Rubens Barrichello.

'Before Casino Square, I was hit from behind, perhaps by Coulthard or Frentzen. The car came down with a hard bump, but I kept going until Rascasse, where it just went, and I was into the barrier...'

One lap down, 77 to go, and already five of the 21 starters were gone. Monsieur Panis, at this stage of the game, was 12th, with but four cars behind him. Who says you need to start at the front in Monaco? Soon he began to make his moves. On lap seven he passed Brundle, and on lap 16 he was by Hakkinen, then Herbert.

And no one else, it should be noted, was doing much overtaking at all.

In the first part of the race, Hill and the Williams looked at least one class above the rest, drawing away by huge amounts every time around. After the first lap, Damon led Alesi by 4.3 seconds, after which the gap grew like this: 6.1, 9.5, 11.6, 13.3. This was a rout.

Close behind Alesi in the early laps was Berger, and in the slippery conditions Gerhard, perhaps surprisingly, seemed the quicker of the two: 'I could have gone a little

# IN HINDSIGHT

At the end of the Monaco Grand Prix, as Olivier Panis stood unbelieving on the rostrum, there was one question on everybody's lips – how on earth did that happen? The Frenchman had started 14th, after all, and was driving a Ligier, so how had he ended up winning on the most tortuous, demanding track of all?

The answer was a combination of a superb drive, a little bit of luck, and some clever, quick thinking.

Given that Damon Hill and Jean Alesi were to retire, the Monaco GP win was up for grabs for many drivers. Heinz-Harald Frentzen (right) should have won it, but he threw most of his chances away when he drove into the back of Eddie Irvine's Ferrari. Even then, though, he could have won, had he gone on to slick tyres when he pitted to change his wings. Frentzen asked for them, but the team either didn't hear or refused to fit them, and he had to come back in again a few laps later.

When he did, he was still the first to fit them, and his split times before he had completed his first flying lap – the Sauber was seven seconds faster in the second segment of the lap than ever before – convinced Ligier that they should call Panis in immediately. That gave him the crucial advantage.

McLaren also acted quickly, but they called in Mika Hakkinen first, which seemed an odd decision, given that David Coulthard (below) was running ahead of him, and if the Scot had come in early, he would have made up the time necessary to stay ahead.

But McLaren said it wasn't the case – Coulthard used marginally more fuel than Hakkinen, they said, and if he had been called in first, he would have run out of fuel just before the end of the race. On such fine threads does Grand Prix success sometimes hang.

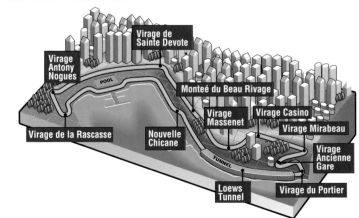

quicker,' he mischievously said, 'but I didn't want to create unnecessary pressure within the team. My main concern was not to spin.' Alas, it was to be another disappointment for Berger, for he stopped for good on lap 10 when a gearbox sensor failed.

That left Alesi clear in second place, for Irvine, who had made a brilliant start, was third, and had a traffic jam behind him, headed by Frentzen, whose frustration became more overt by the lap. At one particular spot – immediately beyond the swimming pool complex – the Ferrari seemed almost to stop, so that the Sauber was all but going over the top of it. Blue flags seemed thin at the ground, it must be said, but this was nothing unusual for Monte Carlo, where flagging is traditionally lamentable.

It was inevitable that the Irvine-Frentzen tussle was going to end in tears, and on lap 18 the distracted Heinz-Harald – who could well have been threatening Alesi's second place – took a run at Eddie on the approach to Ste Devote. The Ferrari driver robustly defended his place, and the consequence was that the Sauber needed a new nose, which it received at the end of the lap.

By now the track was swiftly drying, and this should have presented Sauber with an ideal opportunity to put their man onto slicks, several laps ahead of the game. Instead, unfathomably, they sent Frentzen back out on new wets. Within 10 laps, he would be back in again for more appropriate rubberwear, but in the mean time he ran off a whole series of fastest laps.

By lap 28, with a 25-second lead, Hill was in for his routine stop, and duly took on slicks. Alesi went momentarily ahead, but recognised that Damon was now much quicker, and let him by on the hill up to Casino Square, knowing that he, too, was stopping shortly. At the end of lap 30, Jean came in, rejoining without losing his second place.

Panis, meantime, had pitted at the same time as Hill, and the stop was a quick one, for he had begun the race with a heavy fuel load, and taken only

**Mika Salo finished sixth**

a splash. This may have been crucial, for in the swiftly drying conditions, McLaren unaccountably brought in Hakkinen first, leaving the higher-placed Coulthard stuck out there on worn wet tyres. Before the stops, David had been ahead of Panis; after them, he was behind.

Now, suddenly, the Ligier was fourth, and Olivier began to lap substantially faster even than the leader, taking nine seconds off third-placed Irvine in four laps. Funny, with a French car now stuck behind his Ferrari, Eddie began to see blue flags at every corner...

On lap 36 Panis put the time-honoured move on Irvine at the Loews hairpin. The man in front is always vulnerable in these circumstances, and Eddie found himself spun and stalled, while Olivier, his steering slightly damaged by the impact, got on his unimpeded way at last. Irvine, thinking himself out on the spot, undid his belts, and prepared to alight, but the marshals pushed him, and he got going again.

'I was sure I'd be disqualified, because the rules about outside assistance are quite clear,' he said, but in the pits the Ferrari mechanics did up his belts again, and sent him back into the race, having also – thanks to a communication failure over the radio – unnecessarily changed the car's nosecone. By now he was two laps down.

More and more fastest laps came from the inspired Panis, who found his Ligier working as well in the dry as it had in the wet, but a setback was in store for him. On lap 41, he spun at the entrance to the chicane, and the initial assumption was that he had

lost it on oil...from Hill's Williams.

Poor Damon. After five victories from the last six Grands Prix, it was on the cards that he was due a mechanical failure, but why did it have to happen here, in his father's stamping ground, in the race that mattered to him more than any other? And why, Renault folk will have pondered, did one of their famously reliable V10s have to come unglued in this, the most prestigious Grand Prix of all? 'The red light came on the lap before,' Hill said, commendably calm in the circumstances, 'and then it let go in the tunnel.' The Williams, with a brief crack of flame from its underside, coasted into the escape road by the chicane.

Although marshals began to put down cement dust in the area, Panis later denied that his spin had anything to do with oil from Hill's car.

Whatever, the incident cost him 10 seconds, and he now trailed the new leader, Alesi, by more than half a minute. Immediately, more fastest laps followed, and Olivier found himself behind Irvine once more. It might have been tempting to Eddie, given what had happened earlier, to keep the Ligier back, but he commendably let Panis through.

Now Alesi responded, setting a series of new fastest laps himself, even though spots of rain were coming down again. It seemed that Jean, after his performances at the Nurburgring and Imola, had put the troubled times behind him, but on lap 60 he was into the pits, and it was unscheduled. 'I felt something wrong at the back of the car,' he said, 'and came in to have it checked over. They changed the tyres, and sent me back into the race, but the problem was still there.' A lap later, the Benetton was back in for good, and later it was discovered that a rear spring on the B196 had broken.

Eighteen laps to go, therefore, and perhaps fewer than that, given the 'two-hour' rule. Almost unbelievably, Panis and the Ligier-Mugen Honda now led, albeit by under three seconds, from Coulthard's McLaren-Mercedes. 'Having raced against Olivier in Formula 3000,' David said, 'I knew that he didn't make many mistakes. And once we'd changed to

---

## MONACO GP

### ROUND 6

**19 May 1996**
**FIA Formula 1 World Championship**

**Race data:** 75 laps of a 2.06-mile circuit
**Weather:** Wet and drying
**Distance:** 154.5 miles

**Winner:** Olivier Panis, Ligier-Mugen Honda JS43, 77.06 mph
**Previous result:** Michael Schumacher, Benetton-Renault B195, 85.51mph
**Fastest lap:** Jean Alesi, Benetton-Renault B196, 1m25.205s

## *Monte Carlo*

Virage de Sainte Devote
Virage Antony Nogues
Montée du Beau Rivage
Virage Massenet
Virage Casino
Virage de la Rascasse
Nouvelle Chicane
Virage Mirabeau
Virage Ancienne Gare
Loews Tunnel
Virage du Portier

## STARTING GRID

| | DRIVER | |
|---|---|---|
| 1 | Schumacher | 1:20.356 |
| 2 | Hill | 1:20.866 |
| 3 | Alesi | 1:20.918 |
| 4 | Berger | 1:21.067 |
| 5 | Coulthard | 1:21.460 |
| 6 | Barrichello | 1:21.504 |
| 7 | Irvine | 1:21.542 |
| 8 | Hakkinen | 1:21.688 |
| 9 | Frentzen | 1:21.929 |
| 10 | Villeneuve | 1:21.963 |
| 11 | Salo | 1:22.235 |
| 12 | Verstappen | 1:22.327 |
| 13 | Herbert | 1:22.346 |
| 14 | Panis | 1:22.358 |
| 15 | Katayama | 1:22.460 |
| 16 | Brundle | 1:22.519 |
| 17 | Diniz | 1:22.682 |
| 18 | Fisichella | 1:22.684 |
| 19 | Lamy | 1:23.350 |
| 20 | Rosset | 1:24.976 |
| 21 | Badoer | 1:25.059 |
| 22 | Montermini | 1:25.393 |

slicks, he was quicker than me. I gave it a go in the last few laps, but essentially it was just a matter of trying to get my car home.'

A slightly unsettling aspect of the duel was that Panis appeared to be fending off a McLaren driven by Schumacher. 'I'd had a problem in the warm-up with my visor misting up all the time,' said Coulthard, 'so I asked Michael if I could borrow one of his helmets, and he said sure...'

If the battle at the front was essentially resolved, further back there remained issues at stake. Johnny Herbert had established himself in a relatively safe third place, after an excellent, if unobtrusive, drive in the

Sauber-Ford, but behind him Messrs Villeneuve, Hakkinen and Salo were energetically contesting fourth.

Jacques had a curiously downbeat weekend in Monte Carlo, putting in by far his least impressive performance since arriving in F1. He admitted that the fault was his, that he had never truly got to grips with the place, particularly its ultra-slow corners, but now he began strenuously to defend fourth place.

On lap 67 the trio encountered Luca Badoer's Forti, which was dragging itself around, laps behind. The Italian has never been a co-operative sort, when it comes to mirrors, and at Mirabeau chopped

across Villeneuve, squeezing him onto the sidewalk, then into the unyielding masonry. The Williams and the Forti were out on the spot, and in the confusion Salo nipped by Hakkinen, to take fourth place.

'It was annoying,' Jacques said, 'that the race ended the way it did, although I'm sure Badoer didn't see me – you never do that on purpose.' Later the Stewards found the Italian guilty of careless driving, and fined him US$5000, and a suspended ban. He couldn't holler.

The last act in the drama came on lap 70, when Irvine spun at precisely the corner which had accounted for his team-mate on the first lap.

As he prepared to take off again, Messrs Salo and Hakkinen arrived, and found themselves with nowhere to go. The Ferrari, the Tyrrell and the McLaren concertinaed together, and now there were just four cars circulating.

After the finish, Panis looked like a man in a trance, unable to take in that he had won this, the Monaco Grand Prix. 'I have nothing to regret about having won this way,' he said, 'because I pushed hard all the way to bring home a Ligier victory.'

The last one was 15 years ago, by Jacques Laffite, in Montreal, also in the wet. That day, as this, the win was entirely deserved. ■

## RACE RESULTS

| | DRIVER | CAR | RACE | LAPS | RESULT |
|---|---|---|---|---|---|
| 1 | Olivier Panis (F) | Ligier-Mugen Honda | 1m25.581s | 75 | 2h00m45.629s |
| 2 | David Coulthard (GB) | McLaren-Mercedes | 1m26.236s | 75 | 2h00m50.457s |
| 3 | Johnny Herbert (GB) | Sauber-Ford | 1m26.852s | 75 | 2h01m23.132s |
| DNF | Heinz-Harald Frentzen (D) | Sauber-Ford | 1m25.608s | 74 | stopped in pits |
| R | Mika Salo (FIN) | Tyrrell-Yamaha | 1m26.461s | 70 | accident |
| R | Mika Hakkinen (FIN) | McLaren-Mercedes | 1m26.482s | 70 | accident |
| R | Eddie Irvine (GB) | Ferrari | 1m26.120s | 68 | accident |
| R | Jacques Villeneuve (CDN) | Williams-Renault | 1m26.682s | 66 | accident |
| R | Jean Alesi (F) | Benetton-Renault | 1m25.205s | 60 | suspension |
| R | Luca Badoer (I) | Forti-Ford | 1m33.305s | 60 | accident |
| R | Damon Hill (GB) | Williams-Renault | 1m28.523s | 40 | engine |
| R | Martin Brundle (GB) | Jordan-Peugeot | 1m35.477s | 30 | spin |
| R | Gerhard Berger (A) | Benetton-Renault | 1m49.966s | 9 | gearbox sensor |
| R | Pedro Diniz (BR) | Ligier-Mugen Honda | 1m53.469s | 5 | transmission |
| R | Ricardo Rosset (BR) | Footwork-Hart | 1m58.465s | 3 | accident |
| R | Ukyo Katayama (J) | Tyrrell-Yamaha | 1m55.722s | 2 | throttle/accident |
| R | Michael Schumacher (D) | Ferrari | | 0 | accident |
| R | Jos Verstappen (NL) | Footwork-Hart | | 0 | accident |
| R | Rubens Barrichello (BR) | Jordan-Peugeot | | 0 | accident |
| R | Pedro Lamy (P) | Minardi-Ford | | 0 | accident |
| R | Giancarlo Fisichella (I) | Minardi-Ford | | 0 | accident |
| DNS | Andrea Montermini (I) | Forti-Ford | | – | crash |

## CHAMPIONSHIP POSITIONS

| | DRIVER | PTS | CONSTRUCTOR | PTS |
|---|---|---|---|---|
| 1 | Hill | 43 | Williams-Renault | 65 |
| 2 | Villeneuve | 22 | Ferrari | 25 |
| 3 | Schumacher | 16 | Benetton-Renault | 18 |
| 4 | Panis | 11 | McLaren-Mercedes | 16 |
| 5 | Alesi | 11 | Ligier-Mugen Honda | 11 |
| 6 | Coulthard | 10 | Jordan-Peugeot | 8 |

FIA FORMULA 1 WORLD CHAMPIONSHIP

# SCHUMACHER REIGNS IN SPAIN

Michael Schumacher was able to shine through the torrential rain that knocked out two-thirds of the pack, including championship leader Damon Hill.  It was one of the greatest wet weather drives in history

> **"After qualifying we were nowhere, so I wasn't expecting much from today when I woke up and saw the rain"**
>
> *Michael Schumacher*

Appalling weather swiftly cut into the pack at Barcelona. Six of the 20 cars were gone within a lap, and at the finish only half a dozen were still rolling. As a race, therefore, the Spanish Grand Prix was less than memorable, and for some drivers, notably Damon Hill, it was better forgotten. The world championship leader started from pole, but retired on lap 11, after going off the road a third time.

In the torrential rain Hill's Williams-Renault team mate Jacques Villeneuve took the lead at the start, and for several laps rejected the attentions of Jean Alesi. Both, however, were swiftly overwhelmed by Michael Schumacher, who had made a

disastrous start, but soon settled into a pace utterly beyond any of his rivals. The Ferrari may not have much pleased Michael in dry qualifying, but in the wet he pushed hard and found the car near perfect.

Once into the lead, Schumacher pulled away at the rate of four seconds a lap. 'He just left me standing,' Villeneuve shrugged afterwards. It was, in truth, one of the great wet weather drives in history, worthy of comparison with Ayrton Senna's performances at Estoril in 1985 or Donington in 1993. So mesmeric, in fact, you forgot it was supposed to be a race.

After traditional Spanish early summer weather for practice and

qualifying, the rain battered down from early on raceday morning, and two days of hard work, of conserving tyres, perfecting set-ups (or not), were shot to hell.

In the soaking warm-up, Hill and Schumacher set the fastest times, which was hardly a surprise, but Olivier Panis, winner at Monte Carlo in the rain, was third fastest with the Ligier-Mugen Honda, ahead of Alesi's Benetton-Renault, Eddie Irvine's Ferrari and Heinz-Harald Frentzen's Sauber-Ford. The last-named, in fact, caused the session to be cut short, when he had a sizeable accident out of the last corner.

Fortunately, the Sauber spun into the tyre wall backwards, but the

Clockwise from above: Pedro Diniz stayed out of trouble to claim his first world championship point. Michael Schumacher dives down the inside of Jacques Villeneuve to take the lead. So Damon, how was it for you? Mika Salo had hoped for an upturn in performance with Tyrrell's new suspension, but was once again disappointed

impact was nevertheless considerable, and three corners were torn off. Frentzen looked pale and shaken as he walked away, but a medical check revealed nothing awry, and he was passed fit to race.

Villeneuve took the warm-up very easily, but certainly got to it when the race began. 'My start went very well, and I was happy with that – it seemed like Damon just didn't go anywhere. Of course it's always good to get the lead at the start of a wet race, because at least you see something – the guys behind don't!'

Hill indeed hesitated when the lights went out, trailing Villeneuve and Alesi into the first turn, but his getaway was scintillating compared with Schumacher's. The Ferrari appeared almost to stall, before stumbling away.

'My start was a disaster,' Michael said. 'I went for the clutch, and there was nothing. I nearly stalled, then tried it again – I just had an on/off

clutch, for some reason. We've had problems with it before, and thought we were on top of it, but obviously we're not.

'Fortunately, no one went into the back of me, but I don't know how many positions I lost – even Pedro Diniz passed me, I think. Now I know how it is to start a wet race from the back: you just can't see anything. I really was afraid I'd go into someone.'

Although back in sixth at the end of the first lap, Schumacher had already overtaken three or four cars. On the second lap he was up to fifth, team mate Irvine having spun into retirement, and on the fourth up another place, courtesy of Hill, who had made the first of his mistakes. Next, Michael dealt with Berger, before quickly closing on Alesi.

In a single lap, the Ferrari took nearly four seconds from the Benetton, and it was obviously only a matter of time before Schumacher was up to second, up to first, away

into the far yonder.

For now, though, it remained Villeneuve from Alesi, and neither was without his problems. 'I was on the limit,' said Jean, 'and because the ride height of my car was a little bit too low, I was aquaplaning badly everywhere. With these cars, you know, you aquaplane not only with the tyres, but also with the flat bottom of the car. Also, my speed on the straight was terrible whenever I got right behind Jacques, because a lot of water was going into the airbox. Like that, I was only able to get 14,000 revs...'

As for Jacques, he found that his tyres began to go off markedly after only 10 laps. Even had they not, though, there was no way he could have resisted Schumacher. On lap nine, Michael was past Alesi, into second, and on lap 12 he overtook Villeneuve, too, at precisely the same place, into a tight left-hander. On each occasion, he left his braking late,

poked the nose of the Ferrari inside, leaving neither Jean nor Jacques an opportunity to resist. The moves were exquisitely judged, and now all Schumacher had to do was keep his concentration alive for another 53 laps. It was going to be a long day, not least for the spectators.

'I had no chance to follow Michael,' Alesi ruefully admitted. 'Where was Michael's advantage?' smiled Villeneuve. 'Everywhere! He was much quicker in the corners, and that's all there was to it. As long as he was behind me, he couldn't see as well, but once he got in front, he just left me standing.'

Thus, the situation at the front appeared settled only a dozen laps into the race. Behind the leaders, little scraps were going on, and in the paddock many drivers were in civvies, their Spanish Grand Prix already done. Foremost among these was Hill, who had gone off the road on laps four, eight and, finally, 11.

# IN HINDSIGHT

Michael Schumacher's victory in the Spanish GP will go down in motor racing history as one of the greatest wet-weather drives of all time.

Immediately after the race, comparisons were already being made between the World Champion's performance and Ayrton Senna's

greatest drives in the wet, at the Portuguese GP in 1985 (above) and the European GP at Donington Park in 1993.

But the biggest question after the race was how did he do it? The Ferrari had, after all, been a nightmare in the wet in Brazil, and was not even close to being competitive during qualifying in Spain. How, then, was Schumacher able to lap five seconds faster than anyone else?

The best explanation is a technical one. Knowing that their only hope of victory was a totally wet race, Ferrari put full wet settings (lots of downforce and soft springs), on Schumacher's F310. Most teams, though, seemed to go for the usual practice in the wet — compromise the dry setting as little as possible in case it stops raining, because a car set up for the dry is quicker in the wet than a car set up for the wet is on a dry track.

And Williams's senior operations engineer, James Robinson, admitted that the team did not go far enough with its wet settings, partly because in the race morning warm-up, Hill and Villeneuve worked towards a set-up, but the session was cut short by an accident to Frentzen's Sauber.

But none of this is to take anything away from Schumacher's genius. As Robinson said: 'The Ferrari looked like it was on ice. The guy is just something else.'

The last of these adventures had occurred out of the last corner, Damon spinning across the road, as Frentzen had done in the warm-up, but this time fortunately the impact was small, the front of the car grazing down the pit wall.

'I made three mistakes,' said Hill, 'and I had the wrong set-up on the car. What happened today was really down to me.' Damon had opted for 'compromise' settings, gambling on a dry track later in the race, which seemed curious, to say the least, given the meteorological forecasts. But he was not the only front runner to make this choice: both the Benettons were similarly set up.

'Obviously, it's a bad day for the championship, as far as I'm concerned,' Hill said. 'I made a bad start, but normally I reckon I'm as good as anyone in the wet. The biggest problem was visibility. On the first lap there were cars left and right of me, and I couldn't see them until I was on top of them. As for the road ahead, you couldn't see that at all. I actually felt that the race should have been started behind the pace car, but I don't know what the other drivers wanted.'

Schumacher, for one, agreed with Hill. 'That's what the pace car's here for, and I can't understand why it wasn't used.' Certainly, had it been employed, there might have been more for the few spectators to watch,

but the powers-that-be had decreed otherwise, and that was that.

Others unemployed early on included David Coulthard, who went out on the first lap after contact with he knew not whom. 'I just couldn't see anything at the start, so I pulled to the inside to watch the white line, in order to see the track. The next thing I knew was that my right front corner had gone – I've no idea who I hit, because I couldn't see him, anyway...'

McLaren, after a recent spell of good performances, were nowhere. Mika Hakkinen ultimately finished fifth, but way off the pace, lapped. His car, he said with some tact, had been 'very difficult to handle'.

At Monaco, to Giancarlo Minardi's consummate disappointment, his two drivers contrived to collect each other on the opening lap; two weeks later it happened again, Giancarlo Fisichella running blindly into the back of Pedro Lamy. 'Bad luck – and an excess of enthusiasm – have spoiled another race that could have been favourable to us,' the boss growled.

The Minardi boys, though, were bit players at Barcelona – as indeed, relatively, were all the drivers save Schumacher. Once Michael had got into the lead, the rate at which he went away was simply stupefying. Usually lapping four clear seconds faster than anyone else, he increased his lead from two to 34 seconds in a matter of 10 laps.

As Benetton team mate Jean Alesi drove to second place, Gerhard Berger spun off as he tried to lap Pedro Diniz

Moreover, there was not the hint of a mistake. Sometimes the tail of the Ferrari would kick out into a glorious powerslide, but one had the impression that Michael was doing this almost for fun, as if trying to give the spectators something to keep them – and himself – amused. It was not quite so, of course, for Schumacher is way too intelligent to put a race victory at unnecessary risk. More to the point was that, by continuing to drive hard, he was keeping his ferocious concentration level topped up.

The car, unquestionably, was working with him. 'After qualifying,' he said afterwards, 'we were nowhere, in comparison with Williams. In Brazil and Monaco the car didn't feel good in the wet, so I wasn't expecting anything from today, when I woke up and saw the rain. But in the warm-up the car was handling well, which really surprised me, and in the race I pushed it, and the car was superb, especially at the beginning.'

Yes, but why was he so much quicker than everyone else? 'I've no explanation for it,' he replied, a touch modestly, one thought. 'Our car seems to be very sensitive to certain weather conditions, and today it was handling well. We made some final changes after the warm-up, which suited the car even more, and our strategy – two stops – was perfect.'

The stops came on laps 24 and 42, and both were perfectly carried out. Given his advantage, of course, there was no question of Schumacher losing the lead on either occasion, and he simply drove on through the murk and gloom, circulating at a speed beyond the dreams of any rival.

It was noticeable, too, that he played with lines far more than anyone else. 'I tried some different lines, yes, and they paid off very well. There were three or four points on the circuit which were very critical – every time you went over them, you nearly lost the car. There were streams across the track, and their positions changed over the course of the race, so it was necessary to adapt.'

Simple as that.

The rain continued to bounce off the road, and even Alesi, who had not

---

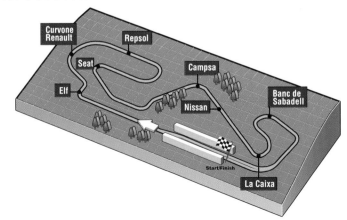

## SPANISH GP
### ROUND 7

**2 June 1996**
**FIA Formula 1 World Championship**

**Race data:** 65 laps of a 2.93-mile circuit
**Weather:** Wet
**Distance:** 190.45 miles

**Winner:** Michael Schumacher, Ferrari F310, 95.56mph
**Previous result:** Michael Schumacher, Benetton-Renault B195, 121.37mph
**Fastest lap:** Michael Schumacher, Ferrari F310, 1m45.517s

## *Barcelona*

Curvone Renault · Repsol · Seat · Elf · Campsa · Nissan · Banc de Sabadell · Start/Finish · La Caixa

## STARTING GRID

| | DRIVER | |
|---|---|---|
| 1 | Hill | 1:20.650 |
| 2 | Villeneuve | 1:21.084 |
| 3 | Schumacher | 1:21.587 |
| 4 | Alesi | 1:22.061 |
| 5 | Berger | 1:22.125 |
| 6 | Irvine | 1:22.333 |
| 7 | Barrichello | 1:22.379 |
| 8 | Panis | 1:22.685 |
| 9 | Herbert | 1:23.027 |
| 10 | Hakkinen | 1:23.070 |
| 11 | Frentzen | 1:23.195 |
| 12 | Salo | 1:23.224 |
| 13 | Verstappen | 1:23.371 |
| 14 | Coulthard | 1:23.416 |
| 15 | Brundle | 1:23.438 |
| 16 | Katayama | 1:24.401 |
| 17 | Diniz | 1:24.468 |
| 18 | Lamy | 1:25.274 |
| 19 | Fisichella | 1:25.531 |
| 20 | Rosset | 1:25.621 |
| DNQ | Badoer | 1:26.615 |
| DNQ | Montermini | 1:27.358 |

thought a 'pace car' start necessary, believed that the vehicle should have been brought out as the halfway stage approached. It was not, however, to be seen at any stage.

While Schumacher disappeared, Villeneuve continued to run second, with Alesi third, and Berger fourth. Then it was Barrichello, in another fine drive for Jordan-Peugeot, Frentzen, showing remarkably well after his morning accident, Verstappen, Hakkinen and Diniz. And that, long before half-distance, was it.

In the Ferrari pit, they had the simple agony of waiting out time. Quite obviously, Schumacher was beyond threat from anything but the reliability of his car. And on lap 33, as it came by the pits, it sounded rough, the crisp bark of the V10 suddenly flat, as if it had dropped a cylinder.

'From that point on,' Michael said, 'I was on eight or nine cylinders, which wasn't too pleasant. I lost some power, of course, but that wasn't too

much of a problem in these conditions. My worry was that I wouldn't finish. I think it must have been an electronics problem, because it cleared up a couple of times, but then it came back for the last 20 laps. In the last part of the race I wasn't even at the rev limit in fifth, let alone using sixth.'

Not much happened on the track from there on in, although there were three significant retirements in the last part of the race. On lap 45 Barrichello made an unscheduled stop, for attention to a slipping clutch, which the engineers were able to fix only temporarily. And at the same time Berger went missing from fourth place.

Gerhard had recently made his one and only pitstop, but the mechanics had been unable to release his left rear wheel, sending him back into the race with only three new tyres. Soon afterwards he spun off.

'It was my mistake, and that was a

shame, because the car was very good throughout the race. I was trying to lap Diniz, and I had to do it on the straight because there was no way to stay close behind him in the spray. I tried to show him I was alongside, and he should let me through, but he didn't realise. I left my braking too late, and spun.'

Two laps later, so also did Verstappen. 'I seemed to follow Frentzen for the whole race, and I think maybe I was a bit quicker, if not enough to get by him. Then I went over a puddle, got sideways, and simply lost it...' We were down to six, and those six, mercifully, made it to the finish.

Alesi and Villeneuve each made a single stop, Jean on lap 32, Jacques four laps later, and in the course of the stops the Benetton got ahead of the Williams, where it stayed until the end. 'My first set went off after 10 laps,' Villeneuve said, 'but on the second set the car was very good, and

I could catch Jean a bit, but not enough to fight with him.' The Williams trimmed the Benetton's advantage from 10 to two seconds in the closing laps, but Alesi always looked likely to keep ahead.

Three very wet and cold drivers presented themselves at the press conference. 'I was freezing in the car,' said Schumacher, 'and it was so cold on the podium that my teeth were chattering louder than an engine.'

'Four or five times,' Alesi muttered, 'I came so close to putting it into the wall. I think the team made a big mistake, choosing to stop only once, but at least at the stop I was able to get ahead of Jacques – to overtake him on the track, would have been impossible in the conditions today.'

Not for Schumacher, though, who drove as great a race as we have seen from him.

'It was okay for the first few laps,' Villeneuve grinned, 'until Michael got in my mirrors. Then he flew by...' ∎

## RACE RESULTS

| | DRIVER | CAR | RACE | LAPS | RESULT |
|---|---|---|---|---|---|
| 1 | Michael Schumacher (D) | Ferrari | 1m45.517s | 65 | 1h59m49.307s |
| 2 | Jean Alesi (F) | Benetton-Renault | 1m46.509s | 65 | 2h00m34.609s |
| 3 | Jacques Villeneuve (CDN) | Williams-Renault | 1m48.707s | 65 | 2h00m37.695s |
| 4 | Heinz-Harald Frentzen (D) | Sauber-Ford | 1m48.955s | 64 | 2h00m05.321s |
| 5 | Mika Hakkinen (FIN) | McLaren-Mercedes | 1m49.771s | 64 | 2h00m57.086s |
| 6 | Pedro Diniz (BR) | Ligier-Mugen Honda | 1m50.636s | 63 | 2h00m33.439s |
| R | Jos Verstappen (NL) | Footwork-Hart | 1m48.302s | 47 | spin |
| R | Rubens Barrichello (BR) | Jordan-Peugeot | 1m47.735s | 45 | transmission |
| R | Gerhard Berger (A) | Benetton-Renault | 1m49.097s | 44 | spin |
| R | Johnny Herbert (GB) | Sauber-Ford | 1m48.845s | 20 | spin |
| R | Martin Brundle (GB) | Jordan-Peugeot | 1m49.026s | 17 | transmission |
| R | Mika Salo (FIN) | Tyrrell-Yamaha | 1m51.734s | 16 | black flag |
| R | Damon Hill (GB) | Williams-Renault | 1m50.987s | 10 | accident |
| R | Ukyo Katayama (J) | Tyrrell-Yamaha | 1m55.116s | 8 | electrics |
| R | Eddie Irvine (GB) | Ferrari | 1m59.611s | 1 | spin |
| R | Olivier Panis (F) | Ligier-Mugen Honda | | 1 | accident damage |
| R | Giancarlo Fisichella (I) | Minardi-Ford | | 1 | accident damage |
| R | David Coulthard (GB) | McLaren-Mercedes | | 0 | accident |
| R | Ricardo Rosset (BR) | Footwork-Hart | | 0 | accident |
| R | Pedro Lamy (P) | Minardi-Ford | | 0 | accident |

Brazilian brothers in arms: (from left to right) Rubens Barrichello, Pedro Diniz and Ricardo Rosset

## CHAMPIONSHIP POSITIONS

| | DRIVER | PTS | CONSTRUCTOR | PTS |
|---|---|---|---|---|
| 1 | Hill | 43 | Williams-Renault | 69 |
| 2 | Schumacher | 26 | Ferrari | 35 |
| 3 | Villeneuve | 26 | Benetton-Renault | 24 |
| 4 | Alesi | 17 | McLaren-Mercedes | 18 |
| 5 | Panis | 11 | Ligier-Mugen Honda | 12 |
| 6 | Coulthard | 10 | Sauber-Ford | 10 |

FIA FORMULA 1 WORLD CHAMPIONSHIP

# HILL FIGHTS BACK TO DENY JACQUES WIN

After the disasters of Monaco and Barcelona, Damon Hill savoured the sweet smell of success again in Canada to deny local hero Jacques Villeneuve the home victory that the capacity crowd so wanted

**A**fterwards Damon Hill said it had been a great race, and you could see his point of view, for he controlled the Canadian Grand Prix from first to last, put his fifth victory of the season on the board, and added another 10 points to his tally on a day when world champion Michael Schumacher failed to score.

For Hill, therefore, of course it was a great race, and for Jacques Villeneuve, too, it was a pretty good one, for he made it a 1-2 for Williams-Renault, set fastest lap, and had the capacity crowd cheering, if not ecstatic, at the end. Really, though, it was good for the spectators that their boy finished well, for there was little else to hold their attention through the afternoon.

The race amounted to another demonstration of superiority by

Williams-Renault. There had been hopes that Schumacher might give them a run, but his Ferrari refused to fire up on time, which meant starting from the back. Although Michael predictably made up places quickly, brake problems mired him in midfield, and he was never a factor, eventually retiring with a spectacularly broken driveshaft.

Jean Alesi took the third step on the podium, after a consistent drive in the Benetton-Renault, but was never a threat to the Williams. Both McLaren-Mercedes drivers took points, David Coulthard again heading Mika Hakkinen, but they might well have

been beaten – given a trouble-free run – by the Jordan-Peugeot of Martin Brundle, who had the best race of his season to date, and took the final point on offer.

A great race, though, Damon? Only if you won it, to be honest.

Raceday in Montreal was near perfect for motor racing, warm, sunny and blue, with low humidity. Possibly the only man in the place disappointed was Schumacher, who so revelled in the rains of Barcelona. He was only 13th fastest in the morning warm-up, but no one read too much into that.

For Montreal, Ferrari produced a Benetton-style high nose, and sinfully ugly it was, too, utterly disfiguring a once elegant car. It is the first step in a new aerodynamic package, the rest of which is to follow, and in the warm-up Michael, who ran both his own car and the spare, at one point tried a revised version of the original low nose, to check its compatibility with the rest of the set-up, the high noses being in short supply.

If Schumacher made no attempt to set a quick time, Hill and Villeneuve assuredly did, finishing up one-two, as in qualifying. Both Damon and Jacques declared themselves well content with the handling and balance of the Williams-Renaults. Even the world champion, it seemed clear, would be hard put to push them.

At Montreal, 12 months before, virtually all the leading runners made only one stop for fuel and tyres, but this time, with a softer compound Goodyear on hand, the speculation was that most would stop twice, and that one or two – notably Schumacher – might even make it three. Never trust pre-race mutterings in the paddock was what we learned in Canada. Again.

In fact, the thing faded into insignificance even before the start, for when the cars went away on the parade lap, Schumacher's Ferrari, almost certainly the only threat to the Williams-Renaults, remained stationary on the grid, engine dead. Low fuel pressure was the explanation for the V10's refusal to start, but eventually the mechanics got it fired up, and Michael howled away, now destined to start from the very back. All things being equal, his charge through the field would be worth watching, but

any thoughts of his bothering the Williams pair were already dispelled.

Tooling round on the parade lap, Hill and Villeneuve could scarcely believe their good fortune. 'There was still plenty at stake, though,' Damon said. 'Jacques and I had no idea how many stops the others were planning, of course, but obviously we knew each other's strategy.'

Hill had decided to go for two stops, Villeneuve for only one. 'Obviously, I had to try to get ahead of Damon at the start, and stay there until the first of his stops,' said Jacques, 'to prevent him from doing the lap times he was capable of, running with a lighter fuel load. That was the plan, anyway.' Hill, for his part, was hardly unaware of this, and well understood the importance of a clear track.

'My start was good, a little bit better than Damon's,' Villeneuve said, 'but I'm sure he was looking pretty hard in his mirrors, because he went right, then left, so I had to go across the track twice, and he was on the inside for the first turn. Once we were at the turn, understandably he got wider, and I had to back off. I was on the outside, locked my brakes, slowed a little too much...'

The fact that the Williams drivers were on different strategies became swiftly obvious to onlookers by the rate at which Hill put distance between himself and Villeneuve. The gap was two seconds by the end of the opening lap, and thereafter increased steadily every time round. As well as carrying a heavier fuel load, Jacques was treating his brakes with circumspection, mindful of this track's fearsome reputation for eating them. 'In fact,' he said, 'that was my mistake, I think. I could have gone harder in the early part of the race, and I should have done.'

For a while the second Williams came under pressure from Alesi (also on a one-stop strategy), but as Villeneuve settled in, began to use his brakes a little harder, so the Benetton became a speck in his mirrors. Alesi, indeed, was soon caught by team mate Berger, and appeared for a time to be holding him up. 'I was having a bit of trouble with the rear tyres at that point,' Jean explained, somewhat enigmatically, 'so I slowed a bit.'

In fact, he kept up a remarkably

good clip, given that he was in some pain, a legacy of his heavy qualifying accident the day before, when he had brake failure, and had to put the Benetton into a spin, before hitting a tyre barrier. Where did he hurt? 'Everywhere! But not during the race, because I was too busy to think about it. The main thing was that my neck gave me no problem at all, and that was what worried me before the race. The headrest and the new high cockpit sides really helped.'

In Montreal, a year before, Alesi scored his first – and so far only – Grand Prix victory, in a Ferrari, but it was evident that the red cars were no sort of factor this time. Eddie Irvine, after qualifying well, lasted but a single lap, pulling off with a disturbing suspension failure. 'The right front pushrod broke on the straight, for no obvious reason,' he said. 'A real shame, because I could easily run with Alesi.'

Schumacher, meantime, had dispensed with five cars in the course of the opening lap, then another two on the next one, but after that the charge rather petered out, Michael reaching 14th place, but apparently going no further. He was unable to challenge Mika Salo's Tyrrell-Yamaha, which had to mean that something was awry.

Into the first turn Schumacher was plainly backing off early, and from his wheels there was no trace of carbon brake glow. He had gone into the race with a heavy fuel load, planning only one stop, so the Ferrari was not in

Clockwise from above: There was no repeat victory for Jean Alesi. Michael Schumacher could only look forward to better times. Rubens Barrichello tried but failed to get around the outside of Heinz-Harald Frentzen. Five out of eight for Damon Hill so far

# IN HINDSIGHT

The dreadfully dull race that was the Canadian Grand Prix once again focused attention on exactly why the sport's governing body is looking hard into ways of improving the spectacle of Formula 1.

As early as the Argentinian Grand Prix, it became known that FIA president Max Mosley (below) was trying to find ways of changing F1 cars to make them more raceable.

It is a complicated problem. When a car closes in on another, the airflow over the front wings is disturbed, robbing downforce, and making it understeer. This, in turn makes it slow through the corners, and therefore impossible for a driver to follow another too closely. On top of that, it was agreed, braking distances were too short, reducing the time and space in which a driver could pass a rival.

The easiest solution would be to take off the wings, but as ever, commerce ruled over all, and it was decided that this would result in sponsors losing exposure space.

Attention initially focused on creating more grip from the underside of the car and less from the wings. But when that project ran into a hitch, the FIA hit on the idea of running grooved tyres.

These would reduce grip, the theory went, increasing braking distances. It would, however, make little difference to the cars' senstivity to changing downforce levels, while Goodyear and leading designers were far from convinced the idea would work at all. Whether it works in practice, only the 1998 season, when the grooved tyres are set to be introduced, will tell.

ideal condition to chop through traffic, anyway. Had he, in these circumstances, used his brakes too much too soon?

Michael said not. 'The problem was that I couldn't rely on them, because, for some reason, the front-to-rear brake balance kept adjusting itself! I wasn't touching it, but it changed all the time, and I never really knew what I was going to get. Like that, there was no way to push hard. If you have a brake problem at this circuit, you're finished.'

For lap after lap, therefore, we beheld the strange sight of Schumacher running in convoy with Olivier Panis's Ligier and Salo's Tyrrell. Worse was to follow. On lap 16 Villeneuve set the fastest lap to date, and for the first time succeeded in trimming back Hill's lead, if only by three-tenths or so, to 6.7s. Perhaps, if their pit stop strategies were indeed different on this occasion, Jacques had made the right decision. Either way, there wasn't going to be much in it, although Damon lost little time in pulling it out to nine seconds again.

Behind them, at one-third distance, ran Alesi, Berger – and Brundle. Martin has always excelled in Montreal, and was running true to form, aided at first by a light fuel load, Jordan having opted for two stops. After an excellent start, which gained him a couple of places, Brundle quickly dispensed with Hakkinen's McLaren, moving up to fifth, then

proceeding to close on the Benetton pair. Behind him, it took team mate Rubens Barrichello decidedly longer to get by Hakkinen; for the first time in 1996 Martin was the Jordan-Peugeot pacesetter.

On lap 28 the lead changed, when Hill came in for fuel and tyres. It was a routine stop, with nothing untoward, but Damon was now seven seconds behind Villeneuve, and as Jacques continued to stay out, quite obviously his strategy was different from his team mate's. At the end of lap 36 he made his one and only stop, rejoining 20 seconds behind Hill – who had still another stop to come. Maybe this wasn't as cut-and-dried as it had seemed.

Down the field, Schumacher was having a terrible time. Being unable to pass Johnny Herbert's Sauber-Ford was one thing, being caught by the Ligier of Diniz quite another. Pedro got right on the tail of the Ferrari, and must have thought that reality had been suspended. What was he to do in these circumstances? Should he try to pass the world champion, or should he play safe and keep back?

Before Diniz could make a decision on this, Schumacher's brake balance readjusted itself in a manner more acceptable to him, and he drew away again, but it had been a nasty moment. On lap 41, though, his nightmarish afternoon concluded. He made his stop, then took off from the pit in a cloud of tyre smoke. 'There was a problem with the clutch,' he said, 'which was why I got so much

**Mika Hakkinen and David Coulthard ran nose to tail for much of the race**

wheelspin.'

The violence of the getaway was more than the Ferrari could tolerate. As the car went down the pit lane, it began shedding bits and pieces, the most crucial of which was a driveshaft, which was retrieved by a Forti mechanic. 'It was a really bad day,' he said, with consummate understatement, 'but the important thing is not to be discouraged.'

Nor would he be. But later he looked at his situation as realistically as always. 'The world championship,' he said, 'is as good as settled now.'

In recent weeks something dire had happened to reliability levels in

# CANADIAN GP
## ROUND 8

**16 June 1996**
**FIA Formula 1 World Championship**

**Race data:** 69 laps of a 2.748-mile circuit
**Weather:** Dry and sunny
**Distance:** 189.612 miles

**Winner:** Damon Hill,
Williams Renault FW18, 118.40mph
**Previous result:** Jean Alesi,
Ferrari 412 T2, 107.06mph
**Fastest lap:** Jacques Villeneuve,
Williams Renault FW18, 1m21.916s

*Montreal*

## STARTING GRID

| | DRIVER | |
|---|---|---|
| 1 | Hill | 1:21.059 |
| 2 | Villeneuve | 1:21.079 |
| 3 | Schumacher | 1:21.198 |
| 4 | Alesi | 1:21.529 |
| 5 | Irvine | 1:21.657 |
| 6 | Hakkinen | 1:21.807 |
| 7 | Berger | 1:21.926 |
| 8 | Barrichello | 1:21.982 |
| 9 | Brundle | 1:22.321 |
| 10 | Coulthard | 1:22.332 |
| 11 | Panis | 1:22.481 |
| 12 | Frentzen | 1:22.875 |
| 13 | Verstappen | 1:23.067 |
| 14 | Salo | 1:23.118 |
| 15 | Herbert | 1:23.201 |
| 16 | Fisichella | 1:23.519 |
| 17 | Katayama | 1:23.599 |
| 18 | Diniz | 1:23.959 |
| 19 | Lamy | 1:24.262 |
| 20 | Badoer | 1:25.012 |
| 21 | Rosset | 1:25.193 |
| 22 | Montermini | 1:26.109 |

Through all this, the Williams duo continued to circulate serenely. At the end of lap 50, Hill came in for his final stop, getting on his way again after 8.6 seconds. 'All through the race,' Damon said, 'I knew that the critical thing was to come out ahead of Jacques at the last stop. If I got behind him, I knew there wouldn't be much chance of getting past.'

He had no real cause for worry. Villeneuve was still 12 seconds adrift, and although he began to close the gap, sometimes quite substantially, in the last few laps, Hill ultimately maintained a cushion of around eight seconds, backing off only on the final lap when he knew he was safe.

Back on lap 48, Villeneuve had lapped Herbert, then immediately suspected that he might have done it under a yellow flag. 'I let Johnny through again,' he said, 'thinking that otherwise I might get a stop/go.' In less than a lap, he repassed the Sauber, but lost more than three seconds in the process at what could have been a crucial moment in the afternoon's activities.

'After that, I kept pushing,' Jacques went on. 'Damon wasn't far enough in the lead for me to back off, and I figured that if I kept going hard, I'd be close enough to benefit if he made a mistake or got caught out by some backmarkers later in the race.'

'After two races without scoring, I'm particularly happy to have won here,' said Hill. 'No matter what anyone says, you do start to worry about these things. Jacques and I had different strategies today, and I don't think there was much to choose between them. So it was a tough race, in that I had to drive hard all the way through, knowing – after our battle in qualifying – that it was going to be very close between us. He put pressure on me all the way.' And what of Schumacher's suggestion that the world championship was now effectively over?

Hill grinned at that. 'Well, if you think back to the start of the season, Michael said he wasn't even thinking about the championship this year! I think Ferrari's goal has always been to get up there in the second half of the season – which begins now. Michael isn't going to go away.' ■

Formula 1. There were very few finishers at Monte Carlo and Barcelona, in part explained by the high accident rate which invariably accompanies a wet race, but in Montreal the sun shone and the cars continued to fall by the wayside.

Katayama's Tyrrell-Yamaha and Rosset's Arrows-Hart had departed in spectacular fashion in the early stages, Ukyo trying a passing move on Ricardo at the last chicane which was never vaguely on. Engine failures accounted for their respective team mates, Salo and Verstappen, and Frentzen's Sauber, well up in the opening laps, went out with a broken

gearbox. Add in the Ferraris, the Fortis and the Ligiers, and the field was looking pretty thin as the race came towards its conclusion.

Brundle's Jordan came close to joining the retirements, too. Team mate Rubens Barrichello had earlier gone out with a broken clutch (troublesome from the start), but Martin was running up in fourth place when he made his final stop, on lap 44. Accelerating out of the pit lane, he reached the first turn immediately behind Lamy, and believed the Minardi driver was letting him through. This was not the case, and Brundle was back in the pits next

time round, this time for a new nosecone to be fitted.

If the McLaren-Mercedes were not exactly on the pace, still they ran like watches all afternoon, much of the time nose to tail. Hakkinen was marginally ahead of Coulthard until he spun at the hairpin, trying to lap Fisichella's Minardi.

Mika did, however, keep the engine alive, which was more than could be said for Berger, who spun fourth place away on lap 43, trying to catch team mate Alesi. Typically, Gerhard made no excuses: 'It was my mistake, unfortunately. I was going hard, and simply braked too late.'

## RACE RESULTS

| | DRIVER | CAR | RACE | LAPS | RESULT |
|---|---|---|---|---|---|
| 1 | Damon Hill (GB) | Williams-Renault | 1m21.957s | 69 | 1h36m03.465s |
| 2 | Jacques Villeneuve (CDN) | Williams-Renault | 1m21.916s | 69 | 1h36m07.648s |
| 3 | Jean Alesi (F) | Benetton-Renault | 1m22.824s | 69 | 1h36m58.121s |
| 4 | David Coulthard (GB) | McLaren-Mercedes | 1m22.941s | 69 | 1h37m07.138s |
| 5 | Mika Hakkinen (FIN) | McLaren-Mercedes | 1m23.070s | 68 | 1h36m19.585s |
| 6 | Martin Brundle (GB) | Jordan-Peugeot | 1m22.958s | 68 | 1h36m36.934s |
| R | Johnny Herbert (GB) | Sauber-Ford | 1m23.907s | 68 | 1h36m55.183s |
| R | Giancarlo Fisichella (I) | Minardi-Ford | 1m24.349s | 67 | 1h36m44.064s |
| R | Pedro Lamy (P) | Minardi-Ford | 1m24.855s | 44 | accident |
| R | Luca Badoer (I) | Forti-Ford | 1m26.007s | 44 | gearbox |
| R | Gerhard Berger (A) | Benetton-Renault | 1m23.102s | 42 | spin |
| R | Michael Schumacher (D) | Ferrari | 1m24.163s | 41 | driveshaft |
| R | Olivier Panis (F) | Ligier-Mugen Honda | 1m23.399s | 39 | engine |
| R | Mika Salo (FIN) | Tyrrell-Yamaha | 1m23.648s | 39 | engine |
| R | Pedro Diniz (BR) | Ligier-Mugen Honda | 1m24.332s | 38 | engine |
| R | Rubens Barrichello (BR) | Jordan-Peugeot | 1m23.028s | 22 | clutch |
| R | Andrea Montermini (I) | Forti-Ford | 1m24.621s | 22 | loose ballast |
| R | Heinz-Harald Frentzen (D) | Sauber-Ford | 1m24.082s | 19 | gearbox |
| R | Jos Verstappen (NL) | Footwork-Hart | 1m24.844s | 10 | engine |
| R | Ricardo Rosset (BR) | Footwork-Hart | 1m26.347s | 6 | accident |
| R | Ukyo Katayama (J) | Tyrrell-Yamaha | 1m25.769s | 6 | accident |
| R | Eddie Irvine (IRL) | Ferrari | 1m33.016s | 1 | suspension |

## CHAMPIONSHIP POSITIONS

| | DRIVER | PTS | | CONSTRUCTOR | PTS |
|---|---|---|---|---|---|
| 1 | Hill | 53 | | Williams-Renault | 85 |
| 2 | Villeneuve | 32 | | Ferrari | 35 |
| 3 | Schumacher | 26 | | Benetton-Renault | 28 |
| 4 | Alesi | 21 | | McLaren-Mercedes | 23 |
| 5 | Coulthard | 13 | | Ligier-Mugen Honda | 12 |
| 6 | Panis | 11 | | Sauber-Ford | 10 |

FIA
FORMULA 1
WORLD
CHAMPIONSHIP

# HILL'S SIXTH WIN BOOSTS TITLE HOPES

He may have had 'the warm-up from hell', but for Damon Hill, the French Grand Prix was manna from heaven as he once again led home team mate Jacques Villeneuve.

Damon Hill probably wouldn't agree, but this is another of those years when the Williams-Renaults were simply too good. In Magny-Cours, Hill did not win the pole, but effectively he started from it, and thereafter lost the lead only briefly, following the first of his planned pit stops. So long as his car kept running, Damon was not to be threatened, and now had six victories from nine races.

After a sizeable accident in qualifying, Jacques Villeneuve did well to finish second again, which made it a fourth 1-2 for Williams in 1996, and the Benettons of Jean Alesi and Gerhard Berger, third and fourth, made it a clean sweep for Renault's latest RS8B V10 engine. In France, of course. The symmetry was perfect.

Hill inherited pole position on the formation lap, in the course of which, unthinkably, Michael Schumacher's Ferrari blew up. After unexpected reliability in the early part of the season, Ferrari preparation had fallen to pieces in recent times (too often literally), and when the disgusted World Champion took off his helmet and balaclava, his face was a colour match for his car. The title was not yet irretrievably lost, but Damon's hold on it was becoming more secure

## "How did I feel? Er, amazed and disbelieving and...delighted"

*Damon Hill*

by the day.

Damon's mood, though, was less than light on Sunday morning. 'That,' he declared, 'was the warm-up from hell.' First, he collided with Frentzen's Sauber-Ford at the hairpin, and it was hardly justice that Heinz-Harald's car was significantly the more damaged of the two. Typically, Hill made no excuses, and went to apologise. 'I was fiddling with an adjustment in the cockpit, and simply didn't see him,' he said. Then he went out in the T-car, and promptly straight-lined a sandtrap, this after a brake problem on which he did not elaborate.

His team mate, by contrast, was a markedly happier man than the day

before. Villeneuve's qualifying accident, at the exit of the first corner, meant a virtual all-nighter for his mechanics (who built up a car for him from a new monocoque), but also left him feeling stiff and sore. On raceday he wore a surgical collar, but said that the Williams physio, Erwin Golner, had worked miracles on him: 'The most important thing is that I can move my neck OK, although the muscles are pretty stretched, I guess.'

Important, too, was that the race set-up of his new car delighted him in the warm-up, and he set the fastest time, followed by Jean Alesi's Benetton, and the McLaren-Mercedes of Mika Hakkinen and David

Coulthard, with Schumacher fifth. A near accident was avoided, incidentally, when David's car was plucked by crane from a sand trap a handful of seconds before Michael's Ferrari arrived, both having gone off after locking their brakes.

After qualifying, Schumacher, while naturally pleased to be on pole position, had doubted he could sustain a Williams sort of pace for very long. In point of fact, he was somewhat fortunate to be in that position, for halfway through the qualifying session the FIA technical delegate, in response to an earlier request from Patrick Head, had checked Ferrari's bargeboards - on

Eddie Irvine's car - and found them to be mounted a little too high. That done, all three of the red cars disappeared behind the closed doors of the Ferrari garage for a while.

Before the check, Schumacher had done the lap which would give him the pole, and while there was no proving that his car, too, had been similarly 'in contravention of the rules' at the time, wicked cynics had their suspicions. As it was, the hapless Irvine had all his times disallowed, and would start from the very back.

Thus, as the cars departed on the formation lap, there was a Ferrari at either end of the pack, but this state of affairs was not to last. Out of the hairpin, Hill noticed that Schumacher's car was smoking.

'Before the start you have all sorts of permutations in your head,' Damon said, 'but then when you go off on the formation lap, and the guy's engine blows up...I mean, it's not what you expect, really, is it? How did I feel? Er, amazed and disbelieving and...delighted!'

For a long time, Hill has been on the receiving end of sundry contemptuous remarks from his German rival, and none could begrudge him a smirk or two on this occasion. 'Of course it made the race a whole lot easier for me,' he said,

'and it rather changed my thinking for it, you could say that.

'In fact, I was worried that Michael's engine was going to blow up in a big way, and leave a huge oilslick, so I had to back off. His car was spraying a lot of oil out on the track, and also onto my visor. Actually, it's easy to get distracted by something like that, and I still had to concentrate on making a good start.'

Schumacher, meantime, alighted from his stricken car, momentarily unable quite to cope with enormity of what had happened. 'I was,' he said, 'very angry at first. In a few seconds, I saw all the hard work I've done with

the team go up in smoke.' Literally, as well as metaphorically. Then the ice man in Michael reasserted itself. 'It's at times like this that you must control your emotions, and stay cool and rational. We must not get discouraged. We must grit our teeth, and continue to push on.' Light-hearted stuff. And there was more from team director Jean Todt: 'This is the blackest day of my long career in motor sport.'

It didn't help, either, that among the earliest retirements in the race was that of Irvine's sister car, which lasted but five laps before halting with gearbox hydraulics failure. Ferrari's

renaissance may have been underway, but remained on the nursery slopes for the moment. Uncharitable souls recalled the events of the previous day, and one or two murmured something about 'justice'.

When the red lights went out, Hill got the start he wanted, and confidently led Alesi and the rest into the first turn, quickly pulling out a comfortable lead. Behind Jean ran Hakkinen, under immediate pressure from Villeneuve, Berger, who had not got away well, Brundle, Coulthard and, amazingly, Diniz, making the most of his Mugen Honda horsepower, together with Ligier's

Above: Michael Schumacher's French Grand Prix was over before it even started. Right: Pedro Diniz had moved up to sixth when his engine failed. Below: This was the roughest ride Flavio Briatore got all weekend – his drivers finished third and fourth

# IN HINDSIGHT

The announcement that Renault was to withdraw its supply of engines from Formula 1 at the end of 1997 was not entirely a surprise, but it nevertheless sent shockwaves through the sport.

Frenzied speculation began as to who would fill the gap. Would Honda return, and if so with Williams or Benetton? What about BMW, whose executives had flown to the British GP the previous year with Frank Williams? Could Mercedes, despite denials, supply Williams instead of McLaren in 1998? Would Williams swap one French engine for another and take Peugeot away from Jordan, even though he had reportedly told Eddie Jordan that he would not? And so on.

Everyone had a point of view, and F1 boss Bernie Ecclestone (above) weighed in in Magny-Cours with the suggestion that both Honda and BMW were indeed working up to a Grand Prix return.

Come the end of the season, though, and the prospects of BMW back on the grid in the near future looked increasingly slim, even if Honda remained a strong tip.

The sub-text to this, however, was the worry that engine suppliers would begin to find F1 less attractive. Although Renault left because it felt it had achieved all it could and could only lose by staying in, others, it was feared, may go for other reasons.

What was appallingly unreliable Yamaha gaining from F1, for example (below)? And very few other manufacturers would stay in indefinitely. And if more than a couple pulled out, what would the teams do for engines? The question remained unanswered at the end of the season.

intimate knowledge of this, their very own test track.

Soon the French Grand Prix settled down. Perhaps, if he had started alongside Hill, Villeneuve might have been able to stay with him, but he had not, and was trapped, to some degree, behind Hakkinen. Mika was pretty quick in the first turn, the quick one,' said Jacques, 'and he had good straightline speed, so it was tough behind him.'

And the pain from the practice shunt? 'Well, it was bad for the first five laps or so, but after that it heated up, and with the adrenaline, I guess, it became a bit numb – until halfway through the race, when it began to hurt quite a lot again.'

By lap 15, Hill ran seven seconds clear of Alesi, with Hakkinen third, a slightly frustrated Villeneuve fourth, then Berger, then Brundle, pushed by Coulthard, and Diniz, Barrichello and Panis running all of a bunch. On lap 18, indeed, Ligier chose to bring Panis in early for his first stop, simply because he was stuck in traffic. The notion was sound, but unfortunately a fault in Olivier's refuelling equipment meant that not a lot of gas went in, and now he would have to stop three times, rather than twice. It was unfortunate because for some of the time he was among the fastest drivers on the track.

The really significant stops began with Alesi, on lap 21, Hill and Hakkinen pitting on lap 27, which allowed Villeneuve temporarily into the lead. Once there, Jacques put in three very quick laps before making his own stop, on lap 30, and this allowed him to get out of the pits ahead of Hakkinen, whom he had been unable to overtake on the track.

Now Villeneuve was in his element. 'After the first pit stop, I was running by myself, and the second set of tyres were really good. I could make up quite a lot of time then.' At a remarkable rate, he began to close on Alesi, whom he passed into the hairpin on lap 37. 'Jean was very clean in letting me by,' Jacques commented. 'I think he had a

problem with his brakes, which made my life easier.'

Alesi confirmed this was so: 'My car was very good at the start of the race, but as the fuel load lightened, I began to have problems at the rear - I couldn't brake as I had at the beginning. When I was caught by Jacques, I didn't really give him any problem. I stayed on the line, and he overtook me on the inside. Then I tried to follow him, but I couldn't.'

Once into second place, Villeneuve settled into a very quick rhythm, sometimes interrupted by uncooperative backmarkers, such as Pedro Lamy. For all that, he began gaining slightly on Hill, who was having his own traffic problems, and taking great care with them. 'It's true I was very circumspect in getting by some people, and it certainly cost me some time, but I didn't want to lose the race by tripping over a backmarker.' Thus, the gap came down, from 12 seconds on lap 37 to seven on lap 49, at which point Villeneuve made his second stop.

After that, he never looked so threatening again. 'My car was definitely at its best on the middle set of tyres,' Jacques said. 'The third set wasn't so good, and I spent a lot of time behind Panis, trying to lap him - I was never quite close enough to overtake him, but I was losing a lot of time behind him in the quick turns.'

Problem was, Panis was locked into his own private battle with Coulthard, whom he was chasing for sixth place. Ultimately, Villeneuve got by the Ligier, and renewed his pursuit of Hill,

who made his own final stop on lap 53, rejoining the race with a nine-second lead over his team mate. Nineteen laps remained to the flag.

Immediately, though, the gap began to grow - not by much, but by enough to show that Hill was firmly in control. 'As soon as I got the message that Jacques had got past Alesi, and was pushing, I had to pull my finger out, and get going,' said Damon.

Villeneuve never gave up, and came out of the race with the fastest lap, but the battle which truly enlivened the closing laps was not the one between the Williams-Renaults, but that between the Benetton team mates, Alesi and Berger, who were scrapping over third place. After a quiet beginning, Gerhard came on ever stronger through the race, and the rate at which he caught Jean suggested that this day he was the quicker of the two. Alesi, though, was never worried about being passed.

'In the battle with Gerhard, he was a bit quicker in the faster parts of the track, but I knew it was impossible for him to overtake, because of the turbulence. Actually I was playing with him a little bit - in some places I was very slow, just to upset him a little bit more! Five years we have been team mates now, and we have a very good friendship...'

Alesi's certainty that, even if Berger was a little quicker, he would not be able to get by him, sounds like a pretty good indictment of the current Formula 1 rules, but there is nothing new here. The phenomenon of 'dirty air', and all that it entails, has been

---

## FRENCH GP

### ■ ROUND 9

**30 June 1996**
**FIA Formula 1 World Championship**

**Race data:** 72 laps of a 2.640-mile circuit
**Weather:** Dry and sunny
**Distance:** 190.08 miles

**Winner:** Damon Hill,
Williams-Renault FW18, 118.17mph
**Previous result:** Michael Schumacher,
Benetton-Renault B195, 115.79mph
**Fastest lap:** Jacques Villeneuve,
Williams-Renault FW18, 1m18.610s

## *Magny-Cours*

Golf course bend
Adelaide curve
Estoril
Grande Courbe
Nürburgring
Imola curve
Château d'eau
Lycée bend
Chicane

RESULTS © 1996 Federation Internationale de l'Automobile, 8 Place de la Concorde, Paris, 75008 France

## STARTING GRID

| | DRIVER | |
|---|---|---|
| 1 | Schumacher | 1:15.989 |
| 2 | Hill | 1:16.058 |
| 3 | Alesi | 1:16.310 |
| 4 | Berger | 1:16.592 |
| 5 | Hakkinen | 1:16.634 |
| 6 | Villeneuve | 1:16.905 |
| 7 | Coulthard | 1:17.007 |
| 8 | Brundle | 1:17.187 |
| 9 | Panis | 1:17.390 |
| 10 | Barrichello | 1:17.665 |
| 11 | Diniz | 1:17.676 |
| 12 | Frentzen | 1:17.739 |
| 13 | Salo | 1:18.021 |
| 14 | Katayama | 1:18.242 |
| 15 | Verstappen | 1:18.324 |
| 16 | Herbert | 1:18.556 |
| 17 | Fisichella | 1:18.604 |
| 18 | Lamy | 1:19.241 |
| 19 | Rosset | 1:19.242 |
| 20 | Badoer | 1:20.562 |
| 21 | Montermini | 1:20.647 |
| 22 | Irvine | 1:17.443 |

the bane of Grand Prix racing for way too long now.

'I think I could have gone faster than Jean,' said Berger, 'but it would have been too risky to overtake, given that we are in the same team, and Benetton can't really afford any risks at the moment. Instead, I stayed behind, but kept the pressure on, waiting for a mistake - which he didn't make...'

**Left: Eddie Irvine failed to finish yet again for Ferrari. This time he lasted five laps. Below: United colours of Benetton**

The chequered flag fell for Hill, with Villeneuve coming in eight seconds later. 'There were no real worries in the race,' Damon said. 'The car behaved well, and the pit stops were good. I can't complain about anything. It's true that this morning's warm-up is something I'd prefer to forget, but maybe it's like they say: if it's a bad rehearsal, it'll be all right on the night. But Jacques is still there, and he'll keep fighting, I'm sure.'

This Villeneuve undertook to do. 'Of course I'll keep pushing. There's no point in giving up until it's over, is

there? For sure, qualifying better would help me a lot. I mean, I'm really happy with the result today, particularly after the big crash we had yesterday. I changed my lines a little bit in the race, and I drove the track a bit better today than in qualifying, so if we could get to that stage on Saturdays, I'm sure it would make a big difference.'

They came in two by two on Sunday: two Williams, then two Benettons, then two McLarens, and each team had cause for some satisfaction: Williams, because their

cars dominated as usual, Benetton, because both their cars, if not currently potential race winners, at least finished in the money, and McLaren, because at last they appear to be climbing the ladder again, albeit at a slower rate than they might wish.

The real nightmare at Magny-Cours was endured by Ferrari, who appeared to be facing a crisis. It was only a month since Schumacher brilliantly won in Barcelona, while Hill crashed out, but it seemed much longer. For now, anyway, the championship looked Damon's for the taking. ∎

"I was playing with him a little bit – in some places I was very slow, just to upset him"

*Jean Alesi*

## RACE RESULTS

| | DRIVER | CAR | RACE | LAPS | RESULT |
|---|---|---|---|---|---|
| 1 | Damon Hill (GB) | Williams-Renault | 1m18.938s | 72 | 1h36m28.795s |
| 2 | Jacques Villeneuve (CDN) | Williams-Renault | 1m18.610s | 72 | 1h36m36.922s |
| 3 | Jean Alesi (F) | Benetton-Renault | 1m19.378s | 72 | 1h37m15.237s |
| 4 | Gerhard Berger (A) | Benetton-Renault | 1m19.206s | 72 | 1h37m15.654s |
| 5 | Mika Hakkinen (FIN) | McLaren-Mercedes | 1m19.632s | 72 | 1h37m31.569s |
| 6 | David Coulthard (GB) | McLaren-Mercedes | 1m19.968s | 71 | 1h36m30.673s |
| 7 | Olivier Panis (F) | Ligier-Mugen Honda | 1m18.712s | 71 | 1h36m48.120s |
| 8 | Martin Brundle (GB) | Jordan-Peugeot | 1m20.414s | 71 | 1h37m07.503s |
| 9 | Rubens Barrichello (BR) | Jordan-Peugeot | 1m20.134s | 71 | 1h37m24.841s |
| 10 | Mika Salo (FIN) | Tyrrell-Yamaha | 1m20.710s | 70 | 1h36m52.589s |
| 11 | Johnny Herbert (GB) | Sauber-Ford | 1m21.262s | 70 | 1h37m43.573s |
| 12 | Ricardo Rosset (BR) | Footwork-Hart | 1m22.095s | 69 | 1h37m00.175s |
| 13 | Pedro Lamy (P) | Minardi-Ford | 1m22.842s | 69 | 1h37m47.135s |
| 14 | Heinz-Harald Frentzen (D) | Sauber-Ford | 1m21.273s | 56 | Stuck throttle |
| 15 | Ukyo Katayama (J) | Tyrrell-Yamaha | 1m20.989s | 33 | Engine |
| R | Luca Badoer (I) | Forti-Ford | 1m22.258s | 29 | Withdrew |
| R | Pedro Diniz (BR) | Ligier-Mugen Honda | 1m20.997s | 28 | Valve pressure |
| R | Jos Verstappen (NL) | Footwork-Hart | 1m21.461s | 10 | Steering |
| R | Eddie Irvine (GB) | Ferrari | 1m21.824s | 5 | Gearbox |
| R | Giancarlo Fisichella (I) | Minardi-Ford | 1m23.448s | 2 | Fuel pump |
| R | Andrea Montermini (I) | Forti-Ford | 1m24.818s | 2 | Withdrew |
| R | Michael Schumacher (D) | Ferrari | no time | 0 | Engine |

## CHAMPIONSHIP POSITIONS

| DRIVER | PTS | CONSTRUCTOR | PTS |
|---|---|---|---|
| Hill | 63 | Williams-Renault | 101 |
| Villeneuve | 38 | Ferrari | 35 |
| Schumacher | 26 | Benetton-Renault | 35 |
| Alesi | 25 | McLaren-Mercedes | 26 |
| Coulthard | 14 | Ligier-Mugen Honda | 12 |
| Panis | 11 | Sauber-Ford | 10 |

FIA
FORMULA 1
WORLD
CHAMPIONSHIP

# VILLENEUVE STEALS HILL'S THUNDER

It was meant to be Damon Hill's day. But a poor start and loose wheel handed his team-mate Jacques Villeneuve a British Grand Prix win and cut his lead in the championship to 15 points

**"There was this curious sensation at the front of the car for three or four laps..."**

*Damon Hill*

**Below: It was a result that none of Damon Hill's fans wanted. Above right: Jacques Villeneuve shares a joke with Martin Brundle**

The battle, if so it may be called, began only after the race. Jacques Villeneuve took the chequered flag at the end of the British Grand Prix, but it was not until three and a half hours later that he was confirmed as winner of the race, a Benetton protest having failed.

If Villeneuve drove to a flawless victory, Damon Hill, of course, was the man the crowd wished to see win at home. Hill narrowly beat his Williams-Renault team mate to the pole, but made a poor start, and was engulfed by several cars in the opening seconds, never getting higher than fourth before spinning out thanks to a loose front wheel.

No points for Damon at Silverstone, then, but joining Villeneuve on the podium were Gerhard Berger and Mika Hakkinen, two stars for whom success had been thin in 1996. In the meantime, Michael Schumacher, who found it hard to lose in 1995, was having a nightmare of a mid-season, his Ferrari again retiring early, this time with a hydraulic leak.

Both the Jordan-Peugeots scored points, which made a refreshing change, and David Coulthard made it two McLaren-Mercedes in the top six. Ferrari, though, had taken not a thing from the last three races. On the face of it, any challenge to Hill's world

championship was coming from Villeneuve alone.

A hot and balmy day had been promised by the forecasters for Sunday, but it hardly looked that at nine o'clock. Already it was muggy in the extreme, but of the sun there was no sign, and shortly before the warm-up a fine mist of rain descended on Silverstone. It soon abated and by the end of the half-hour times were close to those set in qualifying.

Hakkinen emerged fastest, and if that was a surprise, it was not a shock, for he had been markedly happier with the McLaren-Mercedes since its recent aerodynamic reconfiguration, and was in especially fine spirits after Saturday qualifying. 'But you're supposed to hate the "modern" Silverstone, Mika.' 'That was yesterday – today I love it!' David Coulthard, by contrast, was less confident in the McLaren following the changes, and was down in 16th, still dissatisfied with its balance.

Both Williams-Renault drivers – Villeneuve second, Hill third – were quite satisfied with their cars, although Damon pointed out that the changing conditions had made for a pretty inconclusive session. Schumacher, immediately behind them on qualifying times, was fourth, content with his Ferrari, and ready for a good race, to wash away memories of the debacle at Magny-Cours. He was in for disappointment.

The crowd, of course, was rabidly behind Hill, but in the paddock there was a feeling – based on nothing more than widespread hunch – that this might not be Damon's day, that Villeneuve would run him closer than usual, might indeed have the beating of him. Jacques, at last, was on a circuit he knows intimately, and had been uncharacteristically upset after narrowly missing pole position. 'I thought I was going to get it,' he said, 'and I feel I should have got it.'

The Williams drivers went for similar strategies at Silverstone, opting for two stops, although Hill went to the grid with a little more Elf than

Villeneuve. Starting with a heavier fuel load, it was therefore crucial that Hill should start well, and keep ahead of Villeneuve through the early laps, robbing him of the opportunity of running faster in a slightly lighter car.

He did not, though, get away well, to the point that not only Villeneuve got the drop on him before the first corner, but so also did Alesi, Hakkinen and Schumacher. The game was not necessarily lost – Jacques would have to make two stops, where Damon could still opt for one – but it was not a good beginning. 'I don't know why he made a bad start,' Villeneuve grinned. 'I'm just glad he did!

'Thing was, I had the same weapon as Damon – same car, same engine, and basically the same fuel strategy, so I knew it was important to get him at the start.'

Given that overtaking in contemporary Formula 1 is difficult anywhere, at Silverstone, many drivers report, it is especially nightmarish. Twelve months before, Schumacher and his patently quicker Benetton had to sit behind Alesi's Ferrari for 20 laps, Michael having resigned himself to 'waiting for the stops' to move up a place. Now it was Hill's turn.

This time, however, the Ferrari in front was more obliging. As early as lap two, there was smoke from Schumacher's car, and halfway round he backed off, cruised back to the pit, and drove straight into the garage. Down came the door immediately, and behind it Michael presumably expressed his disappointment in

Clockwise from main: And the winner is...Jacques Villeneuve. Silverstone saw Mika Hakkinen take his first podium of the year. It's all about to go wrong for Ferrari again, this time Eddie Irvine. Jean Alesi was another who failed to make it to the finish. Damon Hill stuck behind Michael Schumacher

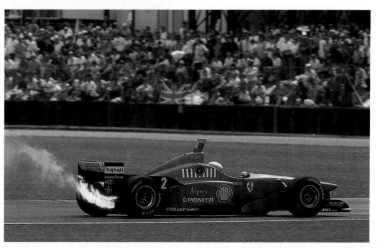

# IN HINDSIGHT

Silverstone was witness to the sad sight of a Formula 1 team in its death throes. Forti owed several suppliers 'a lot of money', according engine builder Cosworth, which was one of them. And a fed-up Cosworth refused to give the Italian outfit engines for the race.

The drivers were able to take part only in qualifying, and then both cars stopped out on the circuit having done just two laps, all the miles their remaining engines had left. The team had only filled the cars with enough fuel to take them up to maximum engine mileage.

Forti claimed it would be able to carry on, it was simply waiting for money from new partner Shannon. But the money never materialised, and that was the end of Forti.

But its problems highlighted the plight of the small teams in F1. Everyone recognised that Forti was a competent racing team — it had done a very good job in Formula 3000 — but it simply never had the money to do F1 properly.

After the demises of Larrousse, Lotus, Pacific and Simtek since the beginning of 1994, it was beginning to look as if starting up a team in F1 had become well-nigh impossible.

The costs involved in setting up a team are enormous. And how do you get a works engine deal, for example? Because without one your car will not be quick enough to attract any serious sponsorship. And what money you get will probably come from pay drivers, who are unlikely to be as good as other available drivers with less sizeable wallets. There, in a nutshell, was the Catch 22 situation.

Help was at hand, though, with the imminent arrival of the new Concorde Agreement, which afforded extra prize money and TV revenue to teams to such an extent that Minardi reckoned it may never have to take on a pay driver again.

But Minardi is an established team, and the concern about new teams being able to make the leap to F1 — and the prospect of an ever-diminishing grid — remained.

words of one syllable. A leak in the hydraulics system - reportedly the consequence of an under-tightened O-ring - had left him stuck in sixth gear. 'This,' he commented, 'is absurd. Since Magny-Cours, we have tested at Monza and Imola, then run here through two days of practice, and all without any failures. Now we come to the race, and we get this. Still, in racing things like this can happen...'

They can indeed, and the Ferrari disasters were not through yet. Irvine, after qualifying poorly, made a superb start, and was up in sixth by lap three; by lap five, though, there was smoke from the back of his car, too, and it was the same story as before: straight into the garage. This time the fault lay with a broken differential bearing.

While the Ferrari mechanics began packing up early once more, Villeneuve was at the front, and making hay. A second and a half up on Alesi at the end of the opening lap, he was 2.8s clear on the second, then 3.9, 5.2, 6.4, and like that. As early as lap three, he set a time which stood as fastest for much of the race.

Hill must have been cursing himself for his poor start, but there was little he could do about his predicament now. Villeneuve continued to put distance between himself and Alesi, who was a couple of seconds ahead of Hakkinen, and then came Damon.

'The McLaren was at its best in the early part of the race,' Mika said, 'because my first set of tyres was the best. I found I could hold Damon off, because, although his car was incredibly fast in the first part of the lap, it was not so quick further round - which is where the overtaking opportunities are. A couple of times he got really close, but not enough to get by me.'

For lap after endless lap, there was stalemate virtually throughout the field. By lap 15 Villeneuve was 17 seconds ahead of Alesi, not absolutely beyond reach, perhaps, but driving with a precision and authority which suggested no one would beat him this day. Hill, though, maintained he still had his hopes: 'I didn't consider all was lost, because I could have

changed my strategy, and made just one stop. I was still within 20 seconds of Jacques, and, that being so, I felt there was still a very good chance.'

Behind Hill, Barrichello ran fifth, then Berger, Brundle, Coulthard, and the Sauber-Fords, which circulated in close order, Herbert behind Frentzen, but clearly wishing to be ahead. On lap 17, Johnny made the move, and quickly pulled clear, going well at the circuit where he won in 1995, but with no such illusions this time.

Brundle began the planned stops, on lap 17, followed by team mate Barrichello, but the stop everyone was waiting for, of course, was that of Villeneuve. On lap 21 Jacques set what was to be the fastest lap of the race, and at the end of the 23rd he was in, taking on fuel and tyres, getting on his way in 9.5 seconds, and dropping - temporarily - to fourth place in the process.

Alesi now took the lead, with Hakkinen a couple of seconds behind him, and Hill still hounding the McLaren. Damon, though, was now becoming worried, for Villeneuve - having made the first of his stops - was right behind him, and there was also a rather more immediate concern. 'There was this curious sensation at the front of the car for three or four laps, and eventually I got on the radio, and told them there was a problem. Then, just as I was going into Copse, something seemed to seize at the front...'

On lap 27 the Williams swapped ends, and spun into the gravel trap. It had gone too suddenly to suggest a driving error, and as he waved to the crowds, Hill's body language, too, suggested that there had been nothing he could do about it. Disappointed beyond measure, Damon made his way back to the pits, and not a few spectators began heading home early.

The 'sensation at the front of the car' had been caused by a loosening left wheel nut - a problem which has periodically plagued Williams down the years. A locking device prevented the wheel from coming off, fortunately, but when Damon pressed the middle pedal before Copse, only the right-side brakes worked. Hence the spin.

As Hill retired, so Hakkinen made

his stop, which relegated him to fourth, behind Alesi, Villeneuve and Berger, with both the Benetton drivers still to make their single stops. Running in the lead, Alesi looked very composed, but so also did Villeneuve, who knew he would be back in front. On lap 31 Jean came in (10.4s), then Gerhard (also 10.4s) two laps later, which left Jacques with half a minute's lead over Hakkinen.

What we had at Silverstone, sad to say, was a largely dreary Grand Prix, truly marked only by Villeneuve's consummate domination. Hakkinen's McLaren was working less to the driver's taste on its second set of tyres, and anyway Mika, like Jacques, had another stop to make. Alesi and Berger were now going through to the end, but if Villeneuve's second stop went according to script, he faced no threat from them.

As in Magny-Cours, such entertainment as there was in the second half of the race looked likely to be provided by the rivalry of the Benetton drivers, for Berger, just as in France, was now coming on strongly, and catching his team mate.

'Jean,' said Gerhard, 'was pushing very hard - I could see the dust from his rear brakes, so I played with the brake balance on my car, at first putting too much on the front, but eventually getting it just about perfect.' Unlike Hakkinen, too, Berger found his second set of tyres much better than the first.

Soon the two were circulating as

---

# BRITISH GP

 **ROUND 10**

**14 July 1995**
**FIA Formula 1 World Championship**

**Race data:** 61 laps of a 3.152-mile circuit
**Weather:** Dry and sunny
**Distance:** 192.272 miles

**Winner:** Jacques Villeneuve, Williams-Renault FW18, 124.02mph
**Previous result:** Johnny Herbert, Benetton-Renault B195, 122.30mph
**Fastest lap:** Jacques Villeneuve, Williams-Renault FW18, 1m29.288s

## Silverstone

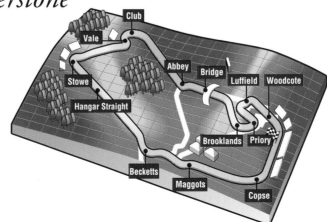

## STARTING GRID

| | DRIVER | |
|---|---|---|
| 1 | Hill | 1:26.875 |
| 2 | Villeneuve | 1:27.070 |
| 3 | Schumacher | 1:27.707 |
| 4 | Hakkinen | 1:27.856 |
| 5 | Alesi | 1:28.307 |
| 6 | Barrichello | 1:28.409 |
| 7 | Berger | 1:28.653 |
| 8 | Brundle | 1:28.946 |
| 9 | Coulthard | 1:28.966 |
| 10 | Irvine | 1:29.186 |
| 11 | Frentzen | 1:29.591 |
| 12 | Katayama | 1:29.913 |
| 13 | Herbert | 1:29.947 |
| 14 | Salo | 1:29.949 |
| 15 | Verstappen | 1:30.102 |
| 16 | Panis | 1:30.167 |
| 17 | Diniz | 1:31.076 |
| 18 | Fisichella | 1:31.365 |
| DSQ | Rosset | - |
| DNQ | Montermini | 1:35.206 |
| DNQ | Badoer | 1:35.304 |

Left: Last year's British GP winner Johnny Herbert finished ninth. Above: Martin Brundle took another point for Jordan on home ground

one, and by lap 43 Alesi's car was smoking. It was not slowing, however. Somewhat churlishly, despite surely realising that the end was nigh, Jean at first declined to let Gerhard through, but ultimately had no option. 'Suddenly,' he said, 'there was a problem with my brakes.' In fact, a rear wheel bearing had failed, and the Benetton coasted back to the pits. Alesi was mortified: 'I am hugely disappointed, because I was on course for a podium finish. The car was really handling well today.'

That left Berger in a secure second place, but no more was in prospect, for Villeneuve had made his second stop on lap 42, and it had gone without hitch, Jacques stationary for only 7.4 seconds. Now, with a clear run to the finish, the Williams was 20 seconds clear of Berger, who held a similar advantage over Hakkinen.

The laps ran out. Villeneuve took the flag for his second Grand Prix victory, after a copybook drive, first to last. Little wonder that Frank Williams had scoffed, the evening before, at fatuous rumours that the team was contemplating exchanging him for Frentzen in 1997.

'I've tested a lot at Silverstone,'

Jacques said, 'so I know the place really well, but it got hot this afternoon, and you hardly ever get that here. It makes a big difference, especially with the tyres, which react very differently in these conditions. But it was great, for once, not to have to spend Friday learning a circuit, and finding where the limit was.'

Berger and Hakkinen were plainly relieved to have finished well, and it was a pleasure to see the Jordans in the points, Brundle finishing sixth, despite having had to make three stops, the unscheduled one brought about by a puncture. 'I'm back on form again,' Martin said, 'and driving well. Normal service is resumed!'

It was only after the celebrations that the controversy began, with Benetton protesting that the front wing endplates of the victorious Williams were illegal. Ultimately, a Stewards' report rejected the protest, pointing out that the endplates had been unchanged since the very beginning of the season, and that, in the opinion of Charlie Whiting, the FIA Technical Delegate, they had been legal from the beginning. Everyone - save Benetton, and perhaps Ferrari - was delighted by the decision. Everyone loves Gerhard Berger, but no one would have wished to see him win this way. Silverstone belonged only to Villeneuve. ∎

## RACE RESULTS

| | DRIVER | CAR | RACE | LAPS | RESULT |
|---|---|---|---|---|---|
| 1 | Jacques Villeneuve (CDN) | Williams-Renault | 1m29.288s | 61 | 1h33m00.874s |
| 2 | Gerhard Berger (A) | Benetton-Renault | 1m29.984s | 61 | 1h33m19.900s |
| 3 | Mika Hakkinen (FIN) | McLaren-Mercedes | 1m30.531s | 61 | 1h33m51.704s |
| 4 | Rubens Barrichello (BR) | Jordan-Peugeot | 1m30.671s | 61 | 1h34m07.590s |
| 5 | David Coulthard (GB) | McLaren-Mercedes | 1m31.282s | 61 | 1h34m23.381s |
| 6 | Martin Brundle (GB) | Jordan-Peugeot | 1m30.552s | 60 | 1h33m17.786s |
| 7 | Mika Salo (FIN) | Tyrrell-Yamaha | 1m31.765s | 60 | 1h33m38.262s |
| 8 | Heinz-Harald Frentzen (D) | Sauber-Ford | 1m32.662s | 60 | 1h33m59.701s |
| 9 | Johnny Herbert (GB) | Sauber-Ford | 1m32.213s | 60 | 1h34m00.496s |
| 10 | Jos Verstappen (NL) | Footwork-Hart | 1m32.080s | 60 | 1h34m05.550s |
| 11 | Giancarlo Fisichella (I) | Minardi-Ford | 1m33.707s | 59 | 1h34m04.161s |
| R | Jean Alesi (F) | Benetton-Renault | 1m30.553s | 44 | brakes |
| R | Olivier Panis (F) | Ligier-Mugen Honda | 1m32.188s | 40 | handling |
| R | Pedro Diniz (BR) | Ligier-Mugen Honda | 1m32.508s | 38 | engine |
| R | Damon Hill (GB) | Williams-Renault | 1m30.264s | 26 | loose wheel nut |
| R | Pedro Lamy (P) | Minardi-Ford | 1m34.372s | 21 | gear selection |
| R | Ricardo Rosset (BR) | Footwork-Hart | 1m33.382s | 13 | electrics |
| R | Ukyo Katayama (J) | Tyrrell-Yamaha | 1m32.699s | 12 | engine |
| R | Eddie Irvine (GB) | Ferrari | 1m31.490s | 5 | engine |
| R | Michael Schumacher (D) | Ferrari | 1m30.944s | 3 | gearbox |

## CHAMPIONSHIP POSITIONS

| | DRIVER | PTS | CONSTRUCTOR | PTS |
|---|---|---|---|---|
| 1 | Hill | 63 | Williams-Renault | 111 |
| 2 | Villeneuve | 48 | Benetton-Renault | 41 |
| 3 | Schumacher | 26 | Ferrari | 35 |
| 4 | Alesi | 25 | McLaren-Mercedes | 32 |
| 5 | Berger/Coulthard/ | | Jordan-Peugeot | 13 |
| | Hakkinen | 16 | Ligier-Mugen Honda | 12 |

FIA
FORMULA 1
WORLD
CHAMPIONSHIP

# HILL CLAIMS BERGER'S GLORY

Title favourite Damon Hill took his seventh Grand Prix win of the season in Germany – but only after Gerhard Berger's Benetton expired with less than three laps to the chequered flag

> **"I heard a strange noise from one of our engines, and I wasn't sure if it was Gerhard's or mine"**
>
> *Damon Hill*

**W**illiams-Renault had clearly the fastest car at Hockenheim, as usual, but this time came close to losing the race. Although Damon Hill ultimately won his first German Grand Prix, a poor start left him behind the Benetton-Renaults of Gerhard Berger and Jean Alesi for the first part of the race, and that, given he was planning two stops to their one, could have cost him the victory. Hill ran a scintillatingly quick middle stint, in the lead, but after his second stop rejoined behind Berger and ahead of Alesi.

In by far his best drive of the season to date, Gerhard was in particularly resolute mood, and although Damon took a couple of stabs at overtaking, the likelihood was that Benetton would score its first win of the season. Sadly for the luckless Berger, however, his Renault V10 expired spectacularly within three laps of the flag and the win was Hill's for the taking.

If Hill's victory owed something to fortune, it nevertheless came after yet another fine drive, and Benetton got something from the day, too, Alesi taking second place, ahead of Jacques Villeneuve's Williams, with Michael Schumacher's Ferrari a distant fourth, tailed closely by David Coulthard's McLaren-Mercedes. The last point went to Rubens Barrichello, but Jordan were not a factor.

Two scorching days for practice and qualifying were followed by cloud on race morning. There were spots of rain before the warm-up, but the track remained dry, and allowed Mika Hakkinen and David Coulthard to set the fastest times in their McLarens, which of course delighted the many Mercedes personnel on hand. Some suggested that perhaps the cars were carrying less than a representative fuel load, but McLaren folk were adamant this was not so.

Whatever else, the cars were strong

indeed on top speed, getting up to more than 211mph on Hockenheim's long straights. It was decided to run the latest-spec engine in Hakkinen's MP4/11, and to run Coulthard's car with the older, more proven, motor. Both drivers declared themselves fairly optimistic about the race.

Pole man Hill, though, was right behind them, with Alesi, Berger and Schumacher next up. Back in ninth was Villeneuve, but he wasn't too despondent about it: 'We found that my car had a broken front damper, which was on it throughout practice and qualifying. Of course it feels a lot better now, but I just think we could have had a better race car than we have. Still, we've worked on the set-up this morning, and it doesn't feel too bad now.'

One man very happy before the start was Berger, whose last Grand Prix win came at Hockenheim, in 1994. 'I wouldn't say that the Benetton feels ideal for my driving style - I just hate nervous turn-in, and natural oversteer - but we found something in testing at Paul Ricard last week, and I feel much more confident in the car as a result. Here it has felt very nice.'

Gerhard looked on form throughout practice, and was starting from the front row, having out-qualified team mate Alesi for the first time all season. In 1995, when both were together at Ferrari, he did that almost as a matter of course.

At mid-morning there was a downpour of almost tropical proportions, which coincided precisely with the drivers' parade. All were thus soaked by the time they got back to the paddock, where it was announced that an additional 15-minute 'acclimatisation' session would be run, at 12.45.

In fact, by the time the cars got out, the rain had long since stopped, but parts of the forest section of the track remained saturated. As two o'clock neared, the skies were clear, and the temperature was steeply on the climb; by race time, there were patches of damp off the line, but no more than that.

Hill had decided on two stops for this race, and the Benetton drivers only one, but the opening seconds might have persuaded you that the

Clockwise from top: Jacques Villeneuve took third thanks to Gerhard Berger's retirement. This had nothing to do with Benetton's upturn in performance. The German Grand Prix is go. Heinz-Harald Frentzen finished eighth, next year it could be first. Berger was just three laps from glory, instead he ended the day with nothing. The paddock gossip centred on Damon Hill's future with Williams.

## IN HINDSIGHT

'Has Hill been dumped?' the cover of AUTOSPORT asked before the German Grand Prix, while inside we ran a story quoting an unidentified source saying that a deal had already been done for Heinz-Harald Frentzen to replace the world championship leader at the best team in F1.

Unsurprisingly, the entire paddock talked about little else throughout the Hockenheim weekend. Was it true, they asked in unison? And in the face of denials from Hill, Frentzen and Williams, most concluded that it was not.

In that case, many spent a long time trying to find out who the source was, in order to test the credibility of the story. But a journalist must never reveal his sources...

Interestingly, most of the Williams team had no problems with the story, although one or two did get very upset about it — as, indeed, did Hill — and given the hassle it had caused them you could see why.

For five weeks the drama played itself out, with most predicting that Hill would indeed stay with Williams, that the story in AUTOSPORT had been planted by Williams to try to persuade Hill that not all the cards were in his hand, and that he should moderate his salary demands considerably.

Then, the week after the Belgian Grand Prix, Hill's manager called a press conference, and given its timing and location it could mean only one thing — Hill had lost his Williams drive.

At Monza the following weekend, everyone was wondering when the deal with Frentzen was done, and many believed the official line that it was after Spa.

But if that was the case, how did AUTOSPORT's source know back in July? Later in the season, he shook his head. 'Like you say,' he grinned, 'never reveal your sources. But two people have told me. It was done in November last year.'

So now you know.

opposite was true, for Hill made a relatively leisurely getaway, and it was Berger - despite his heavier fuel load - who grabbed the initial lead; Alesi, fifth on the grid, started like a bullet, slotting in behind his team mate at the first turn. Even in the fastest car, even at a track like Hockenheim, overtaking is increasingly difficult in Formula 1, and Hill faced work.

'The aerodynamics are so overwhelmingly important these days,' Damon said, 'that when you get close to another car - and you don't have to be really close - the efficiency of your own car is reduced. I found myself behind Jean, and going through turns 10kph slower than when I was running on my own, but there's not a lot you can do.'

While Hill sat behind Alesi in some frustration, Berger began to eke out a slender lead, albeit never more than two seconds. At this stage, of course, Damon had no idea of Benetton's strategy for the race; he hoped that, like himself, Gerhard and Jean would be making two stops. But if they were not, he was losing a valuable opportunity of getting clear away in the lead.

Whatever else, though, it was immediately clear that this was to be a race between the three of them, for Schumacher, fourth, simply could not keep pace, and was losing close to a second a lap, pressured all the way by Coulthard, who may be the best starter in the business, and nipped by a rather surprised Villeneuve on the opening lap.

Jacques ran sixth, initially pushed by Irvine, with Hakkinen down in eighth, after being clinically squeezed towards the pit wall by Schumacher at the start.

After 10 laps the three front runners were separated by less than three seconds, but Schumacher was now nine behind Alesi, and plainly holding up Coulthard and Villeneuve, who were being steadily caught by Irvine and Hakkinen.

In the grandstands there was a sea of German flags, as usual, but they were not being waved with the usual fervour, and many of the traditional fire crackers, mercifully, were being

saved for a more appropriate occasion.

McLaren's race strategy was very soon revealed, Hakkinen coming in after 13 of the 45 laps. The wheel changes and refuelling required only 8.3 seconds, but Mika was ominously slow in getting on his way, and immediately after the first turn pulled off. An engine problem, given that this was the latest Mercedes V10, might have been suspected, but no. 'It was something in the transmission,' he reported. 'I'd been having upshift problems almost from the start, and eventually I couldn't get any gears at all.'

Coulthard, though, was having a trouble-free run. He stopped - 7.6 seconds - on lap 16, but still Schumacher had no respite, for now Villeneuve moved on to his tail.

Like David, Jacques found that overtaking was a different matter. 'I was stuck there,' he said. 'It was just a matter of waiting for the stops, unfortunately.'

Hill was in the same position, although there were those who wondered why, with Damon committed to two stops, and unable to get by Alesi, his team didn't bring him in earlier than lap 20, which was getting towards half-distance. 'Well,' said Adrian Newey, cagily, 'we were relying on a strong middle stint...'

Very well, but why was that 'middle stint' not begun a little earlier? According to Williams calculations, bringing Hill in on, say, lap 15, would have risked sending him out again in traffic, and fairly fast

traffic at that, which would have cost him time.

At least Alesi's Benetton, ahead of him, was running at a good clip.

Damon duly made his first stop (8.1), and was temporarily back to fifth as a result, but his position was soon to improve. At the end of lap 22 Alesi, Schumacher and Villeneuve all came in, and next time round it was Berger's turn. Hill, on fresh tyres and now with a clear road before him, began setting new fastest laps immediately, and took over the lead, with Berger rejoining three seconds behind him.

It was at this point of the race that Hill began the 'strong middle stint' to which Newey referred. Berger may have been at his most resolute at Hockenheim, quickly leaving team mate Alesi behind, but Hill was travelling at another speed altogether, lapping at around 1m46.5s, a clear second and a half faster than Gerhard.

In 10 laps, Damon's lead grew from three to 16 seconds, but even that was not going to be enough to keep him ahead through his second stop.

This he made on lap 34. It went without a glitch, and he was on his way after 8.2 seconds, but if he rejoined ahead of Alesi, Berger had already gone through.

Two seconds ahead, Gerhard now faced the prospect of relentless pressure from Damon, and there were still 45 miles to the flag.

Behind Alesi ran Villeneuve, then Schumacher and Coulthard. Barrichello was next up, but so far behind the front runners as to

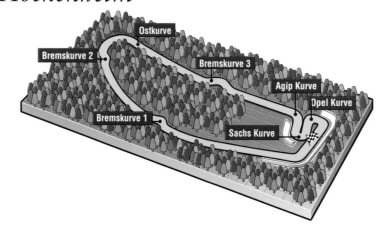

## GERMAN GP
### ROUND 11

**28 July 1996**
**FIA Formula 1 World Championship**

**Race data:** 45 laps of a 4.235-mile circuit
**Weather:** Dry and sunny
**Distance:** 190.575 miles

**Winner:** Damon Hill,
Williams Renault FW18, 140.06mph
**Previous result:** Michael Schumacher,
Benetton-Renault B195, 138.12mph
**Fastest lap:** Damon Hill,
Williams Renault FW18, 1m46.504s

*Hockenheim*

RESULTS © 1996 Federation Internationale de l'Automobile, 8 Place de la Concorde, Paris, 75008 France

### STARTING GRID

| | DRIVER | |
|---|---|---|
| 1 | Hill | 1:43.912 |
| 2 | Berger | 1:44.299 |
| 3 | Schumacher | 1:44.477 |
| 4 | Hakkinen | 1:44.644 |
| 5 | Alesi | 1:44.670 |
| 6 | Villeneuve | 1:44.842 |
| 7 | Coulthard | 1:44.951 |
| 8 | Irvine | 1:45.389 |
| 9 | Barrichello | 1:45.452 |
| 10 | Brundle | 1:45.876 |
| 11 | Diniz | 1:46.575 |
| 12 | Panis | 1:46.746 |
| 13 | Frentzen | 1:46.899 |
| 14 | Herbert | 1:47.711 |
| 15 | Salo | 1:48.139 |
| 16 | Katayama | 1:48.381 |
| 17 | Verstappen | 1:48.512 |
| 18 | Lamy | 1:49.461 |
| 19 | Rosset | 1:49.551 |
| DNQ | Lavaggi | 1:51.357 |

**Left: McLaren showed improved form on Mercedes' home ground. Right: No podium joy for Michael Schumacher after the race**

constitute no threat at all.

A recent retirement was Irvine, with a recurrence of the gearbox hydraulics problem which put him out at Silverstone. For several laps before his retirement, Eddie had run in his team leader's mirrors, giving the impression, in fact, of being a mite quicker than Michael. But whether or not he could – or would – have passed him was now academic.

Villeneuve had got by Schumacher immediately after their stops. 'We came in together, with Michael ahead,' Jacques said, 'but our stop was better than his, and then we had a good battle down to the first chicane.'

In fact, the Williams and Ferrari nearly collided in the pit lane, Schumacher pulling out somewhat abruptly as Villeneuve motored by the Ferrari pit. Jacques stopped in time, but there was a certain resolve about him as he accelerated away behind Michael, and it was not a surprise to see the Williams in front when next they entered the stadium area.

'I was a couple of lengths behind him at the chicane,' said Villeneuve, 'and I don't think he was really expecting me to outbrake him...'

Schumacher, for his part, said that he had braking problems throughout the race. 'Because of that, I couldn't defend myself from Jacques's brave move – he passed me simply because he could brake later. As for the pit lane incident, it wasn't really a dangerous situation - I just had a slight clutch problem as I pulled out, but it wasn't as close as it looked.

'I know it's not evident from our result today,' Michael went on, 'but the car was better here than in the last few races. Apart from the brakes, that is.'

Undeniably, though, he was incidental to the German Grand Prix this time, which came as some disappointment for the impressively massed ranks of his fans, hoping against all reason for a long-overdue result for the Ferrari. All attention was centred on the battle at the front, however, a phenomenon we have not seen in Formula 1 for some little time.

Following his final stop, Hill had closed on Berger at a rate which suggested that the result was a foregone conclusion, but once he got up to the Benetton, it was the old story: 'When you get close to another car, your own car is not as efficient...'

By lap 37, with eight to go, the Williams and the Benetton were effectively tied together, but although Damon jinked around, darting left and right, there is no more doughty an opponent than Gerhard in these circumstances. Making no mistakes at all, he simply made sure that his car was always on the piece of road that Hill would need to put a successful move on him.

'We have the same engines,' Damon said, 'and we were doing exactly the same speed down the straight, so I never got a sufficiently good tow to get alongside him. Every time I tried to draw level Gerhard pulled across in front of me, which he was quite entitled to do. The rules say you can change your position on the track once, which was all he ever did.

'It was a clean fight all the way, and very enjoyable, but it would have taken an error by Gerhard for me to

have passed him, quite honestly, and of course I was trying to pressure him into making one.'

Renault engines, as we know, rarely fail, and almost never in a race. Therefore, it was particularly sad that the one which broke at Hockenheim – the only one – had to be Berger's, for he seemed to be heading for a well deserved victory, after a season of poor fortune.

'With two and a half laps to go,' Hill related, 'as we accelerated out of the first chicane, I heard a strange noise from one of our engines, and at first I wasn't sure if it was Gerhard's or mine. But mine seemed to be all right, so it had to be his, and I moved right just in time, before it erupted. Fortunately, I avoided being covered in oil.'

A scarcely believing Berger pulled off on the grass, and parked. 'Everything,' he said, 'was going perfectly, and I was confident I could hold Damon off. There was absolutely no warning - it just blew. I feel so sad, because I wanted the victory for myself, for the team and for everyone who has worked so hard this year.'

After Hill had gone on to score his

seventh victory of the season, Berger hitched a lift back with Alesi, who had now moved up to second place, but conceded that he had great sympathy for his team mate. If Gerhard came away from Hockenheim empty-handed, however, probably he felt better about himself and his driving than for many a month. 'A real shame, wasn't it?,' McLaren's Jo Ramirez said. 'But - what's that English phrase - it proves that there's life in the old dog yet, doesn't it?'

Behind Hill, Alesi and Villeneuve, Schumacher brought the Ferrari in fourth, but only by strenuous effort, for Coulthard really crowded him in the closing laps, and Barrichello eventually arrived to claim the last point, after another disappointing race for Jordan-Peugeot.

Hill's points lead over Villeneuve is now out to 21, and, with five races to go, his march towards the world championship looked more assured once again.

Apart from his middling start, Damon made no mistakes whatever in Germany, and this time he knew he had been in a fight. ■

## RACE RESULTS

| | DRIVER | CAR | RACE | LAPS | RESULT |
|---|---|---|---|---|---|
| 1 | Damon Hill (GB) | Williams-Renault | 1m46.504s | 45 | 1h21m43.417s |
| 2 | Jean Alesi (F) | Benetton-Renault | 1m47.643s | 45 | 1h21m54.869s |
| 3 | Jacques Villeneuve (CDN) | Williams-Renault | 1m47.903s | 45 | 1h22m17.343s |
| 4 | Michael Schumacher (D) | Ferrari | 1m48.612s | 45 | 1h22m24.934s |
| 5 | David Coulthard (GB) | McLaren-Mercedes | 1m47.856s | 45 | 1h22m25.613s |
| 6 | Rubens Barrichello (BR) | Jordan-Peugeot | 1m49.559s | 45 | 1h23m25.516s |
| 7 | Olivier Panis (F) | Ligier-Mugen Honda | 1m48.288s | 45 | 1h23m27.329s |
| 8 | Heinz-Harald Frentzen (D) | Sauber-Ford | 1m49.773s | 44 | 1h21m50.766s |
| 9 | Mika Salo (FIN) | Tyrrell-Yamaha | 1m50.553s | 44 | 1h22m22.768s |
| 10 | Martin Brundle (GB) | Jordan-Peugeot | 1m49.176s | 44 | 1h23m04.252s |
| 11 | Riccardo Rosset (BR) | Footwork-Hart | 1m51.702s | 44 | 1h23m23.171s |
| 12 | Pedro Lamy (P) | Minardi-Ford | 1m51.654s | 43 | 1h22m08.733s |
| 13 | Gerhard Berger (A) | Benetton-Renault | 1m47.682s | 42 | engine |
| R | Eddie Irvine (GB) | Ferrari | 1m48.336s | 34 | gearbox |
| R | Johnny Herbert GB) | Sauber-Ford | 1m50.304s | 25 | gearbox |
| R | Pedro Diniz (BR) | Ligier-Mugen Honda | 1m49.625s | 19 | engine |
| R | Ukyo Katayama (J) | Tyrrell-Yamaha | 1m50.569s | 19 | accident |
| R | Mika Hakkinen (FIN) | McLaren-Mercedes | 1m48.490s | 13 | gearbox |
| R | Jos Verstappen (NL) | Footwork-Hart | | 0 | accident |

## CHAMPIONSHIP POSITIONS

| | DRIVER | PTS | | CONSTRUCTOR | PTS |
|---|---|---|---|---|---|
| 1 | Hill | 73 | | Williams-Renault | 125 |
| 2 | Villeneuve | 52 | | Benetton-Renault | 47 |
| 3 | Alesi | 31 | | Ferrari | 38 |
| 4 | Schumacher | 29 | | McLaren-Mercedes | 34 |
| 5 | Coulthard | 18 | | Jordan-Peugeot | 14 |
| 6 | Berger/Hakkinen | 16 | | Ligier-Mugen Honda | 12 |

**FIA FORMULA 1 WORLD CHAMPIONSHIP**

# VILLENEUVE PILES ON THE PRESSURE

It was the perfect result for Williams in Hungary, clinching them the constructors' championship. But it wasn't for Damon Hill because, with four races to go, the world title was still up for grabs

The tortuous configuration of the Hungaroring meant that Damon Hill was unlikely to pass Jacques Villeneuve in the closing laps, but still Hill hoped perhaps to usher his Williams team mate into a mistake. It never came. As he showed at the Nurburgring, scene of his first Grand Prix victory, Villeneuve is a resolute man under pressure, and if he locked a wheel a couple of times, he made no error worth the name.

At the flag the two of them were three-quarters of a second apart, and Hill's points lead, with four races to go, was cut to 17. Williams-Renault arrived in Hungary needing only two points to clinch the constructors' championship, so they achieved their aim extravagantly. This made five times that Frank's cars have finished 1-2 in 1996.

Hill made a poor start from his second place on the grid, and it was Villeneuve who gave immediate chase to pole man Michael Schumacher, taking over the lead from the Ferrari driver at the first stops. Hill, meanwhile, lost a lot of time behind Jean Alesi's Benetton, but in the final segment of the race he closed swiftly on Villeneuve, whose car had begun to handle a little less well than before.

Schumacher may have been quickest in qualifying, but in the race only his virtuosity kept the Ferrari vaguely in touch with the Williams-Renaults. Ultimately, with seven laps left, the Ferrari failed. Again.

The first four in the race morning warm-up were exactly as in qualifying: Schumacher, Hill, Villeneuve, Irvine. The Hungaroring has traditionally been a Williams circuit, and Damon – who won his first Grand Prix here, in 1993, and also dominated the '95 race – was considered favourite for pole position. Before the first session, he believed the major opposition would come

> ## "I knew that unless I made a mistake or got caught up in traffic, Damon wouldn't get past"
>
> *Jacques Villeneuve*

from Benetton, but he was wrong.

'McLaren could possibly be contenders for the pole, and certainly Schumacher, as well as Jacques and myself. It's always a big mistake, though, to sit here now – before it all starts – and say what you think might happen. This is quite a tricky circuit to set a car up for. It's quite possible we might not find a perfect balance. The conditions change quite a lot – track temperature, wind blowing sand on the track, and so on.'

In the end, Hill never did get his Williams-Renault quite perfectly balanced, although it was not far away. The surprise of qualifying, though, was the pace of the Ferraris. Recent aerodynamic changes to the cars had been expected to work well at a quick circuit like Hockenheim, but there Schumacher was very disappointed with his car, and he came to Hungary in a pessimistic frame of mind. After only a few laps, though, his mood changed.

'At this track, of course, we run very high downforce, and in this configuration the car is working surprisingly well. I really hadn't expected to go well here...'

Schumacher was brilliant in qualifying. By no stretch of the imagination is the Hungaroring a classic circuit, but, like Buenos Aires, it is a place where a car can be hustled, and no one hustles a car like Michael. His quick laps in practice may not have been pretty to watch, but they made you catch your breath.

Villeneuve's, too. Jacques quickly accustomed himself to the track, and went very much his own way on set-up. After the warm-up, he was especially pleased with his car, but he had no illusions about the task which faced him, if he were to keep alive his championship aspirations. 'It's quite a nice track to drive on,' he said, 'but not for racing.'

Jacques's best hope was that Hill would make another bad start, as at Silverstone and Hockenheim, and here Damon was especially poorly placed, for second on the grid meant starting on the unused – and therefore dirty – right side of the track. In the warm-up he made a point of driving down it, trying to clear some of the sand, but reported afterwards that there was indeed very much less grip there: not only would it make for a

difficult getaway, but it would also militate against effective braking at the all-important first turn.

Out went the lights, and Hill's fears were confirmed. While Schumacher and Villeneuve got away perfectly, he lagged. 'I was pretty disgusted with the start. The way the clutch works doesn't suit me, and I've been working hard to get Williams to supply me with one I can use better.'

Into the first corner Damon was overtaken around the outside by Alesi, which put him down to fourth: 'I could have chopped him,' he said, 'but I don't like to drive that way.'

Hill's decision, laudable as it may have been, almost certainly cost him the Hungarian Grand Prix, for Alesi could run at nothing like the pace of Schumacher and Villeneuve, and now Damon was trapped behind him. 'I lost the race right there,' he said. 'It was over; Michael and Jacques were long gone. I reckon I was two seconds a lap faster than Jean, but getting past him was an impossibility.'

Schumacher and Villeneuve were indeed long gone. Ten laps into the race, they were nose to tail, but Alesi, third, was almost 12 seconds adrift, and behind him languished Hill. Irvine had the second Ferrari in fifth place for a while, with Berger in sixth, but a mistake on lap 15 allowed Gerhard by. Behind the pair of them ran Mika Hakkinen, Rubens Barrichello and David Coulthard. Already heading

Above: He started the year so well, but Jos Verstappen's season continued on its downward spiral. Clockwise from top: No joy for David Coulthard. Monaco GP winner Olivier Panis finished fifth. No smile from Damon Hill after finishing second. A sideways Jean Alesi eventually inherited third place

# IN HINDSIGHT

Williams tied up its eighth Formula 1 Constructors' Championship with Jacques Villeneuve and Damon Hill's one-two finish in the Hungarian Grand Prix, equalling the record set by Ferrari, which has been competing in F1 since the Makes' title was established back in 1958.

Williams was only founded in 1973, and has won all eight titles since 1980. Statistics can be made to tell lies, but this one gives as true a picture as there is.

The result was a fitting award for the supreme skills of the design team of technical director Patrick Head led by his chief designer Adrian Newey — since the latter drew his first Williams in 1991, the team has won all but one of the Constructors' titles — and a perfect illustration of the domination Williams exerted in '96.

But, typically, both Head and Newey were not ones to let success go to their heads. 'At some point, we'll make a point of having a party,' Head said after the race, 'because it's a big reflection on everybody in the team, the reliability of the cars, the quality of the design and so on, but at the moment it's a very critical time for us in terms of getting on with next year's programme. It's an activity that never stops.'

Newey was on holiday when the title was won, but a week later he said modestly: 'We have a tremendously talented bunch of people here at Williams, and their contribution is immense. Patrick and I are the figureheads, we lead the team. But we're very much dependent on their skill.'

'It's a brilliant team effort and I am thrilled about it,' Williams said. 'As far as it being our eighth title is concerned, it's been a wonderful story of success, and it reflects totally and perfectly on what happened at (Williams's old factory) Didcot and now happens at Grove.

'The triumph says that you have done the best job in competition with everyone else up and down the pitlane.' He missed out the words 'by far', but he shouldn't have.

home were Mika Salo and Pedro Diniz, who collided on the opening lap, Martin Brundle, who crashed on lap six, and Jos Verstappen, who had his now customary accident. Later, they would be joined by Coulthard, whose engine seized on the pit straight, sending the McLaren alarmingly out of control.

The pit stops were begun by Heinz-Harald Frentzen as early as lap 14, but the first of the leading runners to come in was Schumacher on lap 19. At the time Michael led Villeneuve by only a couple of tenths, but such was their advantage over the rest that he dropped only to fifth, rejoining right behind Berger.

For some time it had been clear that Villeneuve was potentially quicker than Schumacher, and now, with a clear road before him at last, Jacques got the hammer down for a couple of laps, before coming in at the end of lap 21. Jacques's hurrying served him well, for after his stop he squeezed back out ahead of Berger and Schumacher.

Alesi made his first stop on lap 22, and Hill on lap 25. With the Benetton roadblock gone, Damon should have been able to build up enough of an advantage to get out ahead of Jean after his own stop, but unfortunately he was delayed by both Ukyo Katayama and Giovanni Lavaggi; he did get out fractionally in front of Alesi, but as he came up to speed on his new tyres, Jean forced by again. 'I couldn't believe it,' Hill said. 'Here we were, starting all over again...'

His frustration was not so prolonged this time. On lap 31 Alesi slid wide at the first turn, and Hill was instantly past, then proceeding to leave the Benetton behind. At this point, though, he was 21 seconds behind Schumacher, who himself trailed Villeneuve by 10. It looked like a long afternoon.

Still, Damon was not without hope. He had gone into the race with the option of two or three stops, and at this stage of the game believed he would be making only two. 'We reckoned we would make our plans on the fly,' said Patrick Head, 'dependent on what happened on the

track. His race engineer and other people on the pit wall decided to go for three stops, although perhaps they were tardy in letting Damon know.'

Perhaps, too, Hill misheard the message when it was radioed over to him. Whatever, he was plainly still confused at the post-race press conference. 'The best strategy would have been to make two stops, I believe, but for some reason we ended up making three. I thought I knew what I was doing, but the strategy changed after the first stop.'

In fact, the decision had been taken quite early in the race, when Hill's poor start left him behind Alesi. But it was set in stone at the first stop when the team, eager to save a few crucial seconds to get him on his way in front of Alesi, gave him a reduced quantity of fuel.

When all were gassed up, and back on the track, the revised order was Villeneuve, pulling away from Schumacher at around a second a lap, then Alesi and Hill, then Berger and Irvine. Johnny Herbert - very much the Sauber front runner in Hungary, relishing the latest Ford Zetec R motor – came next, followed by Hakkinen. On lap 31, Hill took advantage of Alesi's mistake at the first turn, and immediately began to take chunks out of Schumacher's advantage, setting a string of new fastest laps.

Lap 32 saw the end of Irvine, victim once more of gearbox hydraulics failure on his Ferrari, and soon afterwards, sadly, Herbert pulled off with engine failure after a spirited run. The same fate would later befall team mate Frentzen.

Having lost 10 seconds in six laps to the pursuing Hill, Schumacher made his second stop on lap 39, getting on his way again in a remarkable 6.9 seconds. Villeneuve was in next time round (7.0s), followed by Hill (6.7s) – and this time Damon rejoined before Alesi could go by, albeit by only a couple of seconds. Now he was able to continue with his efforts to close down Schumacher, and by lap 50 he was right up behind Michael's Ferrari.

Passing, though, was a different matter. The sinewy Hungaroring has no overtaking spot worth the name,

and an additional problem is that the track surface is unusually dirty, for the place is rarely used. That being so, going off line means not only less grip, but also dirt all over your tyres, which takes a while to disperse. Way quicker than Schumacher he may have been at this stage, but Hill could see no means of displacing him. And all the time Villeneuve, Damon's only rival for the world championship, was continuing to extend his lead and he could do nothing about it.

Therefore, when Schumacher came in for his third and final stop on lap 52, Hill, who had been intending to pit at about the same time, radioed in to say, no, he was staying out for a

# HUNGARIAN GP

### ROUND 12

**11 August 1996**
**FIA Formula 1 World Championship**

**Race data:** 77 laps of a 2.465-mile circuit
**Weather:** Dry and sunny
**Distance:** 189.805 miles

**Winner:** Jacques Villeneuve,
Williams Renault FW18, 107.11mph
**Previous result:** Damon Hill,
Williams Renault FW17, 107.48mph
**Fastest lap:** Damon Hill,
Williams Renault FW18, 1m20.093s

*Hungaroring*

## STARTING GRID

| | DRIVER | |
|---|---|---|
| 1 | Schumacher | 1:17.129 |
| 2 | Hill | 1:17.182 |
| 3 | Villeneuve | 1:17.259 |
| 4 | Irvine | 1:18.617 |
| 5 | Alesi | 1:18.754 |
| 6 | Berger | 1:18.794 |
| 7 | Hakkinen | 1:19.116 |
| 8 | Herbert | 1:19.292 |
| 9 | Coulthard | 1:19.384 |
| 10 | Frentzen | 1:19.436 |
| 11 | Panis | 1:19.538 |
| 12 | Brundle | 1:19.828 |
| 13 | Barrichello | 1:19.966 |
| 14 | Katayama | 1:20.499 |
| 15 | Diniz | 1:20.665 |
| 16 | Salo | 1:20.678 |
| 17 | Verstappen | 1:20.781 |
| 18 | Rosset | 1:21.590 |
| 19 | Lamy | 1:21.713 |
| 20 | Lavaggi | 1:22.468 |

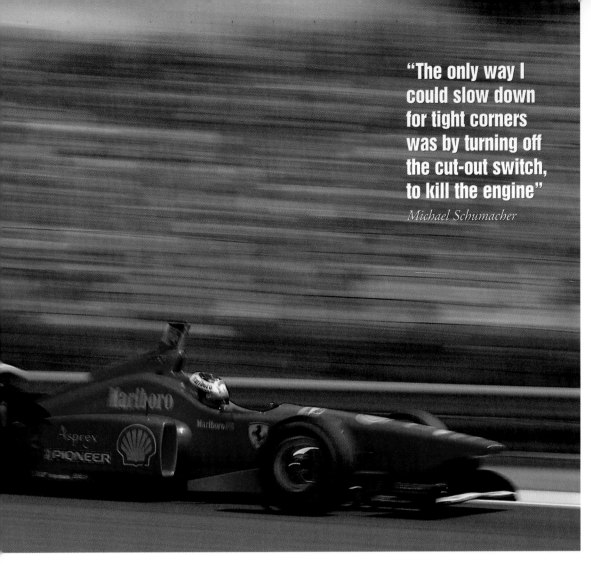

> ### "The only way I could slow down for tight corners was by turning off the cut-out switch, to kill the engine"
>
> *Michael Schumacher*

There were 13 laps to go, and the gap was 6.5 seconds.

Now Hill really went motor racing, swiftly catching Villeneuve just as he had Berger at Hockenheim. Again, though, catching a driver and passing him proved to be two completely different things.

'The last few laps were very tough,' Jacques said. 'My car didn't work quite as well on the last set of tyres, but still I knew, with the layout of this track the way it is, that unless I made a mistake, or got caught up in traffic, Damon wouldn't be able to get past me at all.'

As he demonstrated at the Nurburgring, where Schumacher pushed him for so long, Villeneuve excels in a situation like this. Beyond the odd puff of tyre smoke into a tight turn, there was never the hint of a real mistake. He dealt expertly with the traffic, often snicking by a backmarker into a corner, leaving Hill to follow through.

Jacques was 0.77 of a second ahead at the flag, and the Williams drivers were joined on the podium by a somewhat fortunate Alesi, who benefited not only from the retirement of Berger, but also from that of Schumacher, who pulled off seven laps from the end, with a fault in the throttle control unit.

'A couple of laps earlier, the throttle was getting stiff, and tending to stick open,' said Michael. 'Then the gearbox began to play up on downshifts, and the only way I could slow down for the tight corners was by turning off the cut-out switch, to kill the engine, and then switching it on again. Unfortunately, I eventually made a mistake, and hit the neutral selector switch. That was the end, because the engine cut, and wouldn't fire up again...' An eventful day for the world champion.

A perfect one for Williams-Renault, however, though Hill might have found it lacking in one detail, for this was the first 1-2 in which Villeneuve had preceded him. Behind Alesi, the other points-scorers were Hakkinen, Panis and Barrichello, all of whom were lapped. Schumacher, as usual, had a part to play in this Grand Prix, but mainly this was yet another Williams story. ∎

while, trying to put some distance between himself and the Ferrari. Knowing he had another stop to come, he did not want Schumacher between himself and Villeneuve again.

Before the race, Damon had declared that he had no intention of driving a 'points' race, that such a thing was anathema to him and he wanted to win as often as possible. And while there appeared little chance now of his catching Jacques, still he wanted to go for it.

'It was a very intelligent decision by Damon to stay out,' Head said afterwards. 'A bit of quick thinking. We agreed straight away.'

Behind the three leaders were the Benettons, running in close order, as so often this year. Alesi was ahead of Berger, but Gerhard had caught his team mate at such a rate as to suggest that he was the quicker of the two at this point in the race. For a long time Jean showed no inclination to let him through, which was worrying because both were being caught by Hakkinen's McLaren.

Ultimately, the Benetton pit ordered Alesi to allow Berger through, and if this predictably enraged Jean, he did at least comply. Once by, Gerhard quickly pulled away, but it would do him no good, for on lap 65 his Renault V10 let go massively, just as at Hockenheim. In going on three years, Renault suffered only two race failures, then Berger had two in successive Grands Prix.

On lap 58 Villeneuve, holding a 23-second lead over Hill, came in for his last stop, but this one did not proceed as intended: 'The mechanic changing the right rear realised that the nut was not on correctly,' Patrick Head related, 'so he took it off again, then replaced it properly.' When Jacques took off in a welter of tyre smoke, he had been stationary for 14.8 seconds, and Hill – with his last stop to come – was 14.5 seconds ahead.

Damon's stop, on lap 63, took only 6.6 seconds, but it was enough to allow Villeneuve back into the lead.

## RACE RESULTS

| | DRIVER | CAR | RACE | LAPS | RESULT |
|---|---|---|---|---|---|
| 1 | Jacques Villeneuve (CDN) | Williams-Renault | 1m20.507s | 77 | 1h46m21.134s |
| 2 | Damon Hill (GB) | Williams-Renault | 1m20.093s | 77 | 1h46m21.905s |
| 3 | Jean Alesi (F) | Benetton-Renault | 1m21.932s | 77 | 1h47m45.346s |
| 4 | Mika Hakkinen (FIN) | McLaren-Mercedes | 1m22.257s | 76 | 1h46m43.538s |
| 5 | Olivier Panis (F) | Ligier-Mugen Honda | 1m21.562s | 76 | 1h47m40.381s |
| 6 | Rubens Barrichello (BR) | Jordan-Peugeot | 1m23.181s | 75 | 1h46m34.466s |
| 7 | Ukyo Katayama (J) | Tyrrell-Yamaha | 1m24.040s | 74 | 1h46m49.846s |
| 8 | Ricardo Rosset (BR) | Footwork-Hart | 1m24.026s | 74 | 1h47m07.362s |
| 9 | Michael Schumacher (D) | Ferrari | 1m20.912s | 70 | 1h37m31.955s |
| 10 | Giovanni Lavaggi (I) | Minardi-Ford | 1m25.626s | 69 | 1h41m39.024s |
| 11 | Gerhard Berger (A) | Benetton-Renault | 1m21.733s | 64 | engine |
| R | Heinz-Harald Frentzen (D) | Sauber-Ford | 1m21.882s | 50 | engine |
| R | Johnny Herbert (GB) | Sauber-Ford | 1m22.343s | 35 | engine |
| R | Eddie Irvine (GB) | Ferrari | 1m22.099s | 31 | gearbox |
| R | Pedro Lamy (P) | Minardi-Ford | 1m25.006s | 24 | suspension |
| R | David Coulthard (GB) | McLaren-Mercedes | 1m22.760s | 23 | engine |
| R | Jos Verstappen (NL) | Footwork-Hart | 1m24.018s | 10 | accident |
| R | Martin Brundle (GB) | Jordan-Peugeot | 1m23.889s | 5 | accident |
| R | Pedro Diniz (BR) | Ligier-Mugen Honda | 1m40.435s | 1 | accident |
| R | Mika Salo (FIN) | Tyrrell-Yamaha | | 0 | accident |

## CHAMPIONSHIP POSITIONS

| | DRIVER | PTS | CONSTRUCTOR | PTS |
|---|---|---|---|---|
| 1 | Hill | 79 | Williams-Renault | 141 |
| 2 | Villeneuve | 62 | Benetton-Renault | 51 |
| 3 | Alesi | 35 | Ferrari | 38 |
| 4 | Schumacher | 29 | McLaren-Mercedes | 37 |
| 5 | Hakkinen | 19 | Jordan-Peugeot | 15 |
| 6 | Coulthard | 18 | Ligier-Mugen Honda | 14 |

FIA FORMULA 1 WORLD CHAMPIONSHIP

# MICHAEL KEEPS HILL'S HOPES ALIVE

If it wasn't for Michael Schumacher, Damon Hill's title chances would have been looking desperate after the Belgian Grand Prix. As it was, Hill was still in the driving seat…just

It was at Spa-Francorchamps, five years before, that Michael Schumacher made his Formula 1 debut, and at the same place, one year on, that he won his first Grand Prix. Although in Belgium, the majestic Ardennes circuit is closer to Schumacher 's home town, Kerpen, than any German F1 track, and there should be no surprise that he feels a particular affinity for it.

He excels on it, too. Although beaten by the Williams-Renaults in qualifying, he felt he was in with a shout if race day should turn out wet, as the forecasters suggested. In the event, the rain held off, yet still Schumacher came through to score his second victory of the season and the joy was there for all to see.

Although Schumacher drove brilliantly, however, his win owed something to luck, for without the 'full course yellow' brought about by an accident to Jos Verstappen, it is unlikely that he would have beaten Jacques Villeneuve, pole man and early leader.

Confusion over Williams's pit stop strategy lost time for both Villeneuve and Damon Hill, and this proved crucial in the later stages of the race, when Villeneuve rejoined behind Schumacher after his final stop, and was unable to get by him.

Mika Hakkinen took a good third in the improving McLaren-Mercedes, while Jean Alesi had a quiet run to fourth, ahead of Hill, whose race was a difficult one, and Gerhard Berger, whose afternoon was marred by a costly spin.

Villeneuve, startling in qualifying, did not close on Hill's points total as much as he might have liked, but still the gap was down to 13, with three races left. And the momentum, for the moment, seemed to be with him.

In Hungary, Villeneuve confounded everyone by excelling on a circuit he had not expected to enjoy. Spa-Francorchamps, on the other hand, he had long anticipated with relish for, despite his youth, he has old-fashioned ideas about race tracks, and believes there is still a place for long straights and top-gear corners.

Spa did not disappoint him. 'It's fantastic, magnificent, and it should serve as a model for how Grand Prix tracks should be.' At 4.33 miles, the circuit is unusually long, and Villeneuve spent the morning learning

sections, then piecing them together. 'It might sound a bit childish,' he sheepishly admitted, 'but I've been using a video game which has Spa on it and it meant I knew the way the corners went before I arrived.'

In the race car, he quickly put this rather specialised knowledge to good use, to the point that, at the very end of unofficial practice, he rather stupefied the pitlane with a lap 1.7 seconds faster than anyone else. To prove it was no fluke, he went on to take pole position.

In the raceday morning warm-up, too, he was fastest, and said afterwards that the Williams-Renault felt great. 'Fortunately, it was good right from the first lap of practice here, which really helped with learning the track, and getting to work on the set-up right away.'

Hill's chances of displacing Villeneuve from pole disappeared when rain came down 20 minutes from the end of qualifying, but he remained optimistic about the race. 'Actually, I'm enjoying driving here

more than ever before – this is definitely the best-handling car I've ever had at Spa.'

In the warm-up, though, Hill was only sixth fastest, after spinning at the Bus Stop chicane at the end of the session. In the course of the spin, the Renault V10 briefly counter-rotated, but unfortunately Hill omitted to mention this to the Renault engineers until the race was only an hour away, by which time an engine change was out of the question. Unable to gain assurances that all would be well with

Below: Jacques Villeneuve in admiration of the proud winner. Right: A Mercedes 1-2-3

## "I wouldn't have bet a penny on my chances today"

*Michael Schumacher*

Clockwise from above: Jacques Villeneuve kept his title ambitions alive. Damon Hill had another afternoon to forget. Hear no retirements, speak no retirements, see no retirements – for Tyrrell, anyway. Giovanni Lavaggi failed to qualify after this engine failure on Friday morning

it, Hill opted for the spare car.

Hakkinen finished the warm-up in second, with McLaren-Mercedes team mate David Coulthard fourth, the pair sandwiching the Benetton-Renault of Gerhard Berger, the Austrian bang on form once again.

Michael Schumacher did not go for a time in the warm-up, preferring to concentrate on set-up work. Both he and Eddie Irvine had Ferrari's new seven-speed gearbox for Spa, and Schumacher was pleased with it: 'I wouldn't say it's worth a lot in time

around here – maybe a 10th or two, but it really suits my driving style. I feel I have better control.'

Despite feeling sore after a heavy accident in free practice, Schumacher had his hopes, for he was starting third – and rain was widely forecast for the race. In the late morning, indeed, it was beginning to fall, but by two o'clock the sky was blue, the road largely dry.

Villeneuve, as usual, made an excellent start, but Hill, although departing rather more swiftly than in

recent races, was beaten to La Source by Schumacher. Worse was to come: up the hill to Les Combes, the Williams was also passed by Coulthard's McLaren.

Hill was taken aback, to say the least. 'He just came by me like a train! I just couldn't believe it.

'I was on a two-stop strategy, but now I find that both McLarens were on a one-stop, and David was carrying more fuel.'

Hill was in bad shape in the early part of the race, the Williams T- car

understeering badly on its first set of tyres. Although running fourth, Hill made no real impression on Coulthard, and Hakkinen, fifth, claimed that he was being held up by the world championship leader. 'It wasn't blocking, or anything like that,' Hakkinen said, 'but the old problem of turbulence. As soon as I got near him, my car started understeering in the turns.'

Others had had more immediate problems, however. La Source – being a hairpin immediately after the start –

# IN HINDSIGHT

Behind the action on the track, Formula 1 is played out in murky political waters, and a dispute between the governing body, the FIA, and some of the teams, which became public around the time of the Belgian Grand Prix, provided a striking example of that.

It was a complex argument about a complex subject — and one in which nobody but those directly involved knew the whole story — but in the end it came down to money and control.

Simplistically, F1 seemed set to come into more cash with technological advances in television, and Williams, McLaren and Tyrrell felt they should get more, and F1 commercial boss Bernie Ecclestone less. They also wanted first refusal on running the money side of the sport on the eventuality of 65-year-old Ecclestone's death.

FIA president Max Mosley said that it was the FIA's championship, so it would decide how to organise it. And by mid-summer, he had tired of the two-year long argument that had been raging about the details of the new Concorde Agreement, the document by which F1 is governed, and he promptly settled them with all the other teams, leaving the three dissidents out in the cold.

Morally, it was a deeply dubious move. But politically it was a master stroke, removing the dissidents' bargaining position, and cutting them out of the vast majority of the increased funds.

Within a few days, Ken Tyrrell, Frank Williams and McLaren's Ron Dennis were making noises about wanting to be allowed to back into the fold, but as that would require unanimity among the other teams, and the voluntary sacrifice of a considerable amount of money, their chances looked slim. And with them went their voice in debates about the future of the sport.

Despite their years in F1, it seemed Williams, Dennis and Tyrrell had forgotten one thing. If you get into a fight with Mosley and Ecclestone, the chances are you will lose.

has been the site of many a first lap accident, and there was one this time, which put out the Saubers of Heinz-Harald Frentzen and Johnny Herbert and the Ligier of Olivier Panis out on the spot. Involved, too, was Rubens Barrichello's Jordan, which came in at the end of the first lap. A bent track rod was replaced, but although Barrichello went back into the race, he found that not all was well with the car's handling, and so he decided to retire.

The early laps were all Villeneuve and Schumacher, the pair soon pulling clear of the rest and trading fastest laps, as at the Hungaroring, save that this time it was the Williams ahead of the Ferrari.

At this stage, Villeneuve, while not far ahead, looked serene enough, and later he confirmed this was so. 'No doubt about it, our car was a bit quicker than Michael's. My only problem was that I locked up going into the Bus Stop on one lap, and had vibration through the steering from the flat-spotted tyre – which, of course, made it very easy to lock up again afterwards. Otherwise, everything was okay.'

Not for long, though. At the end of lap 11, Verstappen stopped at his pit to complain of a sticking throttle. Nothing untoward could be found, so he went back into the race, only to crash almost at once, at the exit of Stavelot. The Footwork was severely damaged but Verstappen, although groggy, was able to walk to the ambulance. At the medical centre, a check-up happily revealed no serious injuries, the TWR team later revealing that a stub-axle had broken.

Lucky not to be involved in all this was Hill, who was next on the scene and had to drive through all manner of debris, including bouncing wheels. The worst of Hill's misfortune was to come, however.

Out came the pace car at the end of lap 13, and drivers began to come into the pits. At the end of lap 14, Schumacher stopped, and so did Alesi, but Villeneuve stayed out.

'I was ready to come in,' said Villeneuve, 'and the team was ready for me, but I couldn't hear clearly

what was being said to me on the radio, thought there might be a problem and decided to stay out.'

Thus, Villeneuve came in a lap later – which Hill now expected would be his moment to stop. The team urgently radioed Hill to stay out, but by now Hill was already in the pit entry lane, and had to weave his way slowly through the bollards there, losing time – and places – in the process. Finally, he stopped at the end of lap 16, and although the work was quickly done, by now he was back to a disastrous 13th in the queue behind the pace car.

The field got the signal to go again at the beginning of the 18th lap, and for a time we beheld the unusual sight of two McLarens running at the head of a Grand Prix, for Coulthard and Hakkinen – both running a one-stop strategy – had stayed out on the track throughout the four-lap 'yellow'.

Behind them, at the restart, were Schumacher, Alesi and Villeneuve, but Villeneuve soon dispensed with the Benetton, and at once began to catch the Ferrari. Berger, very much Benetton's pace man at Spa, had been hampered by a slow puncture in the first part of the race, then lost time in the course of the pitstops. If that were not enough, he then spun at the Bus Stop while getting by Irvine, and dropped to 14th place. Now began a great comeback drive.

While Villeneuve caught up to

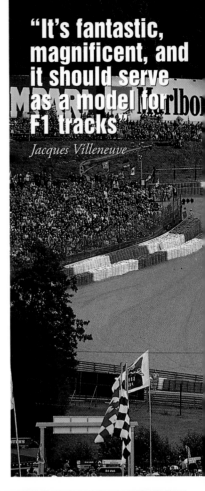

## "It's fantastic, magnificent, and it should serve as a model for F1 tracks"

*Jacques Villeneuve*

Gerhard Berger was once again Benetton's pace man at Spa, ultimately finishing sixth

---

# BELGIAN GP

## ROUND 13

**25 August 1996**
**FIA Formula 1 World Championship**

**Race data:** 44 laps of a 4.330-mile circuit
**Weather:** Dry and sunny
**Distance:** 190.52 miles

**Winner:** Michael Schumacher, Ferrari F310, 129.52mph
**Previous result:** Michael Schumacher, Benetton-Renault B195, 118.19mph
**Fastest lap:** Gerhard Berger, Benetton-Renault B196, 1m53.067s

## *Spa-Francorchamps*

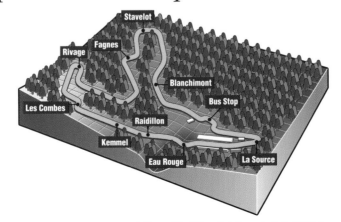

Stavelot · Fagnes · Rivage · Les Combes · Kemmel · Raidillon · Eau Rouge · Blanchimont · Bus Stop · La Source

## STARTING GRID

| | DRIVER | |
|---|---|---|
| 1 | Villeneuve | 1:50.574 |
| 2 | Hill | 1:50.980 |
| 3 | Schumacher | 1:51.778 |
| 4 | Coulthard | 1:51.884 |
| 5 | Berger | 1:51.960 |
| 6 | Hakkinen | 1:52.318 |
| 7 | Alesi | 1:52.354 |
| 8 | Brundle | 1:52.977 |
| 9 | Irvine | 1:53.043 |
| 10 | Barrichello | 1:53.152 |
| 11 | Frentzen | 1:53.199 |
| 12 | Herbert | 1:53.993 |
| 13 | Salo | 1:54.095 |
| 14 | Panis | 1:54.220 |
| 15 | Diniz | 1:54.700 |
| 16 | Verstappen | 1:55.150 |
| 17 | Katayama | 1:55.371 |
| 18 | Rosset | 1:56.286 |
| 19 | Lamy | 1:56.830 |
| DNQ | Lavaggi | 1:58.579 |

Schumacher, the luckless Hill, still down in ninth place, was finding it difficult to get by Brundle's Jordan. On the hill up to Les Combes, he got almost alongside, but the gap narrowed, but the gap narrowed, and he backed off, then following Brundle for four more laps, eventually getting past at the same spot. Once by, he was able to lap two seconds faster, and set off after Salo, whose Tyrrell had made up several places during the stops.

Coulthard surrendered his lead on lap 22, when he made his one and only stop, and Hakkinen did the same two laps later, restoring normality to the order, for now Schumacher led, Villeneuve by a second or so.

In front he may have been, but Schumacher was not without his worries. 'When I'd followed Jacques in the early laps, I was losing time to him at the Bus Stop chicane. I found a way to reduce that, but it meant riding the kerbs very hard. I kept on doing that, and one lap - soon after the restart - I suddenly felt a lot of play in the steering.'

A sensation of this kind would be disturbing at any circuit, but at Spa-Francorchamps it was rather more than that, and Schumacher admitted he was frightened by it. 'The car felt very strange to drive, particularly through Eau Rouge, so I radioed the team, explained the problem, and they told me that everything would be okay if I stayed away from the kerbs from now on. So I did…'

His confidence restored, he continued to keep Villeneuve behind him, but on lap 30 came in for his second stop, rejoining 20 seconds behind Villeneuve. At precisely the same moment, the second Ferrari of Irvine retired - astonishingly, for the fourth consecutive race, with gearbox hydraulics failure.

Now everything depended on Villeneuve's final stop, which he made on lap 32. At 7.6 seconds, it went without hitch, but as he accelerated out of the pits, Schumacher was flashing by on the approach to La Source. He emerged from the pitlane slightly ahead, but Schumacher had momentum on him, and into Eau Rouge the Ferrari was ahead.

There, moreover, it stayed. For many laps, Schumacher and Villeneuve circulated less than a second apart, but eventually the Williams began to fall away. 'On my second and third sets of tyres, the car was very good for two or three laps, but then started to push like a pig. So it was fine when I first got up to Michael, but then I just lost the front end of the car completely, and couldn't turn into corners.

'As well as that,' Villeneuve added, 'I also began to hear something strange from the exhaust, so I preferred to lift off and be sure of second place.'

There was no hiding his disappointment, however. 'I've made up four points on Damon today, but four points a race is not enough. Still, I'm happy about the race, in a way, because the car was very strong, and we lost only because of the pitstop.'

Hill himself was remarkably sanguine after the race, perhaps because, in the end, he felt himself fortunate to have dropped only four points to his rival. 'At one stage it looked as though Jacques was going to win, and I was going to be out of the points, so I can't be too unhappy.

'It was a strange race. I was in the spare car, but although it was set up the same as my race car, for some reason it had a lot of understeer. All in all, I feel relieved that at least I got some points today.'

Hakkinen's fine run deservedly got him on the podium, but Coulthard's good drive went for nothing when he went off the road five laps from the end. 'After my stop,' he said, 'the car was much slower than before, for some reason, and very difficult to drive. It just caught me out.'

Fourth went to Alesi and Hill just held off a charging Berger for fifth. Yet again, Berger was a disappointed man afterwards, having been undoubtedly the fastest man on the track in the closing stages, during which he set several fastest laps.

The fastest of all, though, was Schumacher. 'I think what we managed to do today was fantastic,' he said, 'because although we didn't have the fastest car - I wouldn't have bet a penny on my chances in the dry - we won because we were able to keep at the Williams pace, and did everything right.'

He might also have added that driving genius had something to do with it, too. ∎

## RACE RESULTS

| | DRIVER | CAR | RACE | LAPS | RESULT |
|---|---|---|---|---|---|
| 1 | Michael Schumacher (D) | Ferrari | 1m53.905s | 44 | 1h28m15.125s |
| 2 | Jacques Villeneuve (CDN) | Williams-Renault | 1m53.587s | 44 | 1h28m20.727s |
| 3 | Mika Hakkinen (FIN) | McLaren-Mercedes | 1m54.198s | 44 | 1h28m30.835s |
| 4 | Jean Alesi (F) | Benetton-Renault | 1m54.685s | 44 | 1h28m34.250s |
| 5 | Damon Hill (GB) | Williams-Renault | 1m53.441s | 44 | 1h28m44.304s |
| 6 | Gerhard Berger (A) | Benetton-Renault | 1m53.067s | 44 | 1h28m45.021s |
| 7 | Mika Salo (FIN) | Tyrrell-Yamaha | 1m55.854s | 44 | 1h29m15.879s |
| 8 | Ukyo Katayama (J) | Tyrrell-Yamaha | 1m57.149s | 44 | 1h29m55.352s |
| 9 | Ricardo Rosset (BR) | Footwork-Hart | 1m57.809s | 43 | 1h28m21.974s |
| 10 | Pedro Lamy (P) | Minardi-Ford | 1m57.668s | 43 | 1h28m39.042s |
| R | David Coulthard (GB) | McLaren-Mercedes | 1m54.655s | 37 | accident |
| R | Martin Brundle (GB) | Jordan-Peugeot | 1m55.615s | 34 | engine |
| R | Eddie Irvine (GB) | Ferrari | 1m55.753s | 29 | gearbox |
| R | Rubens Barrichello (BR) | Jordan-Peugeot | 1m56.943s | 29 | handling |
| R | Pedro Diniz (BR) | Ligier-Mugen Honda | 1m58.665s | 22 | misfire |
| R | Jos Verstappen (NL) | Footwork-Hart | 1m56.704s | 11 | accident |
| R | Olivier Panis (F) | Ligier-Mugen Honda | | 0 | accident |
| R | Johnny Herbert (GB) | Sauber-Ford | | 0 | accident |
| R | Heinz-Harald Frentzen (D) | Sauber-Ford | | 0 | accident |

## CHAMPIONSHIP POSITIONS

| | DRIVER | PTS | CONSTRUCTOR | PTS |
|---|---|---|---|---|
| 1 | Hill | 81 | Williams-Renault | 149 |
| 2 | Villeneuve | 68 | Benetton-Renault | 55 |
| 3 | Schumacher | 39 | Ferrari | 48 |
| 4 | Alesi | 38 | McLaren-Mercedes | 41 |
| 5 | Hakkinen | 23 | Jordan-Peugeot | 15 |
| 6 | Coulthard | 18 | Ligier-Mugen Honda | 14 |

FIA FORMULA 1 WORLD CHAMPIONSHIP

# SCHUEY JOINS THE MONZA LEGENDS

They hadn't seen a Ferrari victory at Monza for eight years, but then again they'd never seen Michael Schumacher in a red car. On a day when the title challengers tripped up, Ferrari enjoyed a glorious return to form

A second victory in two weeks for Michael Schumacher and Ferrari guaranteed that the spectators went home from Monza in a delirious frame of mind. But, in terms of the world championship, the Italian Grand Prix was something of a non-event, for errors by both Damon Hill and Jacques Villeneuve meant that neither man scored points. Thus the gap between them remained at 13 points, and now there were but two races to go.

Although Hill, had he won, could have put the championship effectively beyond his team mate's reach, Villeneuve's was the costlier mistake, simply because he missed an opportunity to close the gap. Victories at Estoril and Suzuka were now a virtual necessity – and even then a couple of thirds would seal it for Damon.

For all that, though, Damon will find it hard to forgive himself for what happened in Italy, for this was a victory that he effectively slung away. Only six laps into the race, and looking unlikely to be caught, he clipped a tyre corner marker at the first chicane, and spun away 10 points. Fortunately for him, Jacques made a similar mistake, and ultimately finished a distant seventh.

Following Hill's debacle, Jean Alesi led narrowly from Michael Schumacher, but all the smart money was on the Ferrari driver, and when — at the time of the pit stops — he took over at the front, neither Alesi nor anyone else was going to threaten the red car.

Mika Hakkinen took third for McLaren-Mercedes after a magnificent drive through the field, following an early delay, and unusually good reliability from Jordan-Peugeot saw both Martin Brundle and Rubens Barrichello in the points, with Pedro Diniz — his Ligier-Mugen Honda prodigiously quick in a straight line — taking sixth.

Ah, blessed Monza. Even when Ferrari are nowhere, they pour into the old autodromo on race day, but this time around their numbers were further swelled by Schumacher's recent victory at Spa. Not for six years had Ferrari won two grands prix on the trot, and not for eight years had they won at Monza, but a fully paid-up member of the tifosi is not easily discouraged, and necessarily

understands that to travel is usually better than to arrive.

In their papers on race morning, they will have read that Schumacher, after qualifying third behind the Williams-Renaults, reckoned he might be able to give them a race; it was all a matter, he said, of getting a good start, getting into the leading group, and staying up the front.

The warm-up confirmed his cautious optimism. Again he was third fastest, but he said that the car felt better than the day before, when gusty conditions seemed to affect the Ferrari more than some cars, and he spent most of the session in the spare F310, preferring to conserve the seven-speed gearbox in his race car, the team having only one available.

The two cars ahead of Michael this time, though, were not the Williams-Renaults, but the McLaren-Mercedes, with David Coulthard — pole man here last year for Williams — shading Hakkinen. Through the practice days, David had never been quite as happy with his car as Mika, and he still felt the same way now, but there was little doubt that both men, as at Spa, were contenders.

Inevitably, though, Williams remained favourites. Hill was on the pole, after all, and reckoned, too, that he had improved his starting technique. Fourth fastest in the warm-up, Damon was perhaps more optimistic than Villeneuve, Jacques reckoning that the handling of his car was better than in qualifying, but still not *au point*. The time lost in the Saturday morning session — he was shoved off the road by an inattentive Diniz — had been costly.

Race day brought yet more perfect autumn weather, the sun warm, the shadows long, and shortly before 2pm Hill led everyone away on the parade lap. When they got the signal to go, he made a pretty good start, but Villeneuve's was better, and into the first chicane he began to inch ahead.

Both Williams drivers, however, were outdone by Alesi, who got away like a dingbat from the third row, and was able to snatch the lead before the chicane. 'A Benetton came past me,' said an astonished Schumacher, 'and I thought, "What's going on? Where did he come from?"'

Alesi conceded that 'the start was just magic for me,' but he was not to remain in front for long. 'I was a bit

wide coming out of Lesmo, and Damon passed me. At the Ascari chicane I tried to get by him again, and took a risk – but he took a bigger one! He was very correct, and everything, but I was very surprised. After all, he was going for the championship, yet he was fighting as if we were on the last lap…'

Certainly Hill looked in resolute mood in the opening stages, extending his lead over Alesi by around half a second a lap. Behind these two, though, there was a war going on, and the cause of most of the mayhem was the newly-installed corner marker tyres. The thinking was that these would deter the drivers from running over the new, lowered, kerbs too radically, but in the event, of course, they simply looked upon the stacked tyres as clipping points. And racing drivers have been known to miss the odd clipping point.

The McLaren drivers suffered particularly from this new strain of chicane blight. On the second lap Villeneuve clipped some tyres at the second chicane, and that ended the race for the unfortunate Coulthard. 'The tyres were partially retained by a cable,' said David, 'but still they hit my front wheel heavily, and broke the steering.'

A lap later it was Hakkinen's turn for persecution, this time from Alesi. 'Suddenly there were tyres all over the track, and I couldn't avoid them,' Mika said. 'The nose of my car was broken by the impact, but although I managed to continue for a bit, the understeer was terrible.' Hakkinen came in for a new nose at the end of lap four, taking on new tyres at the same time, and rejoining in an impressive 13.8s.

He was now dead last, but quickly had the hammer down. And coming to his aid, too, was a high attrition rate. On lap five Gerhard Berger — who seems to have had all of Benetton's bad luck this season — slowed at the exit of the Ascari chicane, then pulled off before Parabolica. 'As early as lap two the display showed there was a hydraulic failure, but everything seemed to be OK, so I kept going. Then, just as I was about to pass Villeneuve, the

Top: Damon Hill knew that he could have wrapped up the title at Monza. Bottom: Jean Alesi made a fantastic start from sixth to lead into the first corner. Clockwise from above: Monza is not just about cars. Eddie Irvine falls foul of the tyre chicanes. The championship challengers for 1997? Mika Hakkinen and the tyres that would cost him any chance of victory later in the day

## "I can't blame anyone but myself for what happened. It's just one of those things"
*Damon Hill*

# IN HINDSIGHT

The Italian Grand Prix came close to being reduced to farce with the sight of many of the best drivers in the world ending their race because they hit piles of tyres stacked at the chicanes.

It made an incongruous sight, this high-tech sport having to rely on worn-out old tyres to prevent the drivers riding the kerbs too much in the never-ending quest for that little bit of extra speed.

But in the circumstances, there was little choice. The fact that there was a problem with the chicanes was first noticed in Saturday morning's practice session, when a piece of concrete from the kerbs was thrown into Jacques Villeneuve's path by a Minardi.

As Michael Schumacher (above) said: 'The tyres were not an ideal solution, but we didn't have another one. To risk taking off another concrete block was too dangerous.'

Some blamed the drivers, but, according to Damon Hill, the concrete block came from an area between the kerbs and the gravel traps, which had been covered by gravel during testing. This gravel was removed, so it was not scattered over the track, but that left the concrete exposed.

What the sport's governing body, which launched an enquiry into the situation, wanted to know, was why the problem of 20 powerful F1 cars driving over these blocks and plucking them out was not foreseen.

gearbox stopped working.'

The real drama came on lap six, though; Hill, even at this early stage, appeared to have it made, for although Villeneuve had continued after clobbering the tyre marker on the second lap, his lap times were nowhere, so plainly something had to be awry with the car. Given the upheaval between Williams and himself during the previous week with the announcement of their separation, Damon must have relished the opportunity to clinch the world championship as early as possible, get it out of the way: if he won here, with Jacques not in the first three, it would be over.

At the beginning of lap six, though, he did what Villeneuve — and Alesi — had done before him. At the exit of the second chicane, he clipped the tyre markers, and instantly the Williams was into a spin, in the course of which the engine stalled. That hardly mattered, though, for the car's right front suspension had been bent in the impact, and all Damon could do was abandon ship as swiftly as possible, and pray that Villeneuve would fail to score.

'I can't blame anyone but myself for what happened,' he commented later.

'I think I could have won today — I'd made a good start, and everything was going well — but I made a mistake, and put myself out. No excuses. It's just one of those things.'

Predictably, news of Hill's retirement was received with rapture by the capacity crowd, for now a Ferrari victory became a true possibility. While Alesi was in front, his lead came in for some serious trimming by Schumacher, and Eddie Irvine, having his best run for quite some time, was up into third place.

If neither of the current Williams drivers exactly shone in Italy, neither did the man who will replace Hill in 1997. On lap eight, Heinz-Harald Frentzen, too, was out, and a little vague as to why. 'Either I hit the kerb very hard, or I collided with the marker tyres. Whichever it was, the right hand front suspension broke, and I went into the gravel trap.'

There was a relentless quality about Schumacher now as he closed in on Alesi, with a succession of new fastest laps. But catching the Benetton and passing it were two different things, as Michael acknowledged afterwards. It was the old story, the invisible 'dirty air' barrier. 'I have to say that my car was not great on the first set of tyres,' Michael said, 'but Jean's car was very strong on top speed, and I

knew that I couldn't do anything unless he made a mistake – which he didn't. Fortunately, we had a lot of fuel on board, so I knew we could stop quite late. The only worry was that Benetton had the same strategy.'

Villeneuve's worries were rather greater, rather more immediate. As early as lap 11 he was into the pits for tyres. 'When we hit the tyre markers something was bent in the front suspension, and afterwards the car's behaviour changed completely – one wheel was higher than the other. At first I was concerned that something might break, but after a couple of laps it seemed to be OK, so I pressed on. But the problem was that the car was eating front tyres. On a new set it would be fine for a couple of laps, but then they would blister, and it was very hard to keep a decent pace.'

By lap 14 Jacques was 46 seconds adrift of the leading Alesi, and obviously looking at a minor placing at best. Back in the pits Hill was saying that if he could leave Monza with a 10-point lead, he'd be, if not a happy man, at least a relieved one.

At the front Alesi and Schumacher circulated as one, but Irvine's third place was not to last. On lap 24 he became the latest victim of the tyre markers, clouting one hard enough to break the Ferrari's front suspension.

Jacques Villeneuve escaped this 180mph spin into the barriers after a brush with Pedro Diniz on Saturday

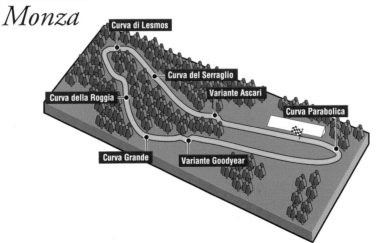

## ITALIAN GP
### ROUND 14

**8 September 1996**
**FIA Formula 1 World Championship**

**Race data:** 53 laps of a 3.604-mile circuit
**Weather:** Dry and sunny
**Distance:** 191.012 miles

**Winner:** Michael Schumacher, Ferrari F310, 146.67mph
**Previous result:** Johnny Herbert, Benetton-Renault B195, 145.29mph
**Fastest lap:** Michael Schumacher, Ferrari F310, 1m26.110s

*Monza*

Curva di Lesmos
Curva del Serraglio
Curva della Roggia
Variante Ascari
Curva Parabolica
Curva Grande
Variante Goodyear

### STARTING GRID

| | DRIVER | |
|---|---|---|
| 1 | Hill | 1:24.204 |
| 2 | Villeneuve | 1:24.521 |
| 3 | Schumacher | 1:24.781 |
| 4 | Hakkinen | 1:24.939 |
| 5 | Coulthard | 1:24.975 |
| 6 | Alesi | 1:25.201 |
| 7 | Irvine | 1:25.228 |
| 8 | Berger | 1:25.470 |
| 9 | Brundle | 1:26.037 |
| 10 | Barrichello | 1:26.194 |
| 11 | Panis | 1:26.206 |
| 12 | Herbert | 1:26.345 |
| 13 | Frentzen | 1:26.505 |
| 14 | Diniz | 1:26.726 |
| 15 | Verstappen | 1:27.270 |
| 16 | Katayama | 1:28.234 |
| 17 | Salo | 1:28.472 |
| 18 | Lamy | 1:28.933 |
| 19 | Rosset | 1:29.181 |
| 20 | Lavaggi | 1:29.833 |

'My car had been nervous from the start,' he said, 'but I'd passed a few cars, and I was due to stop on that lap, so I was pushing very hard…' Schumacher, seeing his team mate's car parked in a gravel trap, worried about it: 'I didn't know what had happened to him - maybe it would happen to me, too.'

After a trip over a chicane on lap 25, Villeneuve was into the pits again for more tyres - and the leaders had yet to stop for the first time. Clearly, the strategy for the front runners at this, a circuit where tyres last well, was to make only one stop - and that well after the halfway mark.

In the concentration on the tussle at the front, it was all too easy to overlook what was happening further down the field. Hakkinen, for example, was simply flying, following his delay early in the race, and set a new fastest lap on lap 29 as he continued his rise up the order. 'The car was fabulous, I have to say, but some guys had better top speed than I had, so overtaking wasn't easy. But I really felt that if we hadn't had to make that stop to change the wing we could have been contenders to win.' By this stage, Mika was up to fourth.

On lap 31 the crucial stops began. Alesi came in (nine seconds flat), and rejoined in second place, behind Schumacher. 'When I stopped,' he said, 'it was already late, and when I saw Michael go on, I thought he would do only one more lap.'

Michael didn't. He did two more, and each of them at a numbing pace. It was a scenario we saw so many times in his Benetton years, this ability to put in blindingly fast laps at crucial moments. He came in at the end of lap 33, and although the actual stop was only a couple of tenths faster than Alesi's, he rejoined the race without losing the lead, and actually had an advantage of five seconds over Jean. The hard work had been in those laps when he had a clear track before him.

Alesi later admitted that he felt powerless in the circumstances. 'After the stops,' he shrugged, 'Michael was just too tough.' Indeed he was, pulling clear of the Benetton all the time, sometimes by half a second a lap, sometimes by more.

Rubens Barrichello watches his rivals during practice. In the race there were no problems for the Brazilian – save for team mate Martin Brundle…

On lap 40, though, he got a shock. At the first chicane, he clipped the tyre markers, as did virtually every driver at some point, and he did it with sufficient force as to have the wheel whipped temporarily from his hands. Being Schumacher, he gathered everything together, but it had been a near thing.

'By then,' he said, 'I had a pretty good lead, and the car was working much better on the second set of tyres. I did most of the race at 90%, I would say, but at this stage I was taking it even easier, and I lost concentration, and made a stupid mistake.' The wheels of the Ferrari were momentarily clear of the ground as the car came off the kerbing, and Schumacher resolved to pick up the pace again, which he duly did.

So the race ran out. In recent years, Ferraris have quite frequently led at Monza in the closing laps, only for the tifosi to be cheated of gratification in the dying minutes of the race. For Alesi, who tried so many times to win the Italian Grand Prix in a red car, and often came close, there must have

been a special irony in following Schumacher home. In defeat, though, Jean was magnanimous, and you almost believed him. 'I have to say that I'm really pleased to see Ferrari win here, but perhaps Michael should prepare his bed in the motorhome, because I don't think he's going to get out of here tonight!'

After Schumacher had taken the flag, there was indeed a crowd invasion of Monza's front stretch such as we have not seen since 1988, when Berger recorded Maranello's last victory here. A win for Ferrari, with Alesi second, is about as good as it gets for the Italian aficionado, after all, and the crush at the foot at the podium had a frightening intensity about it. No surprise, really, that several folk were trampled underfoot in the stampede, some of them needing hospital treatment. Monza, as we have seen countless times before, is strong meat.

Perhaps, for the first time, Schumacher truly came to appreciate what being a Ferrari driver - a winning Ferrari driver at Monza -

means, for a degree of genuine emotion broke through that Germanic calm afterwards. 'It is,' he said, 'something fantastic, isn't it?'

Others celebrated, too. 'I'm not too disappointed, no,' said Alesi. 'After all, I started sixth, and finished second.' And Hakkinen was plainly elated by a wonderful drive to third: 'Without that extra pit stop to change the nose, I really think we might have won.' Brundle much enjoyed his drive — just ahead of team mate Barrichello — to fourth: 'I was absolutely flat out all the way, and I know damn well that Rubens was, too.'

As at Spa, though, it was Schumacher who made the day his own. 'We were lucky that Damon went off,' he said, 'although I think we could have fought Williams today.' If that seemed perhaps a touch fanciful, the irrefutable fact was that Michael again stepped up to the plate, kept his car in one piece, and looked a class above anyone else in the race. He was there at the end, the fastest over the 53 laps, and everything else, frankly, is irrelevant. ■

## RACE RESULTS

| | DRIVER | CAR | RACE | LAPS | RESULT |
|---|---|---|---|---|---|
| 1 | Michael Schumacher (D) | Ferrari | 1m26.110s | 53 | 1h17m43.632s |
| 2 | Jean Alesi (F) | Benetton-Renault | 1m26.652s | 53 | 1h18m01.897s |
| 3 | Mika Hakkinen (FIN) | McLaren-Mercedes | 1m26.827s | 53 | 1h18m50.267s |
| 4 | Martin Brundle (GB) | Jordan-Peugeot | 1m27.831s | 53 | 1h19m08.849s |
| 5 | Rubens Barrichello (BR) | Jordan-Peugeot | 1m27.557s | 53 | 1h19m09.107s |
| 6 | Pedro Diniz (BR) | Ligier-Mugen Honda | 1m27.905s | 52 | 1h17m58.927s |
| 7 | Jacques Villeneuve (CDN) | Williams-Renault | 1m27.027s | 52 | 1h18m14.701s |
| 8 | Jos Verstappen (NL) | Footwork-Hart | 1m28.650s | 52 | 1h18m40.215s |
| 9 | Johnny Herbert (GB) | Sauber-Ford | 1m28.223s | 51 | 1h16m29.260s |
| 10 | Ukyo Katayama (J) | Tyrrell-Yamaha | 1m28.980s | 51 | 1h19m12.208s |
| R | Ricardo Rosset (BR) | Footwork-Hart | 1m30.579s | 36 | steering arm |
| R | Eddie Irvine (GB) | Ferrari | 1m27.687s | 23 | accident |
| R | Pedro Lamy (P) | Minardi-Ford | 1m31.353s | 12 | engine |
| R | Mika Salo (FIN) | Tyrrell-Yamaha | 1m29.418s | 9 | engine |
| R | Heinz-Harald Frentzen (D) | Sauber-Ford | 1m29.945s | 7 | accident |
| R | Damon Hill (GB) | Williams-Renault | 1m27.639s | 5 | accident |
| R | Giovanni Lavaggi (I) | Minardi-Ford | 1m33.189s | 5 | engine |
| R | Gerhard Berger (A) | Benetton-Renault | 1m29.123s | 4 | gearbox |
| R | Olivier Panis (F) | Ligier-Mugen Honda | 1m32.657s | 2 | accident |
| R | David Coulthard (GB) | McLaren-Mercedes | 1m38.080s | 1 | accident |

The cones at the chicanes were replaced with tyres on Sunday – and chaos reigned

## CHAMPIONSHIP POSITIONS

| | DRIVER | PTS | CONSTRUCTOR | PTS |
|---|---|---|---|---|
| 1 | Hill | 81 | Williams-Renault | 149 |
| 2 | Villeneuve | 68 | Benetton-Renault | 61 |
| 3 | Schumacher | 49 | Ferrari | 58 |
| 4 | Alesi | 44 | McLaren-Mercedes | 45 |
| 5 | Hakkinen | 27 | Jordan-Peugeot | 20 |
| 6 | Coulthard | 18 | Ligier-Mugen Honda | 15 |

FIA FORMULA 1 WORLD CHAMPIONSHIP

# VILLENEUVE TAKES TITLE TO THE WIRE

It was a drive worthy of keeping Jacques Villeneuve's world championship hopes alive. The Canadian earned 10 crucial points, while a lacklustre performance from Damon Hill left the title open – with one race remaining

> **"I had nothing to lose. Either I beat Damon or I lost the championship right there anyway"**
>
> *Jacques Villeneuve*

So, it would go to the final race at Suzuka. At Estoril Jacques Villeneuve did what he had to do, and beat Damon Hill fair and square, after the finest race of his Formula 1 career to date. With only the Japanese Grand Prix remaining, the world championship odds remained firmly with Hill, who still led by nine points, but after this performance by Villeneuve he'll have not slept easy.

Hill led away from pole position, and could not have dreamed of a better start, for Jean Alesi and Michael Schumacher both beat Villeneuve to the first corner, and delayed him through the early laps, as Damon raced serenely away.

Villeneuve, though, had clearly not given up on either race or championship, and, after passing Schumacher in perhaps the move of the season, closed in on Hill. Immediately after the last stops, he took over the lead, and the battle between him and Hill was done.

The remaining places, slightly reshuffled, went very much as qualifying had suggested, Schumacher just getting the better of Alesi, and Eddie Irvine holding off Gerhard Berger. The battles were good here, too, but the focus, of course, was on the championship protagonists. Yet again the Williams-Renaults were simply in a different class. Heinz-Harald Frentzen, who came home seventh in the Sauber-Ford, must be counting the days.

Nine-thousandths of a second. It was that close between the world championship contenders in

qualifying, and afterwards Villeneuve shrugged that it was frustrating, but not the end of the world. 'The thing is, if you knew you were that close, and went out again, you'd probably go off, trying to beat it.'

Jacques's frustration stemmed primarily from the fact that the last six minutes of qualifying were rained out, and that he therefore missed what would have been his last run. But so also did every other front runner, including pole man Hill. Could Damon, too, have gone quicker? Yes, he said, he believed so, but not by much.

As is the way of it at Grands Prix these days, Friday meant little to the outside world. The teams learned their lessons, of course, but the list of times was irrelevant, as the elevated position of Ukyo Katayama – third fastest – demonstrated.

Schumacher, fastest on Friday, faced reality on Saturday, and was not surprised. 'I never felt the Ferrari would be really on the pace here,' he said. 'Estoril might have been made for the Williams.'

Although Michael qualified fourth, behind Hill, Villeneuve and the Benetton of Alesi, he felt he needed a wet race to have any real chance of making it three wins on the trot. Not the least of his worries was the abrasiveness of the track; the Ferrari is markedly harder on tyres than the Williams.

That worry was still in his mind on Sunday morning, but a revised set-up pleased him, and he set the fastest time in the warm-up, followed by Villeneuve, Hakkinen and Hill. Both title contenders reported themselves happy with their cars.

Much – of course – was going to depend on the start. Villeneuve was under no illusions in Portugal, knowing that only victory would do, and, given the events of the recent past, one had to favour him, with his hand-operated clutch, to make a better getaway than Hill, with his conventional clutch.

Damon, on the other hand, was starting from the pole, which at Estoril is on the left, clean, side of the track. On paper, it was going to be fraught into the first corner - and that was before you started to consider the likes of Alesi and Schumacher.

Another consideration was the weather, for the race day forecast suggested more of the showers which had plagued the practice days. Fortunately, however, although they shrouded nearby hilltops through the morning, the clouds had lifted by two o'clock, and race conditions were warm and dry throughout.

In the event, the start turned out to be far less frantic than expected. Hill took off well, but Villeneuve got too much wheelspin, and it was Alesi who threatened the leading Williams down towards the first turn. Without hesitation, though, Damon veered right, obliging Jean to do the same, and suddenly the Benetton was running out of race track, and tucking in behind the Williams. 'I never ever saw Alesi,' Hill innocently said

**Top: Hill looked on course for victory early on.
Centre: Irvine was closer to Schumacher.
Above: Out of the way – Lavaggi's Minardi**

**Clockwise from above: Schumacher was unable to match the Williams' pace. The Tyrrells were quick in practice, Katayama third in one of the sessions. Coulthard's gesture says it all, after he was spun by team mate Hakkinen**

afterwards. I was just keeping my eyes on the road...' No prisoners today, his move seemed to say.

During those early laps, Damon pulled out a substantial lead, and – so long as his car didn't let him down – looked to have the world championship on a plate. Alesi was being dropped, at around three-quarters of a second a lap, but more to the point was that Schumacher was losing time to the Benetton – and Villeneuve was still behind the Ferrari.

A couple of times, Jacques took a look into the first turn, but no one

defends his place more resolutely than Michael. Frustrating it may have been, but Villeneuve seemed imprisoned in fourth place, his best hope to get ahead at the first stops.

'The thing wasn't over, though,' he said. 'I knew it was very important to be as patient as possible, not doing anything stupid. All I could do was hope for an opportunity to open up.'

At the end of lap 15 it did. And not a moment too soon, for until this point the Portuguese Grand Prix had been a dreary affair, with but a single order change – Frentzen passing

Verstappen for 14th place - since the first corner of the first lap.

What happened was that Schumacher and Villeneuve came up to a chicane disguised as a Minardi. Giovanni Lavaggi may be a charming fellow, but he really should not be in Formula 1, and for much of the afternoon simply got in the way. He did so now.

At the approach to the last, very quick, corner, Schumacher was obliged to lift off, whereupon Villeneuve showed the instincts of a true racer, and went for an

# IN HINDSIGHT

Jacques Villeneuve's drive to victory in the Portuguese Grand Prix was superb in many ways, but what will make it go down in the history books is the move that initially made it possible.

Had Villeneuve not passed Michael Schumacher on lap 16, the chances are he would never have clawed his way close enough to Hill to beat him. But he did – and how!

Estoril's 140mph final turn is daunting enough by itself, but the prospect of passing Michael Schumacher around it on the outside... Well, the more you think about it, the more unbelievable it becomes.

It left Schumacher impressed, and other drivers merely gulped and looked aghast when informed about it in the paddock afterwards.

The only person not particularly impressed seemed to be the man who executed it. 'It was fun,' he grinned, although another remark betrayed what he really felt: 'I told the team I thought I could do it. They said they would come and pick me out of the guardrail if I tried.'

What they actually said, according to senior operations engineer James Robinson, was practise the move and clean the track if you're going to try.

When he did, his race engineer Jock Clear said, 'he doubted it was possible because the track was dirty. But the opportunity presented itself and he couldn't resist it.'

And what did he say on the radio when it came off? 'I told you it could be done!' It left you wondering what more Villeneuve magic there was to come.

opportunity that he knew might not arise again. What was novel about it was that he went around the *outside* of the Ferrari.

'It was fun overtaking there,' said Jacques. Actually, I think my experience on the ovals helped me – I told the team before the race I was sure it was possible, and they told me they'd come and pick me up from the guardrail when I tried! Actually, I don't think it would have been possible if we hadn't hit traffic. 'The thing was,' he went on, 'I had nothing to lose. Either I beat Damon, or I lost the championship right there anyway, so it was worth it to take a big risk.'

Schumacher admitted to being...surprised by Villeneuve's move. 'I was behind the Minardi, and I knew that if I followed it through the corner, I wouldn't have been able to defend myself against Jacques on the straight, so I pulled up a little bit, to get a gap, and he used the opportunity to come up alongside me. I looked in the mirror, and couldn't see him – and suddenly he was beside me!

'We had a bit of a scary moment, actually, because at one point our wheels were interlocked. I didn't have as much grip as he had through that corner. I couldn't back off, because if I had he would have gone over my front wheel, and we'd have had a big one. So I just hoped my car would grip enough, and fortunately it did...'

Once out on to the straight, Villeneuve slipstreamed past Lavaggi, and was able to hold Schumacher off to the next corner, Michael by now unable to get back on terms. It was, without question, the overtaking manoeuvre of the Grand Prix season, and was effectively to win the Portuguese Grand Prix for Jacques, who now had a clear road, and set off after the Benetton of Alesi.

Benetton and McLaren had decided to go for two stops at Estoril, while Williams and Ferrari favoured three. On lap 17 the pit lane activity began, when Hill came in (7.7 sec), followed next time round by Villeneuve (7.0) and Schumacher (7.2).

In the course of this, Alesi took up the lead, but Hill swiftly closed on

him, and moved in front once more when the Benetton driver pitted on lap 22 (7.9).

Now the crowd had what it had come to see: Hill first, Villeneuve second, and not too far behind. On lap 21 Damon had led Jacques by 14.8 seconds, but two laps later it was down to seven seconds.

True enough, at this point Villeneuve set the fastest lap to date, but more to the point was that Hill was disastrously held up by backmarkers involved in their own battle, and lost more than four seconds in a single lap.

Suddenly the fight looked on, but now it was Villeneuve's turn to hit traffic, and for some laps the gap remained at around nine seconds. Then Jacques really picked up the pace, lapping more than a second faster than Damon, whose lead came down to five seconds.

Lap 34: Hill in, for his second stop, then Villeneuve and Schumacher, who were together again, a lap later. Everything passed without incident, but Jacques's in-lap was much quicker than Damon's had been, and now only three seconds separated them.

Next time round, lap 37, Villeneuve was only two seconds behind, then 1.4, and by lap 40 there was nothing between the two Williams-Renaults. 'I thought, "OK, let's see what he can do,"' said Hill, 'and I began to get away again, and thought everything was under control.'

In fact, Villeneuve had dropped back, because running immediately behind his team mate was robbing his car of clean air, and he worried that the consequent understeer would destroy his front tyres. But Hill never got more than a couple of seconds clear, and the decisive moment of the race was approaching.

'In the early laps, I enjoyed my time at the front,' he said, 'but I knew that Jacques would be able to get through, past Schumacher and Alesi, and that he'd come after me. He caught me pretty quickly, but still I'd hoped to have enough advantage to stay ahead through the last pit stops.'

As he prepared to come in for the final time, on lap 49, Hill was unlucky to be delayed at the last corner by Hakkinen's damaged McLaren. That

cost him a second or so, but the pit stop (8.8) went smoothly enough, and he rejoined in the hope of maintaining his slender advantage through Villeneuve's stop, which followed a lap later.

He was in for a rude surprise. Villeneuve put in a quick lap immediately before pitting, and his stop – eight seconds dead – was also a fraction faster. In perfect symmetry, the Williams-Renaults slotted into formation before the first corner, but now it was number 6 which led.

'I was pretty shocked when that happened,' said Damon. 'When I saw the car coming out of the pit lane, I thought it was a Tyrrell or something, and I was thinking, "Get out of the way, please!" Then I saw "Rothmans" on the rear wing, and I realised it was actually Jacques...'

It seemed logical to expect that Hill would attack on that lap, for his tyres were fully up to temperature, where Villeneuve's were not, but in fact the inspired Canadian actually drew away, and led his rival over the line by a second and a half. Thereafter, the gap was bigger every time they came by.

'At first I thought I'd see what I could do about catching him,' Hill said, 'but he was flying, and there was no way I could stay with him. He just drove a great race today: to come through from fourth, where he was in the early laps, to win at this track is no mean achievement.'

In the last part of the race, too, Hill had a clutch problem. It caused him no real difficulties, he said, but he was anxious about making the finish, and decided to concentrate on that. 'I felt a couple of bad shifts, but that was all. I didn't actually know there was anything wrong with the clutch until they advised me about it over the radio.'

There were other competitors, too, in this Portuguese Grand Prix, even if they received generally scant attention on an afternoon where everything polarised around the Williams-Renaults.

Schumacher and Alesi fought long and hard over third place, Michael getting the verdict by just over a second. 'We touched at one point,' he reported. 'I hit the back of his car, but there was no damage to either of us,

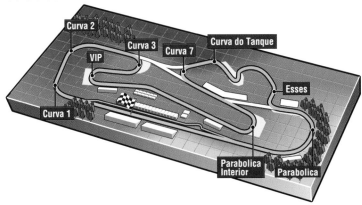

## PORTUGUESE GP

### ROUND 15

*Estoril*

**September 22 1996**
**FIA Formula 1 World Championship**

**Race data:** 70 laps of a 2.709-mile circuit
**Weather:** Dry and sunny
**Distance:** 129.646 miles

**Winner:** Jacques Villeneuve, Williams-Renault FW18, 113.35mph
**Previous result:** David Coulthard, Williams-Renault FW17, 113.29mph
**Fastest lap:** Jacques Villeneuve, Williams-Renault FW18, 1m22.873s

Curva 2
Curva 3
Curva 7
Curva do Tanque
VIP
Esses
Curva 1
Parabolica Interior
Parabolica

RESULTS © 1996 Federation Internationale de l'Automobile, 8 Place de la Concorde, Paris, 75008 France

### STARTING GRID

| | DRIVER | |
|---|---|---|
| 1 | Hill | 1:20.330 |
| 2 | Villeneuve | 1:20.339 |
| 3 | Alesi | 1:21.088 |
| 4 | Schumacher | 1:21.236 |
| 5 | Berger | 1:21.293 |
| 6 | Irvine | 1:21.362 |
| 7 | Hakkinen | 1:21.640 |
| 8 | Coulthard | 1:22.066 |
| 9 | Barrichello | 1:22.205 |
| 10 | Brundle | 1:22.324 |
| 11 | Frentzen | 1:22.325 |
| 12 | Herbert | 1:22.655 |
| 13 | Salo | 1:22.765 |
| 14 | Katayama | 1:23.013 |
| 15 | Panis | 1:23.055 |
| 16 | Verstappen | 1:23.531 |
| 17 | Rosset | 1:24.230 |
| 18 | Diniz | 1:24.293 |
| 19 | Lamy | 1:24.510 |
| 20 | Lavaggi | 1:25.612 |

and afterwards Jean came to apologise for...braking a bit earlier than usual. But it was OK.

'I knew that realistically third place was my best hope today. The Ferrari is never good on circuits where tyre degradation is high - it wears its tyres more than the Williams. At Monza it was fine, because there's a lot of grip in the track, but here we were sliding too much.'

Ferrari beat Benetton, therefore, in the scrap for third place, and the same was true in the dispute over fifth. Irvine, much closer than usual to team mate Schumacher at this race, got the best of Berger, whose car had

a throttle problem. At the last corner of the last lap, Gerhard (above), making a final attempt to get by, locked his brakes, and slid into Irvine. The Ferrari spun, but Eddie was still able to get to the line ahead of the damaged Benetton.

For McLaren, it was an appalling day. Not only were Hakkinen and Coulthard off the pace; on lap 46 they contrived to collide with each other! 

'David had just come out after his final stop,' commented an abashed Hakkinen, 'so he wasn't fully up to speed, and at the corkscrew turn I ran into him...'

Mika's damaged car - the one

which had delayed Hill momentarily - eventually retired, but for his team mate there was no such luck. Having been pushed into a spin, Coulthard made a precautionary stop, to have the McLaren checked over, but a slow puncture was missed, and so David had to come in again on the next lap. If that were not enough, he then exceeded the pit lane speed limit, and received a 10-second stop/go penalty. Last year, in the Williams, Coulthard won at this track.

This time, though, all the plaudits were for Villeneuve, after what had been a quite brilliant drive, the most convincing yet in the young man's 15-

race F1 career. 'I'm still nine points behind Damon,' he said, 'so it doesn't look very good, with one race to go.

'You never know, though, do you? Anything can happen in Japan - Damon could make a mistake, or his car could break, and the same things can happen to me, too. But until the last lap of the last race, I will believe we can do it.'

Even if Villeneuve won at Suzuka, a sixth place finish would be enough to give the title to Hill. After this virtuoso display, though, the odds on Jacques shortened. In Portugal he really looked like a man who wanted the world championship. ∎

## RACE RESULTS

| | DRIVER | CAR | RACE | LAPS | RESULT |
|---|---|---|---|---|---|
| 1 | Jacques Villeneuve (CDN) | Williams-Renault | 1m22.873s | 70 | 1h40m22.915 |
| 2 | Damon Hill (GB) | Williams-Renault | 1m23.762s | 70 | 1h40m42.881 |
| 3 | Michael Schumacher (D) | Ferrari | 1m24.059s | 70 | 1h41m16.860 |
| 4 | Jean Alesi (F) | Benetton-Renault | 1m24.331s | 70 | 1h41m18.024 |
| 5 | Eddie Irvine (GB) | Ferrari | 1m25.206s | 70 | 1h41m50.304 |
| 6 | Gerhard Berger (A) | Benetton-Renault | 1m24.647s | 70 | 1h41m56.056 |
| 7 | Heinz-Harald Frentzen (D) | Sauber-Ford | 1m24.869s | 69 | 1h41m13.769 |
| 8 | Johnny Herbert (GB) | Sauber-Ford | 1m25.786s | 69 | 1h41m17.057 |
| 9 | Martin Brundle (GB) | Jordan-Peugeot | 1m25.028s | 69 | 1h41m21.217 |
| 10 | Olivier Panis | Ligier-Mugen Honda | 1m25.008s | 69 | 1h41m34.267 |
| 11 | Mika Salo (FIN) | Tyrrell-Yamaha | 1m26.199s | 69 | 1h41m37.838 |
| 12 | Ukyo Katayama (J) | Tyrrell-Yamaha | 1m26.447s | 68 | 1h41m50.550 |
| 13 | David Coulthard (GB) | McLaren-Mercedes | 1m25.362s | 68 | 1h41m24.157 |
| 14 | Ricardo Rosset (BR) | Footwork-Hart | 1m26.863s | 68 | 1h40m44.958 |
| 15 | Giovanni Lavaggi (I) | Minardi-Ford | 1m28.911s | 65 | 1h40m33.410 |
| 16 | Pedro Lamy (P) | Minardi-Ford | 1m27.754s | 65 | 1h41m05.173 |
| R | Mika Hakkinen (FIN) | McLaren-Mercedes | 1m24.747s | 52 | accident damage |
| R | Jos Verstappen (NL) | Footwork-Hart | 1m25.913s | 47 | engine |
| R | Pedro Diniz (BR) | Ligier-Mugen Honda | 1m25.791s | 46 | spin |
| R | Rubens Barrichello (BR) | Jordan-Peugeot | 1m24.954s | 41 | spin |

## CHAMPIONSHIP POSITIONS

| | DRIVER | PTS | CONSTRUCTOR | PTS |
|---|---|---|---|---|
| 1 | Hill | 87 | Williams-Renault | 165 |
| 2 | Villeneuve | 78 | Benetton-Renault | 65 |
| 3 | Schumacher | 53 | Ferrari | 64 |
| 4 | Alesi | 47 | McLaren-Mercedes | 45 |
| 5 | Hakkinen | 27 | Jordan-Peugeot | 20 |
| 6 | Berger/Coulthard | 18 | Ligier-Mugen Honda | 15 |

FIA FORMULA 1 WORLD CHAMPIONSHIP

# DAMON'S DREAM FULFILLED IN STYLE

He'd kept the nation waiting, but when it came down to the final hurdle Damon Hill produced a commanding drive. In doing so he seized the Championship in the best possible fashion with race victory

When they radioed him that Villeneuve was out, that now his World Championship was secure, Damon Hill admitted that he momentarily lost his composure. 'It was almost too much to take in while I was driving,' he said, 'but then I told myself to get on with it, win the race for Williams on my last drive with the team.'

Hill drove a perfect race to the title, taking the lead at the start, and keeping it all the way. It was not a flashy victory, in any sense, for he pushed no harder than necessary on such a crucial afternoon, but he drove faultlessly, and stayed out of reach of Michael Schumacher, second, and Mika Hakkinen, third.

None can dispute that the right man has become world champion in 1996, but it was Villeneuve, rather than Hill, who was favourite to win the race. Jacques took a storming pole position, and seemed the more relaxed of the title contenders throughout the practice days.

When it mattered, though, Damon better coped with the pressure. When the lights went out, Villeneuve made an atrocious start, and fell to sixth by the first corner.

Thereafter, he was the fastest man on the circuit, but overtaking is notoriously difficult at Suzuka, and he faced a frustrating afternoon. On lap 37, while running fifth, his Williams shed its right rear wheel, not long after a pit stop.

'Jacques's been an exceptional newcomer to Formula 1,' Hill said of his rival afterwards, 'and a very good team mate. His day will come.'

Damon's day, meantime, had come. Of course there was sympathy for Villeneuve, but at 25 he has many chances ahead of him, not least because he – unlike Hill – keeps his place in the best racing team in the world. Damon's last day in a Williams was also his best.

Villeneuve had dominated qualifying, and there was no surprise when he also set the fastest time in the race morning warm-up. Perhaps you could couldn't read too much into a session in which Rubens Barrichello was second and Ukyo Katayama fifth, but the important thing was that both Villeneuve and Hill were absolutely problem-free.

In fact, the times meant little, for

PHOTOS: ACTION IMAGES

the session began on a circuit still very damp in places from the heavy overnight rain. Over the half-hour it of course dried out significantly, but many drivers didn't bother to go for a time.

Damon and Jacques had two cars each at Suzuka, Williams determined to do right by both drivers, and by Sunday morning each had his race car set up for the dry, his spare for the wet. Some forecasts suggested rain for the afternoon, but whatever the weather the team was prepared. If it turned out wet, there would be no

need to fiddle with the set-up; Hill and Villeneuve would simply step into their T-cars.

Attention was of course polarised on the two championship contenders, but you had to consider the role Schumacher and Ferrari might play. After qualifying, he said that third, behind the two Williams-Renaults, had been his best realistic hope. 'Nothing to do against those two,' he shrugged. 'The Williams is simply too quick. Still,' he went on, 'we still have some more things we can do to improve the car. But obviously for me

it would be better if we had a wet race.'

It stayed dry, though. Through the morning the sun broke through, and as race time neared the sky was hazy. Villeneuve led the 19 starters away on the formation lap, and did it a fair clip, too, working as much heat as possible into his tyres.

When they got back to the grid, though, it seemed they were held for an unusually long time, and the reason soon became clear: Coulthard's arm was in the air, his McLaren stalled.

"If I'm honest about it, I knew that for me it was now or never."

*Damon Hill*

Clockwise from above: Let the celebrations begin. Damon found a few friends ready to party. Hill seized the initiative from the start. The moment of glory. A family affair. The end of Jacques' challenge.

Eight minutes later they gave it another go, and this time the race got on its way. Villeneuve, so composed up to this point, made, in his own words, 'A horseshit start,' spinning the wheels way too much, and getting very sideways away from the grid.

Generally, Jacques's getaways have been a strong part of his game this season, but this time he blew it, and paid a high price, his Williams instantly engulfed by such as Berger, Hakkinen and Schumacher.

Hill's starts, on the other hand, have often compromised his races in 1996, but this time he made no mistake, and confidently led away, followed by Berger, Hakkinen, Schumacher and Irvine.

Jean Alesi was also up there, but by the second corner his race was over. 'I found myself trapped between the Ferraris, and ran out of space,' he explained later. The Benetton's left rear wheel went over the kerb, and then the car spun across the road – right in front of Villeneuve – and hit the inside barrier very hard. It was fortunate that the car went in backwards, and Alesi stepped from the wreckage unhurt. Scratch one Benetton.

The other one, Berger's, looked a potential race winner at this early stage, for Gerhard was keeping his car up with Hill's Williams, and the two of them began to ease away from Hakkinen and Schumacher.

'I was going faster than Damon,' Berger said, 'and I wanted to get past as soon as possible, because we were on a three-stop strategy, and I thought maybe he was only going to stop twice, in which case I wanted to build a lead over him.'

At the end of lap 3, coming into Suzuka's fatuously tight chicane, Gerhard went for it, in what seemed like an extremely ambitious move, for he was some way back of the Williams.

'Unfortunately,' he said, 'the move didn't come off.' No arguments there. As Berger lunged for the inside, Hill came across to take his line, and the two cars almost touched. As it was, the Benetton went over the inside kerbing, to the severe detriment of its front wing. At the end of lap 4, Gerhard was into the pits for a new

# IN HINDSIGHT

While the world was applauding Damon Hill's deserved world championship, there was one man in the centre of the storm who you might have thought would feel a little sorry for himself.

Jacques Villeneuve's had been a superbly impressive first season in Formula 1, and although it became clear reasonably quickly after the start that he would not beat Hill to the title, that trip into the gravel trap was still a less than fitting end to his year.

The accident was not his fault, indeed at the time of writing, Williams did not know either, but he could still have fought for second place, which would have given a nice rounded feel to the race.

But Villeneuve refused to be downcast. 'When the wheel came off,' he said, 'I wasn't very happy, because I saw the wheel going into the crowd, and I was worried someone might be hurt.'

Asked if he had any thoughts for himself, he said: 'No. It's not only in the last race that you win the championship, it's over the whole season. Both Damon and I have made mistakes this year, but he did a better season that we did. He's done a great job the whole season.'

A gracious loser, and a man with a great future. For Villeneuve, there will be other years.

Hill said: 'Jacques has been an outstanding newcomer to Formula 1. He's taken to it like a duck to water, he's done a great job all season, and he's been a great team mate. I'm certain that he is a future world champion.'

nosecone, rejoining in 14th place. Smiles in the Benetton pit were hard to find afterwards.

Hill was unaware of how close he had been to disaster. 'I heard another engine, for the first time since my motorbike days,' he said, 'but I never saw Gerhard. Then, at the exit of the corner, I looked in my mirrors, and saw that he'd dropped back...'

Now Damon began to pull away from Hakkinen and Schumacher, but not by leaps and bounds, for this was a day for consolidation, not excess. All he needed to do was keep clear of possible problems.

Villeneuve, on the other hand, could afford no such luxury. Trapped behind Irvine's patently slower Ferrari, he tried several times to find a way by into the chicane, Suzuka's only realistic overtaking spot, but was never quite close enough. 'In the end,' Eddie said, 'I decided it wasn't fair to hold him up, so I let him pass me at the chicane.'

It was now the end of lap 12, and Jacques was nine seconds behind the leader. Next time round, he set a new fastest lap, and closed quickly on Schumacher, at which point he came in for his first stop. The timing was perfect, but the stop was a lengthy one, indicating that a goodly measure of fuel had gone in, that the Williams strategy was indeed two stops.

Villeneuve rejoined in ninth place, immediately behind Berger, who swiftly let him by. Jacques then passed Panis, and moved up to fourth as others began to make their first stops.

An assertive Berger ensured British hearts were firmly in their mouths with his move on Hill on lap 3

Schumacher was in at the end of lap 16, and two laps later both Hill and Hakkinen, running first and second, stopped. Damon's stop required 11.6 seconds, but Mika's, although less lengthy, was more costly, for he lost a place to Schumacher in the process, Michael having made the best of his two laps on new tyres.

This also had the effect of drawing him significantly closer to Hill. Although Damon kept his lead through the stops, his advantage over Michael was only a couple of seconds, with Hakkinen a second or so behind the Ferrari, and Villeneuve a similar distance behind Mika.

At this point Jacques was only five seconds adrift of Hill, so perhaps the game wasn't over yet. He had clawed his way back into the reckoning by virtue of several new fastest laps, but in fact he was as close to Damon as he was to get. If he was potentially faster than Hakkinen, given a clear road, getting by the McLaren was a different matter. On any straight worth the name, Mercedes horsepower seemed to assert itself.

For many laps the first four cars circulated in reasonably close order, but little by little Hill edged away. 'In the early laps, of course I was pleased that Jacques had made a bad start,' he said, 'but then I thought the same thing at Monza, and look what happened there. So I said to myself, "This is all very well, Hill, but you've got to stay calm and see it through to the finish." I decided to drive nice and

easy, but I kept reminding myself all through the race.'

At 30 laps he was four seconds ahead of Schumacher, but more important to him was that Villeneuve, still running fourth behind Hakkinen, was now more than 10 seconds behind.

On lap 32 Schumacher, Hakkinen and Villeneuve all made their second stops, Jacques's taking a little longer than the others' since, in addition to taking on fuel and tyres, he also requested a front wing adjustment on the Williams.

Barring an unlikely series of disasters for the three drivers ahead, Villeneuve's world championship chances were now done, but he had said before the race that he would believe he could win it until the last lap, and he continued to drive by that creed. On lap 34, as Hill came in for his final stop, Jacques set another new fastest lap, and this one was to stand for the rest of the race.

On the following lap he was absurdly baulked by Katayama. Nothing new there, but what was new was that something was done about it, the stewards imposing a 10-second stop/go penalty on the local hero for 'blocking.'

The world championship was settled at the beginning of lap 37. Villeneuve had thought that perhaps he had a slow puncture, for the car was feeling unstable, but in point of fact what he had was a loosening right rear wheel. As he approached the second turn, his car began to twitch, and while Jacques was able to control it, there was nothing he could do when the wheel detached itself, then flew on ahead of the Williams, which slid into a gravel trap.

Typically, Villeneuve was utterly calm as he climbed from the car. Walking away, he waved to the spectators, and, at this moment, they were his primary concern.

'When I saw the wheel bouncing away, I thought for sure it would land in the grandstands, and I was worried that it would kill someone,' he said. Fortunately, the debris fence contained it, and no one was hurt.

Had he had no thoughts for himself, for the end of his quest for the title? 'No, not at all. Damon did a

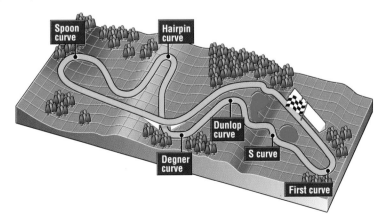

# JAPANESE GP

ROUND 16

13 October 1996
FIA Formula 1 World Championship

**Race data:** 52 laps of a 3.643-mile circuit
**Weather:** Dry and sunny
**Distance:** 189.343 miles

**Winner:** Damon Hill,
Williams Renault FW18, 122.73mph
**Previous result:** Michael Schumacher,
Benetton-Renault B195, 94.321mph
**Fastest lap:** Jacques Villeneuve,
Williams Renault FW18, 1m44.043s

## *Suzuka*

Spoon curve · Hairpin curve · Dunlop curve · S curve · Degner curve · First curve

## STARTING GRID

| | DRIVER | |
|---|---|---|
| 1 | Villeneuve | 1:38.909 |
| 2 | Hill | 1:39.370 |
| 3 | Schumacher | 1:40.071 |
| 4 | Berger | 1:40.364 |
| 5 | Hakkinen | 1:40.458 |
| 6 | Irvine | 1:41.005 |
| 7 | Frentzen | 1:41.277 |
| 8 | Coulthard | 1:41.384 |
| 9 | Alesi | 1:41.562 |
| 10 | Brundle | 1:41.600 |
| 11 | Barrichello | 1:41.919 |
| 12 | Panis | 1:42.206 |
| 13 | Herbert | 1:42.658 |
| 14 | Katayama | 1:42.711 |
| 15 | Salo | 1:42.840 |
| 16 | Diniz | 1:43.196 |
| 17 | Verstappen | 1:43.383 |
| 18 | Lamy | 1:44.874 |
| 19 | Rosset | 1:45.412 |
| DNQ | Lavaggi | 1:46.795 |

better job than I did today, and that's the end of it. I've had a good first season in Formula 1; I want to do better next year...'

A good first season, well, yes, you could say that. The manner of Villeneuve's departure must inevitably have taken some of the gloss from the team's day, but at Williams they appreciate a driver who knows how to control himself, having some experience of those who could not.

From the pits, they radioed Hill the news that he was the 1996 world champion. Damon conceded that initially it threw him. 'It wasn't easy to control my emotions at that moment, but I really tried to put the championship out of my mind, to concentrate on winning the race for the team.'

He did just that, flawlessly, pulling away once more from Schumacher and Hakkinen, who continued to duel. Irvine, who had earlier lost touch with the main group, nevertheless ran fourth, but was being hauled in by Berger, who had run laps at Suzuka bettered only by Villeneuve.

Perhaps it was bound to end in tears. Eddie is a resolute defender of his place, and Gerhard has lately shown signs of some desperation. On lap 40, into the chicane, the Benetton clobbered the Ferrari, which spun into instant retirement.

It didn't help the situation that Berger had also run into Irvine at the last race, in Estoril. 'He said sorry to me,' Eddie said, 'but that is not enough.' If anyone might have smiled at the incident, it was Derek Warwick, who was punted out of the 1993 race in identical circumstances, at exactly the same spot. His assailant? E. Irvine.

Nothing assailed Hill, though. As he began his final lap, he brought the Williams over close to the pit wall, as if the race were already won. 'I was just enjoying myself so much,' he smiled afterwards, 'that I wanted to share it with the boys, and give them a warm-up for the real thing.'

A minute and three-quarters later

he gave them the real thing, and they went nuts. In the paddock there was a sense of rejoicing and relief, too, for Damon is liked inside the sport as by his fans, which is not always the case with world champions.

After thanking everyone he could think of, Hill paid tribute to his team mate and rival, and said that assuredly Villeneuve would be World Champion one day. 'He's young, and he'll have other chances,' Damon said, 'whereas, if I'm honest about it, I knew that for me it was now or never.'

Fortunately for the sport of Grand Prix racing, it was now. A man of greater integrity has never worn the crown. ■

## RACE RESULTS

| | DRIVER | CAR | RACE | LAPS | RESULT |
|---|---|---|---|---|---|
| 1 | Damon Hill (GB) | Williams-Renault | 1m44.753s | 52 | 1h32m33.791 |
| 2 | Michael Schumacher (D) | Ferrari | 1m44.445 | 52 | 1h32m35.674 |
| 3 | Mika Hakkinen (SF) | McLaren-Mercedes | 1m44.852 | 52 | 1h32m37.003 |
| 4 | Gerhard Berger (AUT) | Benetton-Renault | 1m44.350 | 52 | 1h33m00.317 |
| 5 | Martin Brundle (GB) | Jordan-Peugeot | 1m45.882 | 52 | 1h33m40.911 |
| 6 | Heinz-Harald Frentzen (D) | Sauber-Ford | 1m46.407 | 52 | 1h33m54.977 |
| 7 | Olivier Panis (F) | Ligier-Mugen Honda | 1m45.347 | 52 | 1h33m58.301 |
| 8 | David Coulthard (GB) | McLaren-Mercedes | 1m45.613 | 52 | 1h33m59.024 |
| 9 | Rubens Barrichello (BR) | Jordan-Peugeot | 1m46.339 | 52 | 1h34m14.856 |
| 10 | Johnny Herbert (GB) | Sauber-Ford | 1m45.932 | 52 | 1h34m15.590 |
| 11 | Jos Verstappen (NL) | Footwork-Hart | 1m46.977 | 51 | 1h33m22.955 |
| 12 | Pedro Lamy (P) | Minardi-Ford | 1m49.220 | 50 | 1h32m59.965 |
| 13 | Ricardo Rosset (BR) | Footwork-Hart | 1m49.263 | 50 | 1h33m34.338 |
| R | Eddie Irvine (IRL) | Ferrari | 1m45.798 | 39 | accident |
| R | Ukyo Katayama (J) | Tyrrell-Yamaha | 1m47.518 | 37 | engine |
| R | Jacques Villeneuve (CDN) | Williams-Renault | 1m44.043 | 36 | lost wheel |
| R | Mika Salo (SF) | Tyrrell-Yamaha | 1m49.372 | 20 | engine |
| R | Pedro Diniz (BR) | Ligier-Mugen Honda | 1m48.495 | 13 | spin |
| R | Jean Alesi (F) | Benetton-Renault | no time | 0 | accident |

Knowing he'd retire early on Ferrari found Eddie a new job...

## FINAL CHAMPIONSHIP POSITIONS

| | DRIVER | PTS | CONSTRUCTOR | PTS |
|---|---|---|---|---|
| 1 | Hill | 97 | Williams-Renault | 175 |
| 2 | Villeneuve | 78 | Ferrari | 70 |
| 3 | Schumacher | 59 | Benetton-Renault | 68 |
| 4 | Alesi | 47 | McLaren-Mercedes | 49 |
| 5 | Hakkinen | 31 | Jordan-Peugeot | 22 |
| 6 | Berger | 21 | Ligier-Mugen Honda | 15 |

FIA FORMULA 1 WORLD CHAMPIONSHIP

## HOW THEY FINISHED

| | | |
|---|---|---|
| 1. | WILLIAMS-RENAULT | 175 |
| 2. | FERRARI | 70 |
| 3. | BENETTON-RENAULT | 68 |
| 4. | McLAREN-MERCEDES | 49 |
| 5. | JORDAN-PEUGEOT | 22 |
| 6. | LIGIER-MUGEN HONDA | 15 |
| 7. | SAUBER-FORD | 11 |
| 8. | TYRRELL-YAMAHA | 5 |
| 9. | FOOTWORK-HART | 1 |

The 1996 season saw the smallest grids Formula 1 had seen for quite some time. There were 11 teams and 22 cars on the grid in Melbourne in March, and with the mid-season demise of Forti, just 20 cars made it to Suzuka in November. On the driver front, jobs were incredibly secure, with only the cash-strapped Minardi team switching drivers

**Entrant:** Scuderia Ferrari
**Base:** Maranello, Italy
**Chassis:** Ferrari F310
**Engine:** Ferrari V10
**Lubricants:** Shell

## FERRARI

It was all change at Ferrari as Michael Schumacher and Eddie Irvine came aboard and the V12 was replaced by the V10. Much was expected of John Barnard's new F310, but the car arrived late, had some fundamental problems, and the team never really caught up. The gearbox was an Achilles heel and minimised running early on, although somehow Irvine survived to take third in Australia. But Schumacher ignored the problems and wrestled the thing to poles in San Marino, Monaco, France and Hungary – the tightest tracks on the schedule were clearly suited to the F310. Elsewhere, he usually had to make do with third. In the Spanish rain he scored a superb virtuoso win, and after a mid season run of mechanical carnage added sensational victories in Spa and Monza, which saved the team's bacon. His reputation simply grew and grew as the season went on. Unable to do much testing, Irvine struggled in his wake for much of the year, but it was noticeable that when he was allowed some running he would be closer to the German at the next race. An incredible run of nine retirements was finally broken at Estoril – his main task was to hang onto his job, and he did just that.

**MICHAEL SCHUMACHER**
AGE: 27

**1**

**EDDIE IRVINE**
AGE: 30

**2**

**Entrant:** Mild Seven Benetton Renault
**Base:** Enstone, England
**Chassis:** Benetton B196
**Engine:** Renault V10
**Lubricants:** Elf

## BENETTON RENAULT

It was obvious that Benetton would miss Michael Schumacher, but with Jean Alesi and Gerhard Berger coming from Ferrari, the team seemingly had good replacements. And yet Benetton really did struggle to regain its momentum after the world champion's departure, and the cars never looked like matching the Williams duo, despite having similar powerplants. Since the team has long been dominated by Schumacher's input, the new car did not suit Berger's driving style at first, and Alesi beat him consistently in qualifying – at Ferrari they had been evenly matched. Indeed, it wasn't until Germany that Gerhard started ahead of his team mate. That weekend the Austrian was on great form, and could well have hung on in front of Hill and won, had his engine not blown spectacularly in the closing laps. Berger seemed to get the worse of the reliability, retiring several times while running strongly in the top six. In contrast, Alesi's retirements in several early races were self induced, and at one stage relations with the team seemed to be strained. But in the latter half of the year he picked up points with impressive regularity, including several podiums. At no stage however, did he look like a threat for victory.

**JEAN ALESI**
AGE: 32

**3**

**GERHARD BERGER**
AGE: 37

**4**

# GRID STOOD STILL

**Entrant:** Rothmans Williams Renault
**Base:** Wantage, England
**Chassis:** Williams FW18
**Engine:** Renault V10
**Lubricants:** Elf

**Entrant:** Marlboro McLaren Mercedes
**Base:** Woking, England
**Chassis:** McLaren MP4/11
**Engine:** Mercedes V10
**Lubricants:** Mobil

**Entrant:** Equipe Ligier Gauloises
Blondes
**Base:** Magny-Cours, France
**Chassis:** Ligier JS 43
**Engine:** Mugen-Honda V10
**Lubricants:** Elf

## WILLIAMS RENAULT

After his drivers dropped the ball in 1995, Frank Williams was determined to hit back in style, which he certainly did with the FW18. The car just looked right, and the team proved it had got its aerodynamic sums correct by outclassing the similarly powered Benetton for most of the year. Hiring Jacques Villeneuve was a gamble which paid off spectacularly, but old hand Damon Hill responded to the challenge with a superb string of victories early in the season, and he usually had Jacques covered in qualifying. Things fell apart on several occasions when Damon made bad starts, but equally he was let down by the engine when leading in Monaco. Without that he would have been champion well before Suzuka. Villeneuve started with a bang taking pole in Melbourne, but after a few races he was mostly in Hill's shadow, apart from the win at the 'Ring, and was unfathomably off the pace in Monaco. But as it became clear that Damon was on the way out, his confidence blossomed and he was given more freedom to pursue set-ups. Wins in Silverstone, Hungary and Estoril were hard earned and made sure he went to Suzuka with a remote sniff of the title, and effectively less to lose than the outgoing Damon.

**DAMON HILL**
AGE: 36

**5**

**JACQUES VILLENEUVE**
AGE: 25

**6**

## McLAREN MERCEDES

After the disastrous '95 season McLaren and Mercedes were hoping for great things with the new MP4/11, which looked good on early test outings. With Alain Prost on board as test driver and advisor it seemed possible that it could be turned into a winning package. But the car never quite lived up to expectations, and while it gradually improved during the year it was never consistently at the front. The Mercedes was a strong and generally reliable engine, but once again the chassis was the weaker link. A strong rivalry developed between Mika Hakkinen and David Coulthard, but ultimately both did enough to secure their seats for '97. Hakkinen's return from his Adelaide accident was so complete that within a few races we'd all forgotten about it, and good reliability enabled the Finn to be a regular points finisher. Coulthard made some great starts early in the year and briefly ran at or near the front at the 'Ring (where he finished third) and Imola. Over the season he was comprehensively beaten by Mika in qualifying, and their rivalry came to a head when they collided with each other in Estoril. The team was genuinely unlucky at Spa, where its pit stop strategy put them in a strong position until the safety car intervention.

**MIKA HAKKINEN**
AGE: 28

**7**

**DAVID COULTHARD**
AGE: 25

**8**

## LIGIER MUGEN-HONDA

Ligier started the season with less financial support than in previous years, and when Tom Walkinshaw and company upped and left for Arrows after Melbourne, it seemed that the team might fall apart. The car however, was better than many thought and with Mugen-Honda's latest proving one of the best engines in the pitlane, the French team held its own. By the end of the year Flavio Briatore had acquired 100% control of the team, and it remains to be seen what his plans are. At Monaco, Olivier Panis was nothing less than brilliant as he scythed through the field and took a popular and well deserved win, but elsewhere his season was blighted by his apparent inability to qualify well. As a racer he was second to none, as other good drives proved. Pedro Diniz's signing for the team from Forti was greeted with some amusement and cynicism, but the well-sponsored Brazilian was certainly not out of his depth, scoring a point with an impressive drive in the wet in Barcelona, and another at Monza, as well as being particularly good at Magny-Cours. Pedro had more than his fair share of incidents – including his spectacular fireball in Argentina – but is certainly better than last year showed and many people believed.

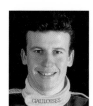
**OLIVIER PANIS**
AGE: 30

**9**

**PEDRO DINIZ**
AGE: 26

**10**

**Entrant:** Benson & Hedges Total
Jordan Peugeot
**Base:** Silverstone, England
**Chassis:** Jordan 196
**Engine:** Peugeot V10
**Lubricants:** Total

# Jordan Peugeot

Jordan scored a coup over the winter by securing major backing from Benson & Hedges, and much was said about how this would be invested in improving the team's technical facilities. Alas, it was too late to make much difference to the 1996 car, which never lived up to expectations. The Peugeot V10 seemed to be doing the job and with its slippery, low cockpit aerodynamics the car was fast in a straight line, regularly timed as one of the quickest through the speed traps, but its weakness was a lack of downforce at the rear. Designer Gary Anderson was rested at mid-season and given a chance to get stuck into the '97 model. Martin Brundle got off to a terrible start with his Melbourne crash, which precipitated a string of accidents and spins. He found his feet with car and team after some productive testing, and in the second half of the year - already written off by some - fought back and regularly outpaced his team mate, securing finishes in the points. After throwing away a great opportunity in Brazil, Rubens Barrichello rarely shone. In his fourth year with the team the partnership had run out of momentum, and Rubens was told to look elsewhere at an early stage of the silly season.

**RUBENS BARRICHELLO**
AGE: 24

**11**

**MARTIN BRUNDLE**
AGE: 37

**12**

**Entrant:** Red Bull-Sauber-Ford
**Base:** Hinwil, Switzerland
**Chassis:** Sauber C15
**Engine:** Ford V10
**Lubricants:** Elf

# Sauber Ford

A new V10 engine from Cosworth seemed set to propel Peter Sauber's team into the big league, such were Heinz-Harald Frentzen's performances with the seemingly outdated V8 last year. But the engine, destined eventually for the new Stewart Grand Prix, was a disappointment in the first half of the year. To make matters worse the latest C15 needed a great deal of development work too, and never lost the understeering trait that Frentzen couldn't live with. Unable to match his '95 times or grid positions, Heinz-Harald seemed to lose faith, and his mistake at Monaco, where he made contact with Eddie Irvine when a more patient approach might well have earned victory, hit him hard. Still he knew from an early stage that Frank Williams wanted him for 1997, and the deal was officially done around the time of Spa. New team mate Johnny Herbert floundered in Frentzen's shadow early in the year, but once he got some testing miles under his belt he improved enormously. A persevering drive to third at Monaco helped his cause, and later in the season he ran Frentzen closer than any previous team mates, outqualifying the German on several occasions. A new two year deal announced in Estoril, was just reward for a good effort.

**JOHNNY HERBERT**
AGE: 32

**14**

**HEINZ-HARALD FRENTZEN**
AGE: 29

**15**

**Entrant:** Arrows-Hart
**Base:** Milton Keynes, England
**Chassis:** Arrows FA17
**Engine:** Hart V8

# Footwork Hart

Arrows began the year in dire financial straits, and with Hart V8 development plans put on hold. But after Australia Tom Walkinshaw ditched his Ligier interests to join forces with Jackie Oliver's team. The car was not a bad little package, as Jos Verstappen showed by qualifying a stunning seventh and finishing sixth in Argentina. But even with TWR's help there was little scope for development and he slid from midfield to the back. Bridgestone joined at mid-season to run a massive tyre test programme, but that did not help the 1996 programme. Verstappen's star waned as the season went on, and a series of spins and offs did not help his cause. A huge crash at Spa caused by a mechanical failure failed to help matters, and by the end of the year he was fed up with the lack of progress. Ricardo Rosset started the year with a solid reputation gained in F3000, but he did little testing and never really got to grips with the Arrows. He struggled at the back of the field, and while the situation improved with experience, he rarely did anything to catch the attention. For 1997 though, the team embarks on a major new partnership with world champion Damon Hill. Only time will tell if the car carrying the number 1 will deliver the goods.

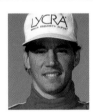

**RICARDO ROSSET**
AGE: 28

**16**

**JOS VERSTAPPEN**
AGE: 24

**17** 

# TECHNICAL IN BRIEF

**THE NEW COCKPIT AND** headrest rules caused controversy. Williams and Jordan's cars appeared with noticeably lower and sleeker solutions which caused grief among teams like Ferrari and McLaren, who claimed their bulky cockpits followed the spirit as well as the letter of the law. The FIA declared all cars legal.

**HIGH COCKPIT SIDES PLAYED** havoc with aerodynamics and most teams found problems in maintaining airbox pressure. By experimenting with crash helmets – and in Sauber's case Heinz-Harald Frentzen's seating position – teams were able to find crucial missing horsepower. Schumacher pioneered the use of Bell's IndyCar helmet in F1.

**FERRARI AND JORDAN WERE** among the teams to try power steering, which was first used in F1 by Williams in 1994, but later dropped. Ferrari was also among the teams pursuing the hand clutch/left foot braking route. Michael Schumacher was initially reluctant to try it, but later followed Eddie Irvine's lead. At Williams Damon Hill preferred to stick to the conventional system, while Jacques Villeneuve opted for a hand clutch. Ferrari and Benetton copied Jordan by trying a seven-speed gearbox, although Ferrari's did not appear until mid-season. The Italian team had

**Entrant:** Tyrrell-Yamaha
**Base:** Ripley, England
**Chassis:** Tyrrell 024
**Engine:** Yamaha V10
**Lubricants:** Elf

# TYRRELL YAMAHA

Tyrrell was at the bottom of the now traditional cycle which sees a year with a big sponsor followed by another with an almost plain white car and a subsequent struggle to make ends meet. The loss of Nokia hit the team hard, but the new car showed great promise in testing. Yamaha's tiny new engine was great for packaging in the chassis, but once the season got underway it failed with alarming regularity. Mika Salo had only a few chances to shine after showing promise by scoring points in the first two races. He was particularly good at Monaco, where he held off Villeneuve and salvaged fifth despite collecting a spun Eddie Irvine. At Spa too he impressed, by which time he'd already been confirmed for next season. Team mate Katayama had a terrible year. He managed to outqualify Salo on a handful of occasions, but in the races the Japanese driver never got near the top six. A mid season spell of engine failures and accidents was at least halted by some reliable finishes later on. Forever a battling outfit, it was testimony to their spirit that Tyrrell was still prepared to try some technical innovations, such as introducing aerodynamically profiled suspension.

**UKYO KATAYAMA**
AGE: 33

**18**

**MIKA SALO**
AGE: 29

**19**

# MINARDI FORD

**Entrant:** Minardi Team
**Base:** Faenza, Italy
**Chassis:** Minardi M195B
**Engine:** Ford Cosworth V8
**Lubricants:** Agip

Minardi's budget was tighter than ever, and the Italian team was forced to race a modified 1995 chassis. The Ford ED engine was totally outclassed, and matters were not helped by poor reliability and a tendency for the drivers to take each other out at races where they stood a chance of a half-decent result! Pedro Lamy did a solid job, but was usually outpaced by new boys Tarso Marques and Giancarlo Fisichella. Both showed promise, but didn't have funds and were replaced by gentleman racer Lavaggi. At the end of the year Flavio Briatore acquired an interest in the team, and as with Ligier, its future is not yet clear.

**TARSO MARQUES**
AGE: 20

**21**

**GIANCARLO FISICHELLA**
AGE: 23

**21**

**PEDRO LAMY**
AGE: 24

**20**

**GIOVANNI LAVAGGI**
AGE: 38

**21**

# FORTI FORD

**Entrant:** Forti Grand Prix Racing
**Base:** Alessandria, Italy
**Chassis:** Forti FGP3
**Engine:** Ford Cosworth V8
**Lubricants:** Elf

Forti lost Pedro Diniz and thus much of its funding over the winter, but made the best of things by trading up from Ford ED to Zetec power in an attempt to beat the new 107% rule. The team also did some work on the car, starting the season with last year's car but introducing a new chassis at the European Grand Prix. With former Ferrari team manager Cesare Fiorio on board and Britain George Ryton handling technical matters, it looked like a sensible effort. Funding from the mysterious Shannon Group seemed to be the icing on the cake, but proved to be disastrous. The sponsor acquired ownership of the team but didn't pay up, and Guido Forti found his hands tied as he tried to regain control. The management's somewhat naive approach landed them in deep trouble, and the team was not seen after Hockenheim, where the cars sat in the garage. It was a shame for long suffering drivers Andrea Montermini and Luca Badoer, who had at least made the cars go reasonably competitively on a couple of occasions when many thought the 107% rule an insurmountable hill to climb. However, the sight of Badoer scrabbling from his upturned car in Argentina sums up the team's season.

**ANDREA MONTERMINI**
AGE: 32

**22**

**LUCA BADOER**
AGE: 26

**23**

---

serious transmission problems for much of the year, and the unique composite spacer on the original F310 was a nightmare.

**YAMAHA BROKE NEW GROUND**
by producing the smallest ever V10 F1 engine, which weighed around 100kgs and left the opposition wondering how it was done. The unit was a chassis designer's dream, yet not surprisingly, proved unreliable. Rivals got the hint,

and by the end of the season Peugeot was testing a tiny engine, and Renault was hard at work on its own project.

**TYRRELL WAS THE FIRST TEAM**
to try aerodynamically

profiled wishbones. Williams and McLaren later introduced versions, but without the all-enveloping shroud used by Tyrrell.

**LIGIER AND BENETTON**
both used electronic handbrakes in 1995, and this season jumped starts were almost non-existent. However, Benetton's system backfired spectacularly at the Nurburgring when both Berger and Alesi found the things stuck on when the race started,

and crawled away with smoke pouring from their rear tyres!

**RACES WERE NO LONGER**
started by a green light following the introduction of a complex new system which saw the field set off when a row of red lights went out. Use of the jump start detection sensors extended to pit stops, which allowed accurate timing of tyre changes and meant that drivers could take stop and go penalties at their own garages.

**TYRRELL TRIED SOMETHING**
very different when it ran front tyres all round in qualifying at Hockenheim, in an attempt to gain straightline speed. The slightly narrower rears did indeed provide an advantage, but lack of testing – because the team did not want Goodyear to know about its ploy – meant that the experiment was inconclusive. The team planned to try again at Monza, but Goodyear told everyone not to try the trick.

*Team-mates*

# CIVIL WARS

Such was Williams-Renault's domination of the 1996 season, it was clear from mid-season that either Damon Hill or Jacques Villeneuve would be the world champion. ADAM COOPER looks at other inter-team title chases

Until this season it had been seven years since F1 had seen a title race develop into a battle between two team mates. But not so long ago such a scenario was the norm rather than the exception. Indeed, between 1978 and '89 the championship was dominated by one marque on seven occasions, although in one of those seasons a third party snuck up on the rails.

In 1978 and again in '79, the contest was resolved in a gentlemanly fashion. The senior driver in both cases finally picked up a long sought title, and his team mate – although quicker over a lap – was happy to stay in his wheel tracks, dutifully complete one-two finishes, and accept that the team position came first.

Ronnie Peterson and Gilles – father of Jacques – Villeneuve deferred respectively to Mario Andretti at Lotus and Jody Scheckter at Ferrari. Ronnie and Gilles were men of honour, had effectively signed as number twos, and had the confidence to believe that their time would come, even though Ronnie was in his ninth season of F1 and getting a little impatient. As fate would have it they each ran out of time, and the two men stand with Stirling Moss as perhaps the greatest drivers never to win the world title. Go back to the Moss's heyday in the fifties and you will find other examples of team chivalry, none greater than Peter Collins's gesture of handing his car to Juan Manuel Fangio at Monza in 1956, thus depriving himself of the title. But that sort of thing doesn't happen any more.

The Damon Hill/Jacques Villeneuve contest was just the latest episode in a series of no holds barred battles within teams. While his father may have been willing to give best to his mate Scheckter, Jacques came into F1 to look after his own interests. Hill was his target, there to be shot down, and the team was happy to see it happen. These days, it can be no other way – if you don't get the job done from the start, somebody else will be there to take your place.

The other recent occasions when team mates were to the fore – in 1984, '86, '87, '88 and '89 – showed just how much times had changed since Ronnie and Gilles followed orders. Three years ago Alain Prost was Damon's first team mate at Williams, and as a multiple world champion provided a valuable marker for the Englishman. Co-incidentally, Prost also figured in all but one of the aforementioned title races. In 1984, he was in the position of the new kid on the block, even though he'd been a GP winner for Renault. Sacked over the winter, he joined

**Villeneuve logged up vital seconds and thirds and stayed in touch with multiple winner Hill**

Hill and Villeneuve had the equipment to dominate in 1996, and the constructors title was sewn up for Williams by August. The drivers' one...

McLaren in a last minute deal to run alongside Niki Lauda. The Austrian veteran was in the middle of his comeback, having largely outpaced previous team mate John Watson. Prost was something different altogether - a young man with limitless ambition, and bloody quick in a racing car. There were no team orders, and it took all of Lauda's guile to wrest the third title he so dearly wanted. He had the brains to accept that Prost was quicker, and he effectively withdrew from the battle for pole. Instead he concentrated on sorting out his car for the race.

In those days of fuel limitations tactics played an important part, and Lauda was the master of stacking up points. They went into the last race in Estoril with Prost on six wins and Lauda on five, but the Austrian had the advantage. Prost won the finale, but second place was enough to earn Niki the title - by the impossibly small margin of half a point. On the podium, he told Alain that 1985 would be his year. He was right, and this time Lauda offered no challenge. Even Prost didn't expect to win again in 1986, not least because history decreed that repeating a championship was all but impossible, but he did it. And mainly because two guys in another team conspired to destroy each other's chances.

While Prost and Lauda were on friendly terms at McLaren, and thus the team could operate with two number ones, such a policy doesn't always work. It failed at Williams in 1986, when the Honda engine gave Nigel Mansell and Nelson Piquet a substantial advantage. Between them they pretty much dominated the '86 season, leaving Prost to pick up the crumbs. But the Frenchman did it to such good effect that when the circus headed to the finale in Adelaide, he was within a race win of taking the title from Mansell, and just a few points behind Piquet. Had either Williams man been a clear number one, he would have clinched the crown long before. As it was, the impossible happened. Mansell retired with a spectacular puncture, Piquet had a precautionary tyre stop and slipped back, and Prost sailed through to victory - and became the first repeat champion since Jack Brabham in 1959-'60.

The '87 season really was only about the two Williams men and even their in-fighting didn't give anyone else a chance to catch up; Prost was left behind. Mansell had more wins, more poles, and as usual more calamities, not all of them self-inflicted. But Piquet racked up more points. Nigel was still in with a shout at Suzuka, until a practice accident saw him out of the race and Nelson declared champ. The 'no orders' policy worked this time, but only because the Williams was in a class of its own, and it was an uncomfortable situation for all concerned. Fed up with the status quo, Piquet headed to Lotus to replace Ayrton Senna, who joined Prost - and Honda - at McLaren. The next two seasons saw the ultimate in fraternal rivalries. For two remarkable years, McLaren enjoyed the services of Senna and Prost, two of the greatest drivers of all time. In '88 Honda made a mockery

**Ronnie and Gilles were men of honour, dutifully completing 1-2s for the team**

Clockwise from above: In 1986 Mansell and Piquet fought throughout – and Prost became champion. Scheckter, winner in '79. Andretti in 1978 and his Lotus 'shadow', Ronnie Peterson

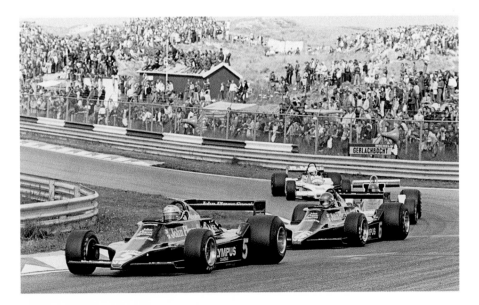

of the last year of the turbo rules and McLaren proved totally dominant. The two drivers got on reasonably well, respectful of each other's talents, although as a double champion and the senior partner Prost could be forgiven for feeling threatened. Senna won their first contest, securing the crown with a brilliant drive at Suzuka, although Prost actually scored more points until dropped scores were taken into consideration. In '89 the uneasy truce came to an end, their relationship deteriorated, and the battle again came to a head in Suzuka. Prost was in front when Senna made a move at the chicane; the Frenchman held his ground, and the McLarens tangled and came to an ungainly halt in the middle of the corner. Senna resumed, but his race win was subsequently denied him by the FIA. So before the final race at Adelaide, Prost was confirmed as champion.

McLaren, Honda and Marlboro had the title comewhat may, but the sight of the two MP4/5s locked together at the Suzuka chicane is the enduring image of the season, and undoubtedly the most extreme example of team in-fighting getting out of hand. Perhaps it was easier for Frank Williams and later Ron Dennis to let their boys fight during those few brief years when Honda reigned

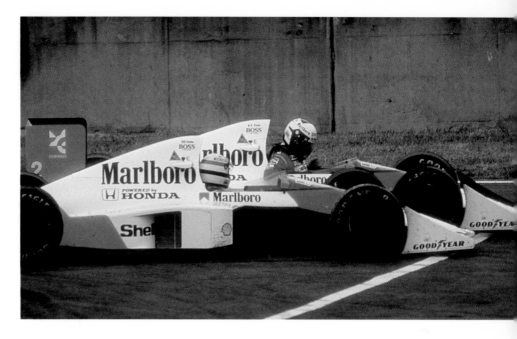

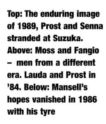

Top: The enduring image of 1989, Prost and Senna stranded at Suzuka. Above: Moss and Fangio – men from a different era. Lauda and Prost in '84. Below: Mansell's hopes vanished in 1986 with his tyre

supreme, but more recently they and others seemed to have learned that such an approach didn't always work. In 1990-'91 Gerhard Berger was rarely a match for champion Senna - and perhaps it was no co-incidence that the two were good friends. When Nigel Mansell finally secured the title for Williams in 1992, Riccardo Patrese was not the force within the team that Piquet had once been. Rookie Hill was very much understudy to Prost in '93, and no one was in a position to threaten Schumacher at Benetton in 1994-95, when the team eagerly succumbed to the driver's wish to build the team around him.

Now, things seemed to have changed once more. In 1995 Williams let Hill and David Coulthard get on with the job, and while they spurred each other on to greater heights, the mistakes they each made ensured that Frank could not even salvage the constructors' title at year's end, despite having a car which was most deemed superior to the Benetton.

However, the policy worked in 1996, and for the first time since '89 we saw two team mates indulge in a private battle. Benetton lost its double world champion, Ferrari had serious technical problems, and thus the FW18 was in a class of its own. As soon as Frank Williams and Patrick Head realised that not even Schumacher posed a serious threat, they could relax, and see which of their guys emerged on top. They upset the delicate balance a little by announcing that series leader Damon was no longer wanted, which gave Jacques a considerable boost. Williams won, but as in 1987, it was messy.

Both Hill and Villeneuve had experience on which to draw. Damon could look back to that remarkable 1994 title race, when everything fell his way in the second half of the season and he got tantalisingly close to the crown at Adelaide. A year later, Jacques was embroiled in a season-long fight for the IndyCar title. In the USA consistent top six finishes are, compared to wins, relatively more rewarding pointswise than in F1. But Villeneuve carried that approach to Europe, logging up seconds and thirds in the first half of the season and staying in touch with multiple winner Hill. By the end of the year, those points meant he was still in a position to win the championship.

Next year Heinz-Harald Frentzen joins Williams. A quick and undoubtedly talented driver, he is used to getting star treatment at Sauber. But he still has to prove himself, and Villeneuve is the target, just as Hill was for Jacques, Prost for Hill and Senna, and Lauda for Prost. Heinz-Harald and Jacques are sure to be at the forefront, but they will undoubtedly be taking points off each other. But what if Williams loses its clear technical edge, and Ferrari gets it right? Michael Schumacher could collect wins on a regular basis, and his designated number two will not be in a position to challenge him, even if he finds the speed with which to do so. It will be interesting to see if the one-car, one-star approach pay dividends again... ■

# WORLD CHAMPI

## DRIVER CHAMPIONSHIP

| NO | DRIVER | AUS | BRA | ARG | EUR | SMR | MON | SPA | CAN | FRA | GBR | GER | HUN | BEL | ITA | POR | JPN | PTS |
|----|--------|-----|-----|-----|-----|-----|-----|-----|-----|-----|-----|-----|-----|-----|-----|-----|-----|-----|
| 1 | DAMON HILL | 2/1 | 1/1 | 1/1 | 1/4 | 2/1 | 2/R | 1/R | 1/1 | 2/1 | 1/R | 1/1 | 2/2 | 2/5 | 1/R | 1/2 | 2/1 | **97** |
| 2 | JACQUES VILLENEUVE | 1/2 | 3/R | 3/2 | 2/1 | 3/11 | 10/R | 2/3 | 2/2 | 6/2 | 2/1 | 6/3 | 3/1 | 1/2 | 2/7 | 2/1 | 1/R | **78** |
| 3 | MICHAEL SCHUMACHER | 4/R | 4/3 | 2/R | 3/2 | 1/2 | 1/R | 3/1 | 3/R | 1/DNS | 3/R | 3/4 | 1/9 | 3/1 | 3/1 | 4/3 | 3/2 | **59** |
| 4 | JEAN ALESI | 6/R | 5/2 | 4/3 | 4/R | 5/6 | 3/R | 4/2 | 4/3 | 3/3 | 5/R | 5/2 | 5/3 | 7/4 | 6/2 | 3/4 | 9/R | **47** |
| 5 | MIKA HAKKINEN | 5/5 | 7/4 | 8/R | 9/8 | 11/8 | 8/6 | 10/5 | 6/5 | 5/5 | 4/3 | 4/R | 7/4 | 6/3 | 4/3 | 7/R | 5/3 | **31** |
| 6 | GERHARD BERGER | 7/4 | 8/R | 5/R | 8/9 | 7/3 | 4/R | 5/R | 7/R | 4/4 | 7/2 | 2/13 | 6/R | 5/6 | 8/R | 5/6 | 4/4 | **21** |
| 7 | DAVID COULTHARD | 13/R | 14/R | 9/7 | 6/3 | 4/R | 5/2 | 14/R | 10/4 | 7/6 | 9/5 | 7/5 | 9/R | 4/R | 5/R | 8/13 | 8/8 | **18** |
| 8 | RUBENS BARRICHELLO | 8/R | 2/R | 6/4 | 5/5 | 9/5 | 6/R | 7/R | 8/R | 10/9 | 6/4 | 9/6 | 13/6 | 10/R | 10/5 | 9/R | 11/9 | **14** |
| 9 | OLIVIER PANIS | 11/7 | 15/6 | 12/8 | 15/R | 13/R | 14/1 | 8/R | 11/R | 9/7 | 16/R | 12/7 | 11/5 | 14/R | 11/R | 15/10 | 12/7 | **13** |
| 10 | EDDIE IRVINE | 3/3 | 10/7 | 10/5 | 7/R | 6/4 | 7/7 | 6/R | 5/R | 22/R | 10/R | 8/R | 4/R | 9/R | 7/R | 6/5 | 6/R | **11** |
| 11 | MARTIN BRUNDLE | 19/R | 6/12 | 15/R | 11/6 | 12/R | 16/R | 15/R | 9/6 | 8/8 | 8/6 | 10/10 | 12/R | 8/R | 9/4 | 10/9 | 10/5 | **8** |
| 12 | HEINZ-HARALD FRENTZEN | 9/8 | 9/R | 11/R | 10/R | 10/R | 9/4 | 11/4 | 12/R | 12/R | 11/8 | 13/8 | 10/R | 11/R | 13/R | 11/7 | 7/6 | **7** |
| 13 | MIKA SALO | 10/6 | 11/5 | 16/R | 14/DQ | 8/R | 11/5 | 12/R | 14/R | 13/10 | 14/7 | 15/9 | 16/R | 13/7 | 17/R | 13/11 | 15/R | **5** |
| 14 | JOHNNY HERBERT | 14/DNS | 12/R | 17/9 | 12/7 | 15/R | 13/3 | 9/R | 15/7 | 16/DQ | 13/9 | 14/R | 8/R | 12/R | 12/9 | 12/8 | 13/10 | **4** |
| 15 | PEDRO DINIZ | 20/10 | 22/8 | 18/R | 17/10 | 17/7 | 17/R | 17/6 | 18/R | 11/R | 17/R | 11/R | 15/R | 15/R | 14/6 | 18/R | 16/R | **2** |
| 16 | JOS VERSTAPPEN | 12/R | 13/R | 7/6 | 13/R | 14/R | 12/R | 13/R | 13/R | 15/R | 15/10 | 17/R | 17/R | 16/R | 15/8 | 16/R | 17/11 | **1** |
| 17 | LUCA BADOER | NQ | 19/11 | 21/R | NQ | 21/10 | 21/R | NQ | 20/R | 20/R | NQ | - | - | - | - | - | - | |
| 18 | GIANCARLO FISICHELLA | 16/R | - | - | 18/13 | 19/R | 18/R | 19/R | 16/8 | 17/R | 18/11 | - | - | - | - | - | - | |
| 19 | UKYO KATAYAMA | 15/11 | 16/9 | 13/R | 16/DQ | 16/R | 15/R | 16/R | 17/R | 14/R | 12/R | 16/R | 14/7 | 17/8 | 16/10 | 14/12 | 14/R | |
| 20 | PEDRO LAMY | 17/R | 18/10 | 19/R | 19/12 | 18/9 | 19/R | 18/R | 19/R | 18/13 | 19/R | 18/12 | 19/R | 19/10 | 18/R | 19/16 | 18/12 | |
| 21 | TARSO MARQUES | - | 21/R | 14/R | - | - | - | - | - | - | - | - | - | - | - | - | - | |
| 22 | ANDREA MONTERMINI | NQ | 20/R | 22/10 | NQ | NQ | 22/NS | NQ | 22/R | 21/R | NQ | - | - | - | - | - | - | |
| 23 | RICARDO ROSSET | 18/9 | 17/R | 20/R | 20/11 | 20/R | 20/R | 20/R | 21/R | 19/12 | 20/R | 19/11 | 18/8 | 18/9 | 19/R | 17/14 | 19/13 | |
| 24 | GIOVANNI LAVAGGI | - | - | - | - | - | - | - | - | - | - | NQ | 20/10 | NQ | 20/R | 20/15 | NQ | |

## CHAMPIONSHIP POSITIONS

| | CONSTRUCTOR | PTS |
|---|---|---|
| 1 | WILLIAMS-RENAULT | 175 |
| 2 | FERRARI | 70 |
| 3 | BENETTON-RENAULT | 68 |
| 4 | MCLAREN-MERCEDES | 49 |
| 5 | JORDAN-PEUGEOT | 22 |
| 6 | LIGIER-MUGEN HONDA | 15 |
| 7 | SAUBER-FORD | 11 |
| 8 | TYRRELL-YAMAHA | 5 |
| 9 | FOOTWORK | 1 |
| - | MINARDI | 0 |

## TOTAL WINS

| | DRIVER | WINS |
|---|---|---|
| 1 | MICHAEL SCHUMACHER | 22 |
| 2 | DAMON HILL | 21 |
| 3 | GERHARD BERGER | 9 |
| 4 | JACQUES VILLENEUVE | 4 |
| 5 | JOHNNY HERBERT | 2 |
| 6 | JEAN ALESI | 1 |
| 7 | DAVID COULTHARD | 1 |
| 8 | OLIVIER PANIS | 1 |

## POLE POSITIONS

| | RACE | DRIVER | TEAM |
|---|---|---|---|
| 1 | AUSTRALIA | VILLENEUVE | WILLIAMS |
| 2 | BRAZIL | HILL | WILLIAMS |
| 3 | ARGENTINA | HILL | WILLIAMS |
| 4 | EUROPE | HILL | WILLIAMS |
| 5 | SAN MARINO | SCHUMACHER | FERRARI |
| 6 | MONACO | SCHUMACHER | FERRARI |
| 7 | SPAIN | HILL | WILLIAMS |
| 8 | CANADA | HILL | WILLIAMS |
| 9 | FRANCE | SCHUMACHER | FERRARI |
| 10 | BRITAIN | HILL | WILLIAMS |
| 11 | GERMANY | HILL | WILLIAMS |
| 12 | HUNGARY | SCHUMACHER | FERRARI |
| 13 | BELGIUM | VILLENEUVE | WILLIAMS |
| 14 | ITALY | HILL | WILLIAMS |
| 15 | PORTUGAL | HILL | WILLIAMS |
| 16 | JAPAN | VILLENEUVE | WILLIAMS |

## FASTEST LAPS

| | RACE | DRIVER | TEAM |
|---|---|---|---|
| 1 | AUSTRALIA | VILLENEUVE | WILLIAMS |
| 2 | BRAZIL | HILL | WILLIAMS |
| 3 | ARGENTINA | ALESI | BENETTON |
| 4 | EUROPE | HILL | WILLIAMS |
| 5 | SAN MARINO | HILL | WILLIAMS |
| 6 | MONACO | ALESI | BENETTON |
| 7 | SPAIN | SCHUMACHER | FERRARI |
| 8 | CANADA | VILLENEUVE | WILLIAMS |
| 9 | FRANCE | VILLENEUVE | WILLIAMS |
| 10 | BRITAIN | VILLENEUVE | WILLIAMS |
| 11 | GERMANY | HILL | WILLIAMS |
| 12 | HUNGARY | HILL | WILLIAMS |
| 13 | BELGIUM | BERGER | BENETTON |
| 14 | ITALY | SCHUMACHER | FERRARI |
| 15 | PORTUGAL | VILLENEUVE | WILLIAMS |
| 16 | JAPAN | VILLENEUVE | WILLIAMS |

Not one to rush things, it took Damon until the last race to confirm the Championship that seemed destined to be his from the very first race of the season. On route he clinched eight wins and nine pole positions, figures that fail to tell the story of a nail biting finale.

It was described as a risk, but in a rookie season of unrivalled brilliance Jaques Villeneuve did more than enough to confirm Frank Williams' faith in him. In the second half of the season he was the man to watch, pulling off some sensational overtaking manouvres.

# SUPERGRID

## DRIVER SUPERGRID

| | DRIVER | CAR | TOTAL TIME | AVG TIME | AVG POS | KMH |
|---|---|---|---|---|---|---|
| 1 | DAMON HILL | WILLIAMS-RENAULT | 23:08.498 | 1:26.781 | 1.44 | 190.781 |
| 2 | JACQUES VILLENEUVE | WILLIAMS-RENAULT | 23:14.018 | 1:27.126 | 3.06 | 190.025 |
| 3 | MICHAEL SCHUMACHER | FERRARI | 23:16.545 | 1:27.284 | 2.63 | 189.682 |
| 4 | JEAN ALESI | BENETTON-RENAULT | 23:26.253 | 1:27.891 | 4.88 | 188.372 |
| 5 | GERHARD BERGER | BENETTON-RENAULT | 23:27.301 | 1:27.956 | 5.75 | 188.232 |
| 6 | MIKA HAKKINEN | MCLAREN-MERCEDES | 23:29.789 | 1:28.112 | 6.63 | 187.900 |
| 7 | EDDIE IRVINE | FERRARI | 23:30.837 | 1:28.177 | 7.88 | 187.760 |
| 8 | DAVID COULTHARD | MCLAREN-MERCEDES | 23:33.921 | 1:28.370 | 8.25 | 187.350 |
| 9 | RUBENS BARRICHELLO | JORDAN-PEUGEOT | 23:35.247 | 1:28.453 | 8.06 | 187.175 |
| 10 | HEINZ-HARALD FRENTZEN | SAUBER-FORD | 23:41.291 | 1:28.831 | 10.56 | 186.379 |
| 11 | MARTIN BRUNDLE | JORDAN-PEUGEOT | 23:41.830 | 1:28.864 | 11.13 | 186.308 |
| 12 | OLIVIER PANIS | LIGIER-MUGEN HONDA | 23:45.967 | 1:29.123 | 12.75 | 185.768 |
| 13 | JOHNNY HERBERT | SAUBER-FORD | 23:49.335 | 1:29.333 | 12.94 | 185.330 |
| 14 | MIKA SALO | TYRRELL-YAMAHA | 23:51.152 | 1:29.447 | 13.25 | 185.095 |
| 15 | JOS VERSTAPPEN | FOOTWORK-HART | 23:53.834 | 1:29.615 | 14.06 | 184.749 |
| 16 | UKYO KATAYAMA | TYRRELL-YAMAHA | 23:57.167 | 1:29.823 | 15.00 | 184.320 |
| 17 | PEDRO DINIZ | LIGIER-MUGEN HONDA | 23:59.333 | 1:29.958 | 16.38 | 184.043 |
| 18 | PEDRO LAMY | MINARDI-FORD | 24:14.808 | 1:30.926 | 18.44 | 182.085 |
| 19 | RICARDO ROSSET | FOOTWORK-HART | 24:17.137 | 1:31.071 | 19.13 | 181.794 |

### NOTES

The SuperGrid is based on a driver's total grid times. Drivers who did not qualify for every race are not included in the SuperGrid.

In the case of Irvine and Rosset, their grid times - later disallowed - of 1:17.443 and 1m30.529 at the French and British GPs respectively have been included if for no other reasons than it is impossible to arrive at any other reasonable time, and they were allowed to start the race. Had the times been allowed, they would have qualified 10th and 17th. For the purposes of the SuperGrid, their positions were rated as 22nd.

The lap distance for the 1996 SuperGrid was 73.583 kilometres. The total pole time was 23m06.646 (average 1m26.665), making the 107% mark 24m43.711 (average 1m32.732).

## LAP LEADERS

| | DRIVER | KMS LED | % TOTAL LAPS |
|---|---|---|---|
| 1 | DAMON HILL | 2,183.619 | 47.436 |
| 2 | JACQUES VILLENEUVE | 1,353.555 | 27.712 |
| 3 | MICHAEL SCHUMACHER | 596.080 | 11.440 |
| 4 | JEAN ALESI | 316.869 | 6.016 |
| 5 | GERHARD BERGER | 211.513 | 3.057 |
| 6 | DAVID COULTHARD | 112.008 | 2.564 |
| 7 | OLIVIER PANIS | 78.272 | 1.578 |
| 8 | MIKA HAKKINEN | 13.936 | 0.197 |

The season started well for Mika Salo, but an engine that showed little inclination to last the course and a lack of development on the car, soon saw the results fail off. Nevertheless Salo coped well enough to maintain his position as one of the most talked about future talents in Grand Prix racing.

Whilst his team mate took the plaudits Eddie Irvine was left standing in the shadows. An appalling run of reliability from the car would have been enough to break other men, but Eddie just shrugged his shoulders and looked to '97.

# SUPER RACE

Ricardo Rosset encountered numerous difficulties on his arrival in Formula One - just what he didn't need when it's so crucial to impress in your rookie season. Faced with having to learn many circuits, as well as the car, he did well to qualify for every race. Whether this was enough to stay in F1 for next year remains to be seen.

Yet another frustrating season for Minardi left Portugal's Pedro Lamy with a disappointing set of results. Against a lack of testing or team mate stability Lamy battled on, but this wasn't enough to bring home any Championship points.

## DISTANCE COVERED

| | DRIVER | KILOMETRES | % TOTAL | AVG. LAP | RETIREMENTS |
|---|---|---|---|---|---|
| 1 | JACQUES VILLENEUVE | 4,493.561 | 92.406 | 1:32.027 | 4 |
| 2 | MIKA HAKKINEN | 4,280.676 | 88.757 | 1:32.101 | 5 |
| 3 | DAMON HILL | 4,016.139 | 82.939 | 1:31.374 | 4 |
| 4 | JEAN ALESI | 3,840.626 | 80.276 | 1:31.643 | 5 |
| 5 | RUBENS BARRICHELLO | 3,846.353 | 77.318 | 1:32.755 | 7 |
| 6 | GERHARD BERGER | 3,791.250 | 76.331 | 1:34.093 | 8 |
| 7 | DAVID COULTHARD | 3,508.905 | 72.781 | 1:32.812 | 7 |
| 8 | OLIVIER PANIS | 3,360.403 | 71.893 | 1:33.614 | 7 |
| 9 | MICHAEL SCHUMACHER | 3,592.833 | 71.105 | 1:32.614 | 6 |
| 10 | JOHNNY HERBERT | 3,307.122 | 70.611 | 1:32.126 | 7 |
| 11 | HEINZ-HARALD FRENTZEN | 3,339.439 | 70.118 | 1:32.134 | 10 |
| 12 | MARTIN BRUNDLE | 3,463.711 | 69.527 | 1:34.366 | 8 |
| 13 | MIKA SALO | 3,331.185 | 68.343 | 1:33.880 | 8 |
| 14 | PEDRO LAMY | 3,205.808 | 63.708 | 1:34.007 | 8 |
| 15 | UKYO KATAYAMA | 3,035.258 | 60.750 | 1:35.554 | 9 |
| 16 | RICARDO ROSSET | 3,076.952 | 60.552 | 1:36.260 | 8 |
| 17 | PEDRO DINIZ | 2,980.756 | 59.862 | 1:36.031 | 10 |
| 18 | EDDIE IRVINE | 2,758.176 | 56.706 | 1:33.752 | 11 |
| 19 | JOS VERSTAPPEN | 2,360.928 | 47.337 | 1:33.275 | 12 |
| | | | | | Starts/Retirements |
| | LUCA BADOER | 1,198.073 | 27.909 | 1:29.253 | 6/4 |
| | GIANCARLO FISICHELLA | 1,221.246 | 25.247 | 1:42.777 | 8/5 |
| | GIOVANNI LAVAGGI | 586.042 | 13.708 | 1:29.242 | 3/2 |
| | ANDREA MONTERMINI | 512.083 | 11.736 | 1:31.173 | 5/3 |
| | TARSO MARQUES | 140.547 | 3.254 | 1:32.925 | 2/2 |

The SuperRace includes drivers who failed to "qualify" for the SuperGrid by not taking part in every Grand Prix.